The Illustrated Directory of
Guitars

NICK FREETH

Colin Gower Enterprises

Colin Gower Enterprises Ltd.,
Cordwainers, Caring Lane,
Leeds, Maidstone, Kent ME17 1TJ
   United Kingdom.
© 2006 Colin Gower Enterprises Ltd.

ISBN: 0-681-44658-7

Designed by Philip Clucas MSIAD
Photography by Neil Sutherland
Edited by Marie Clayton
Color Reproduction by Wyndeham Graphics
Printed and bound in China

CONTENTS

CONTENTS

TOM ANDERSON HOLLOW DROP TOP

A KEEN GUITARIST from the age of eight, Tom Anderson spent several years as a professional musician before becoming involved in designing, maintaining and modifying instruments. Between 1977 and 1984 he worked at Schecter (see separate entry), going on to set up his own, California-based company in 1984. This initially focused only on pickup manufacturing, but, thanks to the success of the Anderson's ProAm electric in the late 1980s, its emphasis soon shifted to guitar production, to which

The one seen here is a "Hollow Drop Top," containing sealed chambers that add extra richness and character to the guitar's tone. There are three pickups, plus a Strat-like 5-way selector, a toggle "splitter" switch, and an additional control, built into the tone knob, giving further permutations of signals from the bridge humbucker and the neck and middle transducers. Like all the company's models, the Hollow Drop Top uses the Buzz Feiten Tuning System: this corrects some of the inaccuracies in intonation suffered by all fretted instruments by means of what Anderson's publicity describes as "visually undetectable structural neck change[s] in combination with slightly altered bridge intonation offsets."

the firm has been exclusively committed since 1990.

The Drop Top—whose name refers to the instrument's maple (or sometimes koa) upper surface, molded over a basswood or alder body—is one of Anderson's enduring classics; launched in 1991, it has subsequently appeared in a variety of different forms.

Left: The rich purple of the Hollow Drop Top's surface is complemented by the instrument's chromed hardware, including an Anderson "vintage tremolo."

Right: Anderson's trade-mark: in its first-ever catalog, the firm described itself as "dedicated to creating the world's finest feeling, playing and sounding" guitars.

TOM ANDERSON COBRA SPECIAL

TOM ANDERSON GUITARWORKS' Cobra line of electrics began in 1993 with the original, maple-topped mahogany Cobra—a single cutaway model, fitted with two powerful humbucking pickups, and featuring the company's usual comprehensive switching options for them. Cobras with chambered bodies followed soon afterward, and among the later incarnations of the instrument (which, according to the company's 1998 catalog, is the guitar considered by Tom Anderson himself to suit his playing style best) has been the stylish Cobra Special shown in our photographs. The Special can be supplied in "TV Yellow" (as here), "Translucent Cherry," and several alternative colors, and it sports a solid, all-mahogany body, contoured for maximum comfort at the waist, and in the area where the elbow of the player's picking arm rests. Like nearly all Andersons (see next two pages), the Special has a bolted-on maple neck; however, its 24¾-inch scale length is slightly shorter than the 25½ inches found on the Anderson Drop Top.

In place of the humbuckers used on earlier Cobras, the Special is equipped with two generously proportioned single-coil "soapbars," clearly inspired by Gibson's classic postwar P-90 units. These transducers,

Below: The Cobra Special has a 22-fret rosewood fingerboard.

named, respectively, "P1" (neck) and "P3" (bridge) by Anderson, deliver what the company has recently characterized as "a much fatter single coil tone than most players are used to...with a wider, less concentrated middle than humbuckers of the same power output." Unsurprisingly, the Cobra Special's combination of great sounds and optimum playability has made it a bestseller.

Left: This pickup selector, like the rest of the Cobra Special's hardware, is reassuringly chunky!

Left: Simplicity and functionality are the order of the day on this model—though a transducer-equipped "X-bridge" can also be fitted to it.

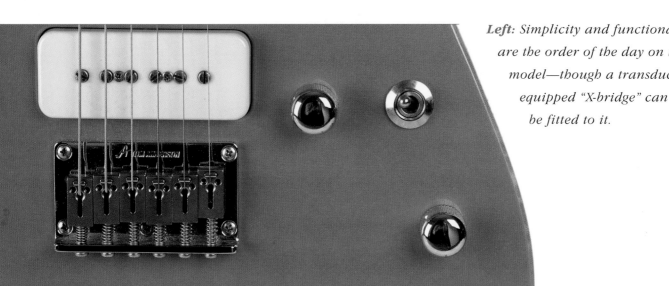

21

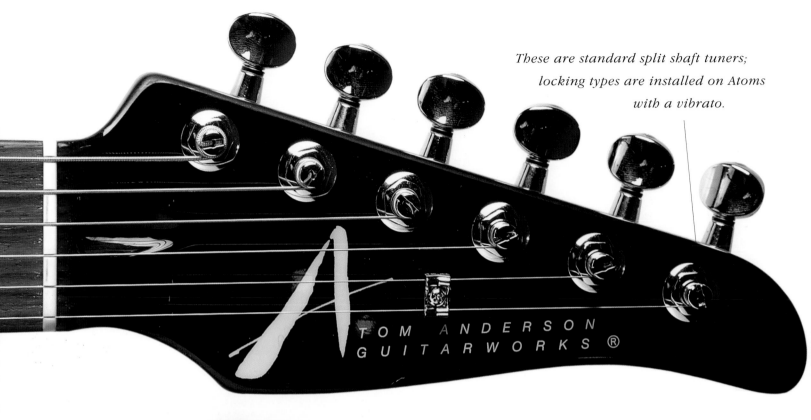

These are standard split shaft tuners; locking types are installed on Atoms with a vibrato.

Below: *Flame maple or walnut tops are available instead of the quilted maple one on this Atom.*

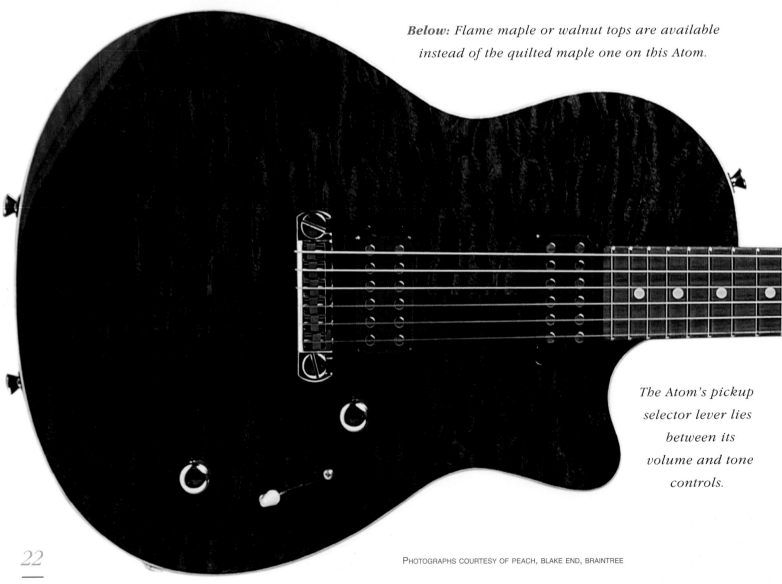

The Atom's pickup selector lever lies between its volume and tone controls.

PHOTOGRAPHS COURTESY OF PEACH, BLAKE END, BRAINTREE

TOM ANDERSON ATOM

FOR MANY YEARS, Tom Anderson has been a devotee of bolted-on electric guitar necks in preference to glued-in ones, or neck-through-body designs. Interviewed by Cliff Suttle for the Harmony Central website in 1998, he expressed his firm faith in the use of neck bolts (with their ability to supply constant pressure) combined with very precise manufacturing techniques (neck-to-body joints on Anderson guitars are milled to tolerances of a couple of thousandths of an inch) to achieve the tone and articulation for which his instruments are renowned. However, in 2005, his company announced a new model, the Atom, that broke new ground by using a different kind of neck joint. Described as "a three-dimensional trapezoidal wedge," it is said to offer unrivalled rigidity and alignment, and to provide a larger contact area between neck and body that maximizes the transfer of vibrations between these two key components.

The Atom has several other intriguingly novel features, including a wraparound bridge and a body shape quite unlike anything previously produced by the firm. It also comes with a remarkably wide range of

Indian rosewood fingerboard, and its two transducers are acticviated—individually, together, and in either humbucking or split-coil modes—via a five-way selector lever (see caption) and a "pull-on" tone knob switch of the same type as the one fitted to the Hollow Drop Top featured earlier.

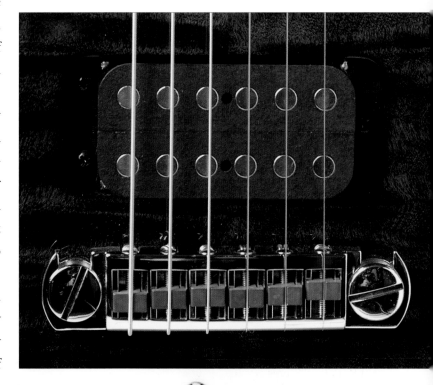

options: customers can choose Atoms with various numbers and types of pickups, alternative woods, and even differing nut widths!

The Atom shown on these pages has a quilted maple top, finished in "Deep Ocean Blue," and laid over a mahogany body. Its neck, too, is mahogany, with an

Since its inception, Anderson Guuitarworks has been based in Newbury Park, California.

Above, top: *A close-up of the Atom's wraparound bridge and one of its humbucking pickups.*

TOM ANFIELD SOLID-BODY

L UTHIER TOM ANFIELD, who is also one of Britain's leading guitar repairers and restorers, as well as a skilled player, is based in the southern English county of Surrey. As a boy, he had been keen to optimize the performance of his own guitars, but explains that he "couldn't afford to have people set [them] up," and decided to learn how to do it for himself. Discovering that he had a natural aptitude for the task, he soon became impatient with the indifferent standards prevailing among some professional guitar technicians at the time: on one occasion, he was so unhappy about

Above: This Kahler vibrato unit includes fine-tuners.

Right: The chrome switch activiates the center/bridge pickup link (see text).

Left: The Anfield's double-cutaway body is made from mahogany.

the quality of the work done on an instrument of his by a music shop that he warned its staff, "One day, I'll be your nemesis!" Anfield pursued his chosen career in Australia for a number of years, going on to establish the highly respected Guitar Tree Luthiery in London in

the late 1990s before starting his current operation.

The Anfield model seen here dates from 1984, and was, in his own words, "put together with and for a close friend." Following his death, Tom "re-inherited" the guitar, and has since re-fretted it and altered its

electronics. It features an ESP neck, three Kent Armstrong pickups (an Alnico at the neck, a Super Distortion in the middle, and a "Motherbucker" at the bridge), plus, as Anfield says, "switches galore for as many sounds as you can think of!" These include series/parallel/coil-tap toggles for each pickup, and an additional control that links the center and bridge transducers in series, providing a major decibel boost. The instrument has LSR machine heads, and a Kahler vibrato, whose arm was removed when our photographs were taken.

TOM ANFIELD "GARY BONER" GUITAR

THIS TOM ANFIELD ELECTRIC carries the Guitar Tree name on its headstock; the Guitar Tree Luthiery was Anfield's previous, London-based business, and for a while, he used its "brand" for some of his instruments. This model was built in 2004 for Gary Boner, guitarist and singer with British blues-rock combo Roadhouse, whom Anfield describes as "one of my great proponents." Its body is made from swamp ash, combined with layers of black sycamore and (on top) flamed alder, and it boasts three pickups: two single-coils, and a humbucker at the bridge. Its original electronics were slightly different, and when they were replaced, Anfield mounted the new transducers on the ebony plate beneath the strings.

Below: Flamed alder and swamp ash provide an ideal combination of good looks and body density.

PHOTOGRAPHS COURTESY OF TOM ANFIELD

These loacking tuners are
made by Gotoh.

*Gary Boner's band
Roadhouse was formed in 1991.*

Above: *Two black "trees"
help ensure a straight path
for the upper strings.*

Bottom: *A sideways view of the instrument's
body, showing how the upper layers of wood
are shaped to follow its contours.*

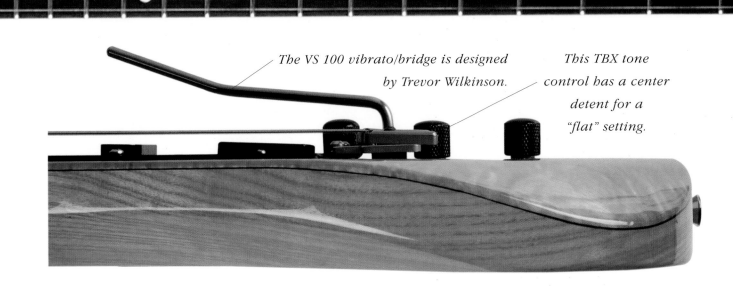

*The VS 100 vibrato/bridge is designed
by Trevor Wilkinson.*

*This TBX tone
control has a center
detent for a
"flat" setting.*

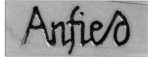

TOM ANFIELD BLACK SOLID-BODY

THE COLOR SCHEME for the Tom Anfield model in these photographs was partly inspired by the space ship control panel, featuring black labels on a black background, described in Douglas Adams' *Hitchhiker's Guide to the Galaxy*! Fortunately, the guitar's layout is easier to navigate than anything encountered by Adams' Zaphod Beeblebrox—although its "Strat-like" appearance conceals some surprises.

The uppermost of the instrument's three black knobs adjusts its overall volume, just as it would on a Stratocaster, but pulling it operates a coil-tap on the humbucking neck pickup (made, like the other transducers, by Kent Armstrong). The middle knob serves both as a tone control and to switch the center

Below: The guitar has an alder body supplied by WD Music; its vibrato is a Wilkinson VS100.

The BJS Legend has a three-piece neck, crafted from flame maple. The same wood is used for its body bindings.

Right: *The Legend's non-flame maple back and sides provide a pleasing visual contrast to its neck timber.*

Left: *European spruce is used for the instrument's top; its single humbucking pickup, which is attached to the pickguard, is designed by British luthier Mike Vanden.*

The Legend's fingerboard is made from ebony.

Below: *These tailpiece inlays, like those on the rest of the guitar, are abalone.*

more than half a century, Jim is believed to have played on over 1,000 hit singles—and is also famous for giving lessons to future Deep Purple axeman Ritchie Blackmore! He remains active as a performer and teacher, and has expressed his delight with Alan Arnold's fittingly named "BJS Legend," commenting recently that "[its] sounds, both electronic and acoustic, are out of this world."

ART & LUTHERIE CEDAR CUTAWAY

THE ART & LUTHERIE line of guitars, designed and manufactured in La Patrie, Canada, is the brainchild of Robert Godin (the creator of several other major guitar brands, such as Godin itself, and Norman—see individual entries for these), who established it to produce what he describes as "entry-level acoustics that would bring the key attributes of pro-quality [instruments] within the reach of novice players." Only a few decades ago, such an aim would probably have been doomed to failure; but recent high-tech developments in manufacturing have helped to bring about dramatic improvements in the once dire quality of many inexpensive flat-tops, and Art & Lutherie models such as the Cedar Cutaway seen here are among the very best of their kind.

Like many of the company's acoustics, it has a solid

Below: The cedar top that gives the model its name is finished in "Transparent Blue."

PHOTOGRAPHS COURTESY OF THE HOUSE OF GUITARS, LONDON

Above: *The nut on this guitar, like its bridge saddle, is made from the bone substitute Tusq.*

Rosewood is used for the A&L's fingerboard.

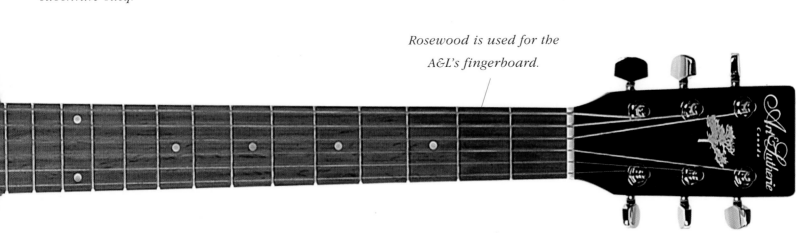

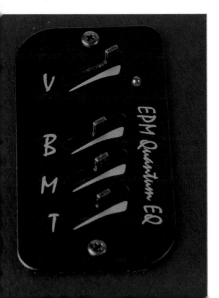

Left: *Pickup systems are now commonly found on cheaper acoustics. This preamp unit is fairly simple, but effective.*

top (a feature once almost unheard of in a modestly priced guitar), and its pleasing sound and easy action will serve as an inspiration and encouragement to the beginner. The silver-leaf maple used for its neck is grown in Canada itself, as are 95% of all A&L's tonewoods, and the Cedar Cutaway also boasts a built-in Godin-designed Quantum undersaddle pickup and preamp. Various finishes are available.

ATKIN OM-DELUXE

ACOUSTIC GUITARS by UK-based luthier Alister Atkin are highly sought after, and his famous customers include major names such as Sinéad O'Connor, singer-songwriter Boo Hewerdine (who first came to prominence in the mid-1980s with The Bible), Eddi Reader, Chris Difford of Squeeze, Amrit Sond, and members of Status Quo.

Atkin first became interested in lutherie while still at school, and after studying the subject at the London School of Furniture, he set up Atkin Guitars in 1994 in the city of Canterbury, some 55 miles southeast of the capital. For a while, he shared premises there with a longer-established local guitar maker, Andy Crockett (an archtop specialist whose instruments are currently used by leading British jazzmen such as Jim Mullen), but now has his own workshop. He produces seven models, all based on classic styles from the 1930s: a 00, 000 and OM, two jumbos, a Dreadnought and a J-45-type flat-top.

A deluxe version of an Atkin OM is shown in our photographs: it sports a sitka spruce top, a back and sides of Brazilian rosewood, and a Brazilian mahogany

Below: The OM (Orchestra Model) is one of Atkin's most popular instruments.

Above: This book-matched back provides an especially attractive effect.

neck with an ebony fingerboard and headstock overlay. The guitar has a nitro-cellulose finish, and its "Atkin" logo is inlaid with mother of pearl. Its gold-plated machine heads are made by Schaller.

Left: These decorations are created using abalone.

BAMBINO GUITAR (19th CENTURY)

MADAME SIDNEY PRATTEN (1821-1895) played a key role in popularizing the guitar among well-to-do Britons during the Victorian era. Born Catherina Josepha Pelzer, she was the daughter of a London-based German guitarist, Ferdinand Pelzer. After building up a reputation as a child prodigy through appearances, often with her father, at concerts and soirées in the capital, she went on to enjoy a highly successful adult career as a recitalist and teacher, and, following her marriage to an English flutist, Robert Sidney Pratten, in 1854, was wealthy enough to set up home in London's fashionable West End. There, pupils drawn from the ranks of the nobility and gentry would come to her for guitar tuition, although she herself would sometimes visit stately homes and palaces to

provide lessons for her highest-born students, who included Queen Victoria's daughters, Princesses Louise and Beatrice. Many of these budding guitarists traveled widely, and would not have wished to carry a full-size guitar with them for practice: it was probably for their convenience that Madame Pratten provided and recommended "bambino" guitars such as the one seen in our photographs.

The name "bambino" (Italian for "child") is somewhat misleading: modern experts are adamant that these little instruments were not intended for very young players, as they would have encouraged incorrect hand placement and other bad technique. They are also dismissive of Madame Pratten's own claim to have invented the "bambino:" as guitar

This bridge is typical of an English guitar of the period.

Right: *Fishman preamps are factory fitted to many Breedloves.*

Above: *The edgings on the SC 25 are plain, but its woods are clearly of the finest quality.*

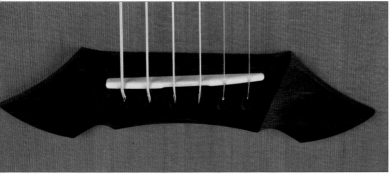

aesthetic," but feature premium tonewoods, as well as meticulous design and construction.

An SC 25 is featured in our photographs: it is a "simplified concert" model, with black bindings and a 15 inch maximum body width, and sports the "soft" cutaway designed in the 1990s by company co-founder Steve Henderson to replace Larry Breedlove's more dramatically angled one.

BREEDLOVE J 25-12

THE J 25-12 jumbo-bodied 12-string that appears on these pages is part of Breedlove's "Premier Line" of acoustic guitars. Premiers are priced above the "S" series described on the last two pages, and form the basis for the Custom Shop models that represent the company's *crème de la crème*. However, many players will be delighted with the "standard-issue" Premier J 25-12, which can be supplied with or without a soft cutaway, and whose sound has been described by Breedlove as "big, but beautifully well balanced—an elegant combination of power and contro." A companion 6-string J 25 is also available.

Since its formation in 1990, Breedlove has developed into what its president, Peter Newport (quoted by Dave Burrluck in his previously mentioned article for *Guitarist* magazine) has described as "the largest custom shop I know of." It currently produces in the region of 1,000 guitars a year in the USA, and, in

Alternative versions of the J 25-12 have included a limited edition all-walnut model, produced in 2006.

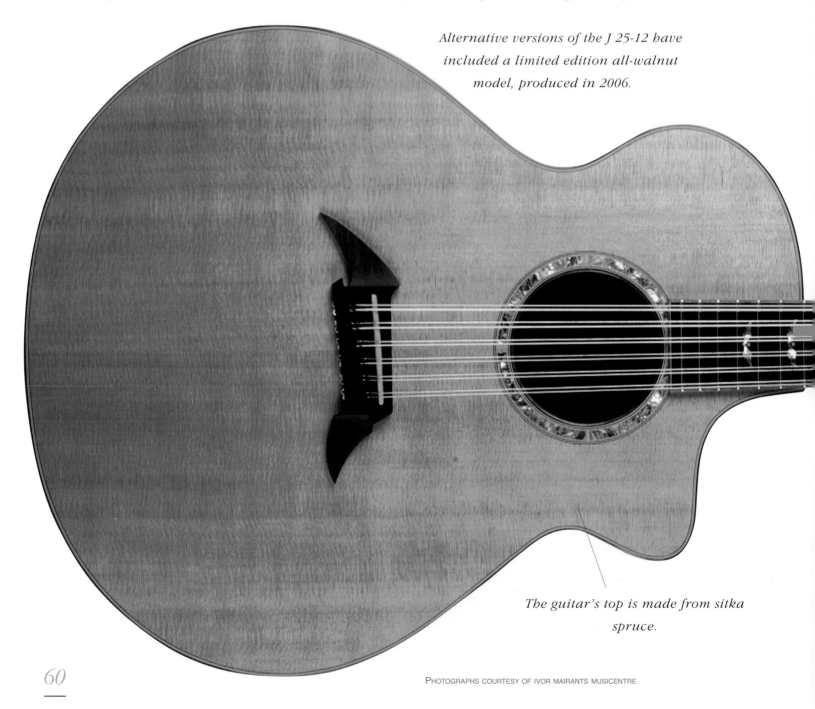

The guitar's top is made from sitka spruce.

Above: The J 25-12's back and sides are made from myrtlewood grown in the region near its Oregon factory.

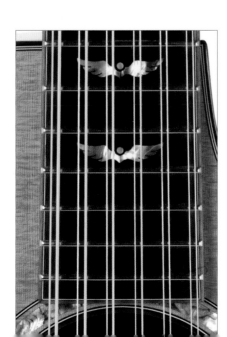

Above right: This soft cutaway gives exceptional access to the upper frets.

Right: "Wings" position markers grace the J 25-12's fingerboard.

2004, launched its new Korean-built "Atlas" acoustic range. This comprises flat-tops, nylon-strungs and basses, all of which are designed by Kim Breedlove, and subjected to careful quality checks at the company's Oregon headquarters before being shipped to dealers. The Atlas line has been highly acclaimed in the press and by players; it includes the AC200/SM, a solid sitka spruce-topped guitar with laminated mahogany back and sides that sells for under $700.

*Some Creedys are made with cedar tops,
instead of the spruce seen here.*

BROOK CREEDY 010

BROOK GUITARS operates from a small workshop in the English county of Devon. Its co-owners, Simon Smidmore and Andy Petherick, are both protégés of luthier Andy Manson (see separate entry); before meeting him and becoming involved in guitar building, Smidmore had been a carpenter, and Petherick an engineer. The two men set up Brook in 1995, and went on to spend a number of years making instruments for Manson, although they now concentrate on producing their own

Above: The Creedy's bridge is rosewood.

designs. These range from dreadnought, jumbo and bass models to small-size travel guitars, each of which is named for a Devonshire river.

The Creedy shown on these pages is a parlor-style flat-top with 12 frets to the body, and a lower bout width of approximately 12.4 inches. It is made from a classic combination of woods: spruce for its top and figured rosewood for its back and sides. Brook guitars are available with two alternative trims: '010'-type instruments like this one have an unbound headstock and fingerboard, mother-of-pearl fingerboard markers, herringbone purfling and chrome hardware, while '015' guitars boast a bound headstock and fingerboard, diamond and dot fingerboard markers, gold tuners, and an abalone rosette.

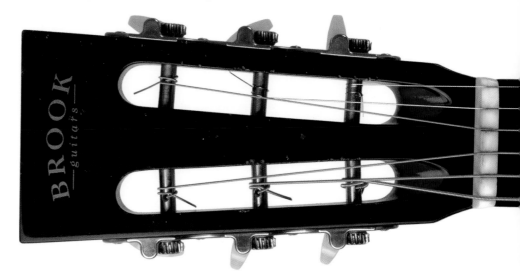

Right: This model dates from 2003, and is still in production at Brook Guitars.

AMALIO BURGUET 1F

V ALENCIA, ON THE MEDITERRANEAN coast of Spain, is an important musical center, and a number of leading guitar makers are based near the city. Alboraya, just to its north, is the home of Esteve Guitars (see separate entry), while in the opposite direction lies the village of Catarroja, the birthplace and headquarters of Amalio Burguet.

Born in 1951, Burguet developed a fascination for the classical and flamenco guitar at an early age, and went on to study both music and instrument building before opening his first, small-scale lutherie workshop. In 1994, he and an expanded staff began operating from their current premises, where, as Burguet explains on his website, they now combine modern production techniques with individual craftsmanship to create guitars that will offer "unsurpassed value to the working musician."

Models such as the "1F" seen here are clear proof of the Burguet company's success. A professional quality, though reasonably priced flamenco guitar, it is available with a spruce or cedar top, while its body is made from cypress, a lightweight wood often chosen to give flamenco instruments their characteristic liveliness and vibrancy.

Below: The 1F has a cedar neck and an ebony fingerboard. A cutaway-bodied version of the guitar can also be supplied.

This headstock has a rosewood overlay.

Left: A vividly patterned rosette and a high-gloss finish add to the Burguet's visual impact.

Amalio Burguet promises his customers "a hand-made Spanish guitar at an affordable price."

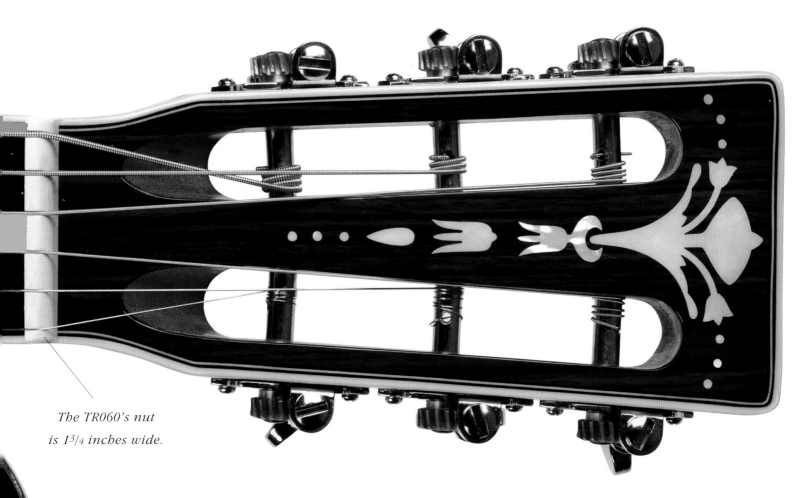

The TR060's nut is 1³/4 inches wide.

Above: *The guitar's attractively decorated headstock and high-gloss finish ensure that it looks as good as it sounds.*

These "antique-style" tuners are made from chrome.

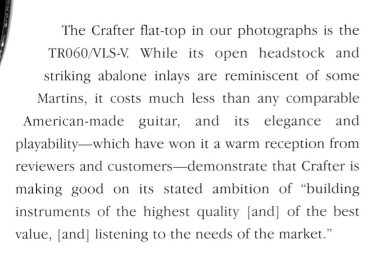

The Crafter flat-top in our photographs is the TR060/VLS-V. While its open headstock and striking abalone inlays are reminiscent of some Martins, it costs much less than any comparable American-made guitar, and its elegance and playability—which have won it a warm reception from reviewers and customers—demonstrate that Crafter is making good on its stated ambition of "building instruments of the highest quality [and] of the best value, [and] listening to the needs of the market."

CRAFTER ACOUSTIC BASS

THE ACOUSTIC BASS GUITAR was originally developed by Californian musician and entrepreneur Ernie Ball in the early 1970s; he considered it a natural companion to the regular acoustic 6-string, and some features of his early designs were inspired by the bass "guitarron" used in Mexican mariachi ensembles. Although it took at least ten more years for the acoustic bass to catch on, it is now widely used by folk and country artists—and also attracts rock players wishing to venture into quieter, "unplugged" ensemble work. Once a somewhat costly and esoteric instrument, it is currently available at all price levels: the Crafter GAB24S/N model shown here, though inexpensive, is impressively specified (a built-in pickup and preamp are fitted as standard), and built from high-quality tonewoods.

The Crafter bass's neck, which has a 32-inch scale length, is mahogany; its fingerboard is made from Indian rosewood.

Gold diecast machine heads with "mushroom"-shaped buttons add to the GAB24S/N's visual appeal.

Pre-amp controls for the instrument's L.R. Baggs pickup are mounted on its shoulder.

The bass's A-braced top is made from solid sitka spruce; its back and sides are rosewood.

Opposite page: *The GAB24S/N bass is part of the Korean Crafter company's "professional series." The N suffix refers to its "natural" finish.*

D'ANGELICO EXCEL, 1949

JOHN D'ANGELICO (1905-1964) was a New Yorker of Italian extraction. After learning his lutherie skills from his great-uncle, an eminent violin and mandolin builder, he established a shop of his own in the Little Italy district of his home city in 1932. There, he and a small number of assistants and apprentices crafted handmade archtop guitars based around four model types, Style A, Style B, Excel and New Yorker—though individual instruments were frequently customized in line with players' requirements. His output was comparatively small: guitar expert George Gruhn, writing in 1980, estimated that "during the late 1930s, when production was at its peak, D'Angelico was able to make approximately 35 instruments per year."

No more Style As or Bs appeared after the 1940s, but D'Angelico continued to make his other two archtop models until his death in 1964. He built his first cutaway-body guitar in 1947, and the new shape proved highly successful; this elegant, lovingly preserved cutaway Excel dates from two years later.

Below: The "finial" ornament within the cutout of this headstock is a characteristic D'Angelico feature.

Above: High quality Grover tuners were John D'Angelico's first choice for his instruments.

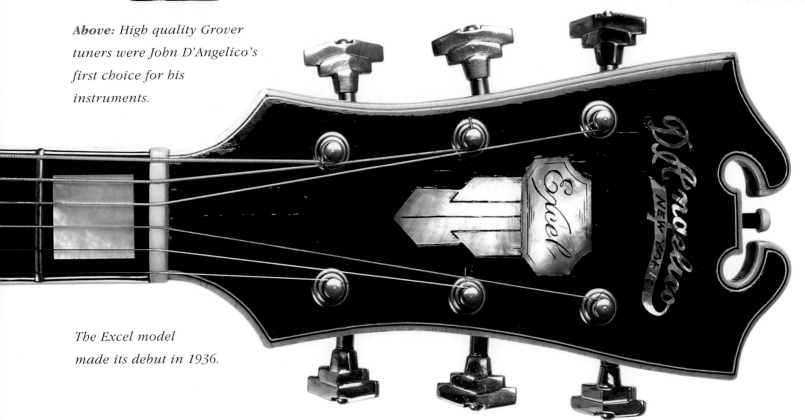

The Excel model made its debut in 1936.

The tailpiece
seen below is
not the original
one fitted by
D'Angelico.

This Excel is
17 inches wide,
and has a solid
spruce top.

The Excel has
a spruce top,
and maple is
used for its back
and sides.

Left: The EXS-1DH
is 16 inches wide—
an inch smaller than
John D'Angelico's own
Excels. However, a
17-inch version is
also available.

D'ANGELICO EXS-1DH

ORIGINAL EXAMPLES OF JOHN D'ANGELICO'S lutherie like the one seen on our previous pages are treasured by collectors, and, if they come onto the market, will often change hands for tens of thousands of dollars. Since 1988, however, high quality, but more affordable D'Angelico replicas have been made in Japan under the supervision of a New Jersey-based firm, D'Angelico Guitars of America. The Excel EXS-1DH is the most inexpensive archtop in the company's current range, but is a loving recreation of John D'Angelico's design. Its name derives from New York's state motto "Excelsior" ("Ever upward"), and it includes characteristic D'Angelico features such as "split-rectangle" fret markers, and the Art Deco-inspired headstock with its "keyhole" cutout and "stairstep" truss-rod cover. The "stairstep" motif can also be seen on the tailpiece and pickguard, and the model is available in a "vintage natural" finish (as shown) or in six alternative shades.

The EXS-1DH's fretboard is ebony.

Above: *The Excel's gold-plated hardware includes a fully adjustable bridge and two humbucking pickups made by Kent Armstrong.*

Right: *Like John D'Angelico's own guitars, this model has a hinged, solid brass tailpiece.*

D'ANGELICO NYL-2 (NEW YORKER)

THE D'ANGELICO NEW YORKER featured here, like the Excel EXS-1DH, is a modern replica made by D'Angelico Guitars of America. The New Yorker, which debuted in 1936, was John D'Angelico's "top of the line" model; and, like his own guitars, this one combines handsome looks with what a reviewer for *Just Jazz Guitar*, Dr. Ken Ciuffreda, described in 2001 as "a rich and deep jazz tone." Its 17-inch top is an inch narrower than D'Angelico's original New Yorkers, but this and other cosmetic and constructional discrepancies do not detract from the appeal of an instrument that, in the words of another critic, Doug Munro of *Jazz Times* magazine, "has all the classic D'Angelico trademarks, with the same headstock and tailpiece we fondly remember."

As John D'Angelico's health declined towards the end of his life, he came to rely increasingly upon the skills and energy of his last apprentice, Jimmy D'Aquisto, whom he had taken on in 1952. Those who knew both men have commented on the strong emotional bond—closer to a father-son relationship than that of an employer and trainee—that clearly existed between them, and there are significant links between D'Angelico's work and the designs produced by D'Aquisto during his own later career. These are explored on the following pages.

Right: The inlay at the center of the D'Angelico New Yorker's headstock is a stylized representation of the Big Apple's Chrysler building.

D'AQUISTO NEW YORKER DQ-NYE

JOHN D'ANGELICO'S LAST GUITARS were assembled by his apprentice, Jimmy D'Aquisto. After D'Angelico's death, D'Aquisto (1935-1995) established his own lutherie business, but continued to produce the Excel and New Yorker archtop models created by his mentor. At first, there was little difference between his versions and the originals, but in time, D'Aquisto—who, as his friend and fellow guitar maker John Monteleone told this author in 1999, "was always torn between living the legacy of John and being himself"—began to invest these classic designs with his own distinctive touches. By the late 1960s, his New Yorkers had acquired reshaped f-holes, and D'Angelico's "Chrysler Building" headstock inlay had been replaced with a scroll-type decoration; and by the '70s, he had abandoned his predecessor's brass tailpieces, substituting ebony ones. These and other modifications are visible on the replica D'Aquisto New Yorker in our photographs—and before long, Jimmy's guitars were to demonstrate more radical new ideas.

Below: The pickguard on this D'Aqusto replica has no D'Angelico-style "stairsteps."

Opposite page: D'Aquisto-style f-holes are elliptical, lacking any center stroke.

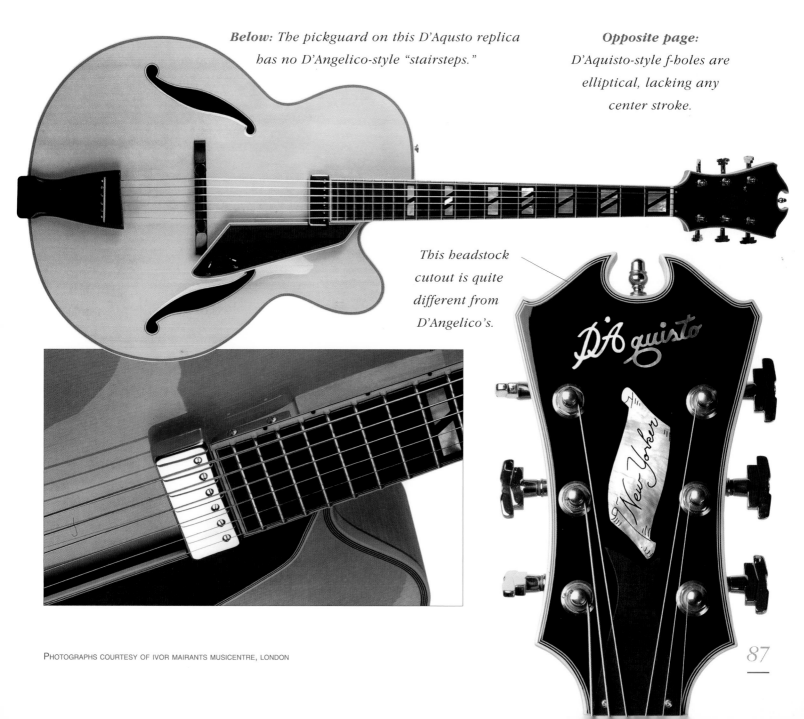

This headstock cutout is quite different from D'Angelico's.

D'AQUISTO CENTURA DQ-CR

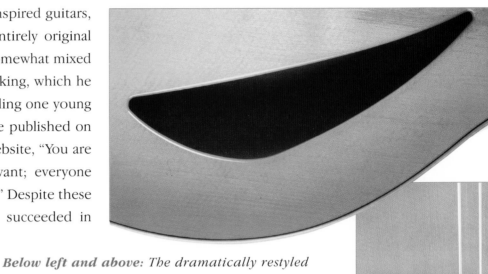

A S WELL AS BUILDING D'Angelico-inspired guitars, Jimmy D'Aquisto created many entirely original instruments. They seem to reflect his somewhat mixed attitude to the traditions of archtop making, which he revered, but often felt inhibited by—telling one young luthier, as Ken Vose reveals in an article published on the Museum of Musical Instruments' website, "You are so lucky. You can do anything you want; everyone expects me to build what I always build." Despite these words, however, D'Aquisto frequently succeeded in

Below left and above: The dramatically restyled openings in the Centura's spruce top can now no longer really be described as f-holes!

Above: The Centura's ebony fretboard has a maple binding.

both surprising and delighting customers and critics with his designs. Among the last instruments he completed before his death, aged only 59, was one of his striking "Centura" guitars, and a recreation of this model is shown here.

Resonator GCE "has exactly what I'm looking for…no matter what kind of gig [I'm doing.]"

In 2004, Dean introduced two new "Heirloom" resonators: like their predecessors, they are proving popular among blues players with limited funds. Both are single-cones: they share the same basic specification, and differ only in their body materials: "distressed brass," and (as here) "distressed copper."

Top left: The neck on this model (and on its brass-bodied companion) is mahogany, with a rosewood fingerboard.

Top right: Dean's distinctive logo graces the Heirloom's headstock.

Below: The Dell' Arte Anouman has a spruce top, and its back and sides are made from Indian rosewood.

DELL' ARTE ANOUMAN

IN THE MID-1930s, the emergence of the great gypsy guitarist Django Reinhardt (1910-1953) brought an exciting new dimension to the international jazz scene. Though he occasionally used electrics in his later career, Reinhardt is most closely associated with the powerful-sounding acoustic models created by an Italian, Mario Maccaferri (1900-1993) and marketed in France by the Selmer company. Instruments of this type remain unrivaled for Django-style playing, and since Selmer ceased producing them in the 1950s, there has been a thriving market for replicas and reworkings of Maccaferri's designs.

Among the very finest Maccaferri-style guitars to appear in recent years are those made by Dell' Arte Instruments in Santee, California. Its owners, luthier John S. Kinnard, a former Taylor staffer who also has experience as a jewelry maker, and French-born guitarist and Maccaferri devotee Alain Cola, have been working together since 1998, and their acoustics attract customers from all over the USA and Europe.

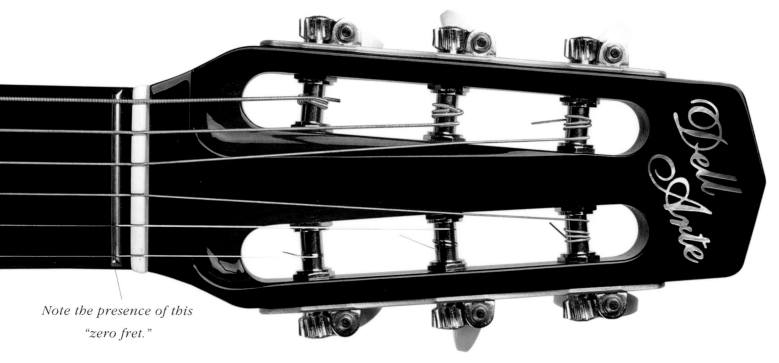

Note the presence of this "zero fret."

Above: Gold Gotoh machine heads are fitted to the Anouman.
Left: The string anchors on Maccaferri-type tailpieces were originally designed to accommodate both ball-ended and loop-ended strings. Today, only the former are used.

These rectangles form one of the standard decorative patterns found on Dobro coverplates.

Below: *The earliest Dobros were all wood-bodied; this model was made under license by the Chicago-based Regal company in the mid-1930s.*

DOBRO (1)

IN EARLY 1929, John Dopyera (1893-1988) resigned from the board of the Los Angeles-based National company. His departure followed a dispute over the ownership of the design for a single-cone resonator providing mechanical amplification for guitars and other instruments (see the National entries).

Like many Regal Dobros, this instrument has 14 frets to the body.

Dopyera and his brother Rudy had previously collaborated on the development of these resonators for National, and, together with their other siblings Emil, Robert and Louis, they now formed a rival resonator guitar making firm named Dobro. Its name is an abbreviation of "Dopyera Brothers," and also means "good" in Slovak, the Dopyeras' native language.

Prevented from using the single-cone resonator they had devised during their time at National, John and Rudy Dopyera invented an alternative one, whose specification is explained overleaf. Rudy filed a patent application for it in June 1929, though, according to some experts, Dobro instruments incorporating the new design were already on the market by this time.

The guitar's fingerboard and headstock facing are rosewood.

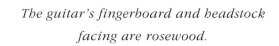

The guitar's engraved body is made from nickel-plated brass.

DOBRO (2)

UNLIKE A NATIONAL RESONATOR—whose convex aluminum alloy cone is positioned rather like a saucepan lid inside an instrument, with a wooden "biscuit" bridge, which transfers energy from the strings, at its apex—the equivalent Dobro unit, though also made from aluminum, is dish shaped. Its bridge, nicknamed a "spider," is metal as well, and has a central section (with a wooden saddle mounted on top of it) making contact with the strings, plus eight radiating "legs" that carry vibrations to the edges of the cone.

The sound created by this system has more resonance and longer sustain than that of a single-cone National, while the latter provides a brasher, punchier quality; however, both designs are more or less equally effective in boosting audibility.

Thanks to the rapid success of their new guitars, the Dopyera brothers were soon struggling to supply potential customers, and in 1932, they signed a licensing agreement with a major Chicago manufacturer, Regal, which began producing Dobro

Below: This Dobro sports floral engravings on its coverplate as well as its body.

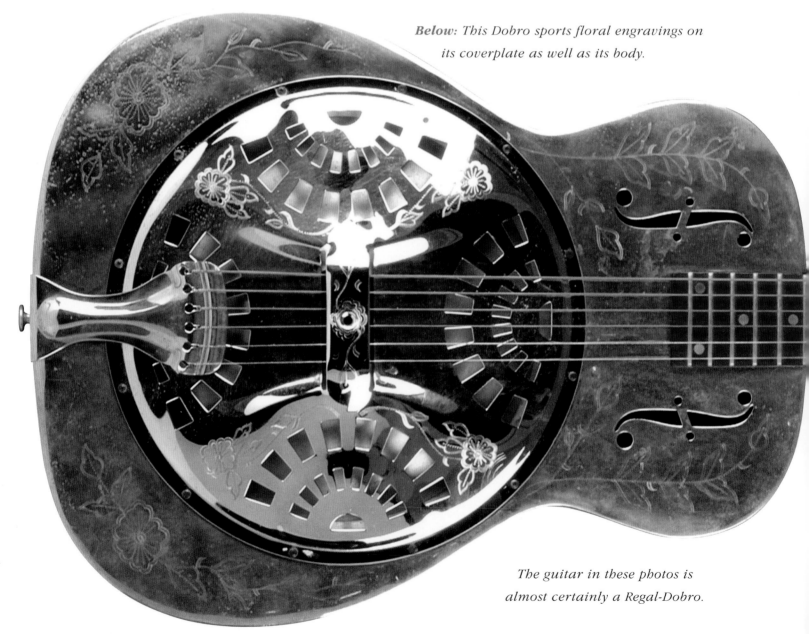

The guitar in these photos is almost certainly a Regal-Dobro.

PHOTOGRAPHS COURTESY OF CHANDLER GUITARS, KEW

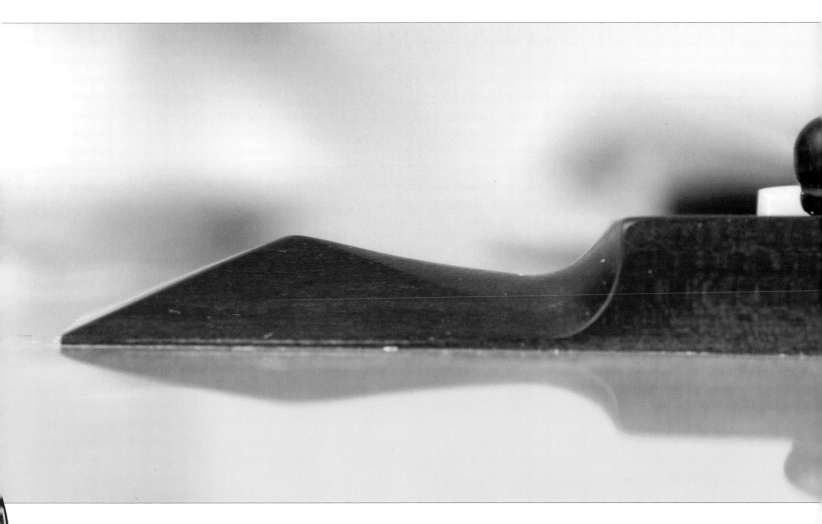

Above: These "pyramid" bridge elevations resemble those on pre-war Martins.

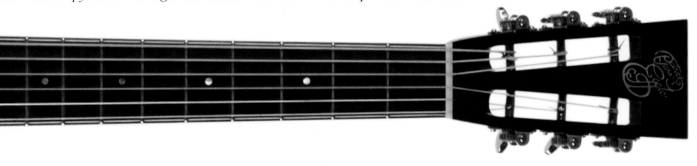

Right: The luthier's name is inlaid with mother-of-pearl.

The Etowah shown here has a sitka spruce top, and a back, sides and neck of Honduran mahogany; it is especially responsive to fingerpicking playing styles, and offers a sparkling high end response as well as deep, resonant bass. Eggle's publicity describes it as "an instant heirloom, [that] will become the guitar you use when you finally write that ballad you've been thinking about."

PATRICK JAMES EGGLE ETOWA CUSTOM

ON THE PREVIOUS two pages, we showed a standard Patrick James Eggle Etowah flat-top; here, we feature a customized version of the same design. The guitar in these photos was awarded the bronze medal in the 2005 "Gear of the Year" contest held by the leading UK music magazine *Guitar & Bass*.

This "luxury" Etowah sports a top made from Adirondack (red) spruce—a highly prized (and very expensive) tonewood that is denser and stiffer along the grain than either sitka or Engelmann spruce, and provides exceptional sonic richness. Indian Rosewood replaces mahogany for the instrument's body and sides, while the mother-of-pearl "snowflakes" decorating its fingerboard, and the abalone "torch" that graces its headstock, were specially created for Patrick James Eggle by Tom Ellis, an Austin, Texas-based craftsman whose work has also appeared on guitars by Taylor, Collings and Paul Reed Smith.

Below: Adirondack spruce, used here for the Etowa's top, was more plentiful in the 1920s and 30s, and appears on many fine pre-war acoustics.

These ebony bridge pins have abalone inlays.

ETOWAH 050604

Patrick James Eggle Custom Guitars
—HANDCRAFTED—
HENDERSONVILLE, NORTH CAROLINA, USA

Patrick James Eggle's signature appears on the Etowah's soundhole label.

Above top and right:
Other optional decorations for custom Etowahs include "tree of life" fingerboard inlays, and "flowerpot," "floral," or "scroll" headstock embellishments.

EKO RANGER XII

THE BOOM IN FOLK MUSIC, largely inspired by Bob Dylan, that swept across much of the Western world in the 1960s led to a massive demand for flat-top acoustic guitars. The finest of these, such as Gibsons and Martins, were US-made, but many players could not afford them—especially overseas, where the instruments' already high prices were raised further by import taxes. Local manufacturers eagerly stepped in to supply less costly substitutes, and among the most successful was the Italian company Eko.

Based in Recanati, on the country's Adriatic coast, the firm was founded in 1960 by Oliviero Pigini (1922–1967). Initially, it imported guitars from Yugoslavia, but in 1964, it opened its own factory in its hometown, from which it was soon turning out a substantial range of electric and acoustic models. An

Below: This Ranger XII dates from about 1969, and has survived over three decades of use with barely a scratch!

Eko Rangers (the name was chosen for its "Wild West" resonances) were produced in 6- and 12-string versions.

Right: The "star-marked" bridge pins were a notable feature of Eko Rangers; sadly, one is missing from the model shown here.

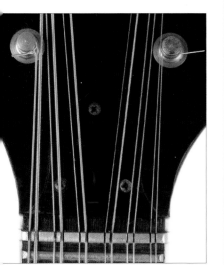

Below: The action, often uncomfortably high on older, less expensive 12-strings, remains very manageable on the Eko Ranger.

The Ranger's "zero fret" prevents excessive "ringing" on its open strings.

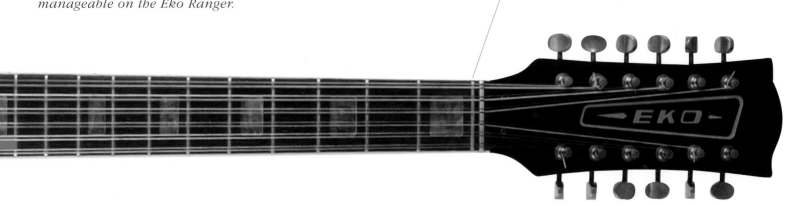

Eko catalog from this period describes these as "the result of years of experience and engineering know-how, coupled with a desire to create exceptionally fine musical instruments." In fact, Pigini's early background had been in accordion making rather than lutherie, and, as music historian Paul Day observes in ***Classic Guitars of the 50s & 60s*** (published by Merchant Books in 2004), the elaborate finishes and multiplicity of controls found on many Eko solid-bodies are strongly reminiscent of those found on squeeze-boxes, or even espresso machines!

Eko flat-tops from the 1960s, like the 12-string shown here, are a little plainer, and all the better for it: their robust construction and powerful tone endeared them to many European pickers, and the guitars even found a ready market in the USA, where they were distributed by the Milwaukee-based LoDuca Brothers. Today, they are widely regarded as collectors' items.

Above: Both single and dual pickup Olympics were available. Each had these distinctive control knobs.

In 1963, the "Mark 1" 1960-style Olympic was replaced by a wholly different design sporting an asymmetrical body, with a Greek "epsilon" Epiphone symbol emblazoned on its pickguard. It retained its old, Melody Maker-like headstock for another year before acquiring a "6-a-side" tuner arrangement. It is this incarnation of the Olympic that is shown here, although our example has lost the epsilon from between its pickups, and its vibrato (added to the model as standard in the mid-60s) has been removed. Both the "regular" Olympic and the Olympic Special went out of production in 1970.

EPIPHONE FRONTIER

THE PRESSURES and impending restrictions of wartime did not prevent Epiphone from launching an extensive range of new instruments in 1942. Among them were several acoustic, dreadnought-style models named with simple catalog codes comprising an FT ("flat-top") prefix followed by a number. One of the most popular of these guitars proved to be the FT-110, the immediate ancestor of the Epiphone Frontier seen here: the FT-30 (later known as the "Caballero") and the FT-79 ("Texan") debuted at the same time.

In its original form, the FT-110 was round-shouldered, and had a comparatively plain finish. Like other Epiphone flat-tops, it acquired a squarer shape when Gibson took over the firm in 1957, and it was also thanks to the bosses at Kalamazoo that it and its cousins were given their "Western"-sounding names. In 1964, the Frontier went on to receive its distinctive "cactus-and-rope"-decorated pickguard, and its "cowboy" image was further emphasized in mid-1960s Epiphone sales brochures, which promoted the

Below: Though the Frontier's appearance has altered over the years, its constituent woods (spruce top, and maple back and sides) have remained unchanged.

Above: The inlays on our 1964 Frontier's pickguard are still in almost pristine condition.

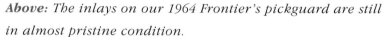

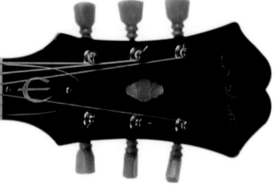

Above: The Frontier has a mahogany neck and a rosewood fretboard.

company's acoustics as "authentically American," and reminded customers that the flat-top guitar itself had "developed out of the need of the early pioneers for a rugged instrument which could stand up under the rough treatment of settling a young and growing country." The Frontier was discontinued in 1970, but has been periodically revived. The example in our photos was made in 1964.

EPIPHONE JOE PERRY LES PAUL

GIBSON'S TAKEOVER by Norlin Industries in 1969 led to major changes for Epiphone. Within a year, Epi manufacturing had been switched from Gibson headquarters at Kalamazoo, Michigan to the Far East, and the few surviving remnants of the brand's former distinctiveness were soon to vanish as it became little more than a conduit for cheap copies of existing Gibson models.

While Epiphone still serves as Gibson's lower-cost "companion marque," it has, nevertheless, recently regained a character of its own, and is currently producing a range of imaginatively designed guitars—some adapted from Gibson instruments, others wholly original. The Joe Perry Les Paul shown here falls into the former category: launched in 2004, it was inspired by a 2003 Gibson Signature Model endorsed by the Aerosmith star, and shares its predecessor's striking "Aged Tiger" finish, which was created by Perry's wife

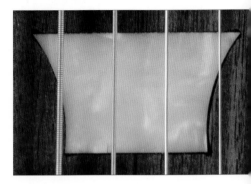

Right: The Joe Perry Boneyard sports classic Les Paul-style trapezoid fingerboard inlays.

Below: The guitar's "Aged Tiger" colored top is made from maple.

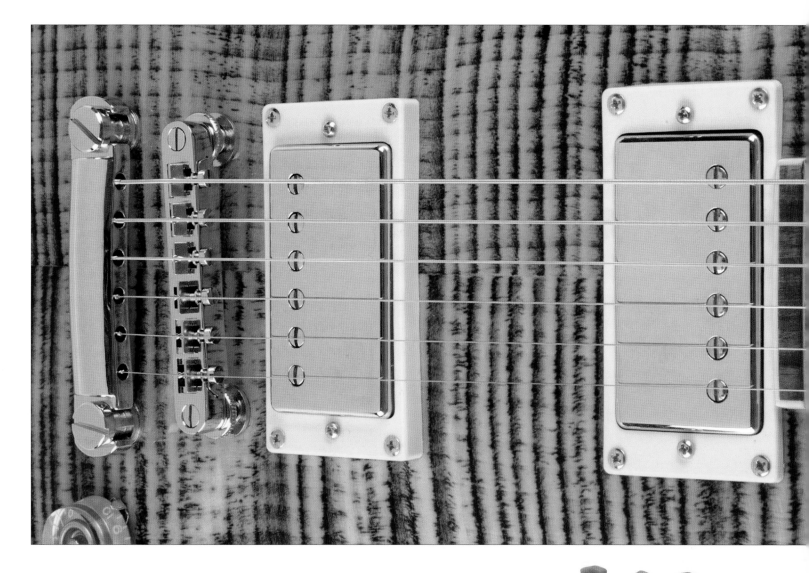

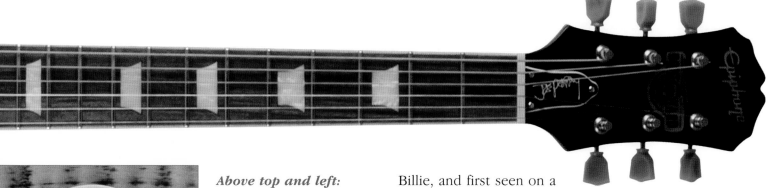

Above top and left:
Cream mountings for the guitar's pickups and selector switch contrast effectively with the surrounding yellow-green body pattern.

Billie, and first seen on a Gibson Custom Shop axe she gave him as a birthday gift. The Epiphone's other distinctive features include a "Boneyard" headstock logo: this can also be found on bottles of Perry's "Rock Your World Boneyard Brew" hot sauces! Its pickups, like those on the Signature Les Paul, are USA-made Burstbucker II and IIIs.

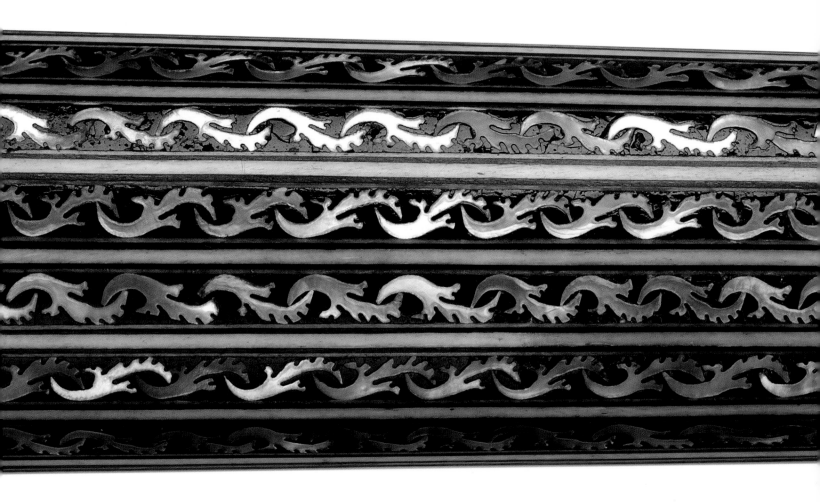

Below: *The instrument boasts an exquisitely decorated 11-fret fingerboard.*

Above: *.The "leaves" on the neck, as well as the lines between them, were produced by embedding pearl in black paste.*

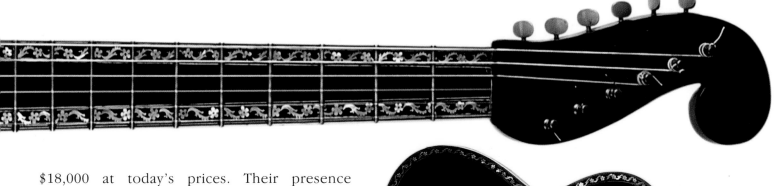

$18,000 at today's prices. Their presence suggests, as James Westbook comments in his book ***The Century That Shaped the Guitar***, that the instrument "may have been made...for a very special person, possibly royalty." There are no records of its original ownership, but it is undoubtedly a "one of a kind" creation.

FENDER "NO-CASTER" REPLICA

LEO FENDER (1909-1991) had been fascinated by electronics since boyhood, and, after a brief stint working as an accountant, he set up a radio repair shop in his hometown of Fullerton, California, in about 1939. One of his customers, local musician Clayton O. ("Doc") Kauffman, was also a skilled inventor and soon he and Fender were collaborating on the production of Hawaiian guitars and amplifiers. These were sold under the K&F brand name, and after the partnership ended in 1946, Leo founded his own Fender Electric

Instrument Company, also based in Fullerton.

Three years later, Fender began developing a solid-bodied electric for "Spanish-style" playing. Unlike the elegant archtop models then being made by other

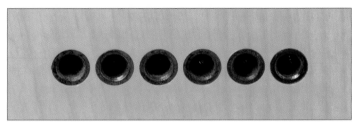

Above: This method of fastening strings inside the Fender guitar's body is straightforward and secure.

The Fender's "six-a-side" headstock was a novelty in 1950.

Above: Ash was used for the bodies on early Fender electrics. The first prototypes had no truss rods; these were added later to prevent the instruments' necks from warping.

firms, this guitar had an almost crude appearance, but, with its wooden-slab body and bolted-on neck, was easy to manufacture and repair. Named the Esquire, and fitted with a single pickup, it was first shown to the music trade in 1950. Leo subsequently changed various aspects of its specification, and added a second pickup; the revised model, rechristened Broadcaster, went into production in late 1950. However, in February 1951 the Gretsch company, which made Broadkaster drumkits, demanded the removal of the word "Broadcaster" from the guitar on the grounds of trademark infringement. For a while, therefore, new instruments left Fullerton with no names on their headstocks: these were later termed "No-casters," and a modern replica of one is shown here.

Right: *The simplicity of the Fender guitar's construction took the firm's rivals by surprise— but many were soon copying Leo's innovations.*

FENDER 1952 TELECASTER REPLICA

THE DISPUTE WITH GRETSCH over the use of the word "Broadcaster" left Leo Fender without a name for his innovative solid electric guitar. The decision to christen it Telecaster is usually attributed to Don Randall, whose Santa Ana-based Radio & Television Equipment Company acted as Fender's distributors. Thanks to the efforts of his sales force, the Tele was soon the talk of the music business—where some traditionalists reacted with distaste (and even outrage) to the spartan simplicity of its design, while others, including many professional players, were thrilled by its convenience and practicality.

Leo Fender himself continued to modify and refine the guitar's features throughout its early life; one significant change, introduced in 1952, removed its "deep soft rhythm" circuit, and the "blend" function for its two pickups, substituting the simpler switching described in the caption below.

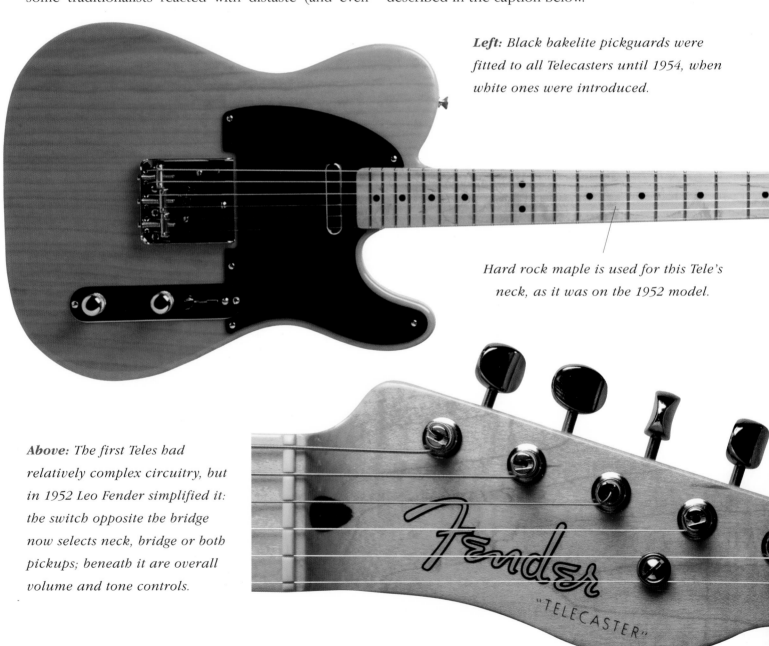

Left: Black bakelite pickguards were fitted to all Telecasters until 1954, when white ones were introduced.

Hard rock maple is used for this Tele's neck, as it was on the 1952 model.

Above: The first Teles had relatively complex circuitry, but in 1952 Leo Fender simplified it: the switch opposite the bridge now selects neck, bridge or both pickups; beneath it are overall volume and tone controls.

Right: Genuine 1952 Fender Telecasters are rare, and sell at many times the instrument's origimal price of just under $190. However, this skilfully aged replica is an effective "stand-in."

One of the Tele's selling points was its "modern styled head...with a stright pull for all strings."

These tuners closely resemble the Kluson units used by Fender in the 1950s.

FENDER PRECISION BASS

THE STAND-UP DOUBLE BASS, played pizzicato, had been a fixture in many popular music combos for much of the first half of the 20th century. However, it had three major drawbacks. The first was its limited volume: against a brass or sax section, let alone a drum kit or an electric guitar, a string bass would frequently struggle to be heard. Secondly, its size and unwieldiness created headaches (and backaches!) onstage—while in transit between gigs, the only space that could often be found for it was on the roof-racks of musicians' cars or tour buses. Last, but not least, were its intonation problems: novice bassists, with no frets to guide their left hands, could play excruciatingly out of tune; and even their more experienced colleagues sometimes struggled to stay in pitch when unable to hear themselves properly amid

Above: The Precision's metal pickup cover is sometimes removed by players who find it obtrusive.

Below: The "Dakota Red" finish on the 1961 model shown here has been expertly renewed.

The Precision Bass's fingerboard is made from rosewood.

PHOTOGRAPHS COURTESY OF GUITAR JUNCTION, WORTHING

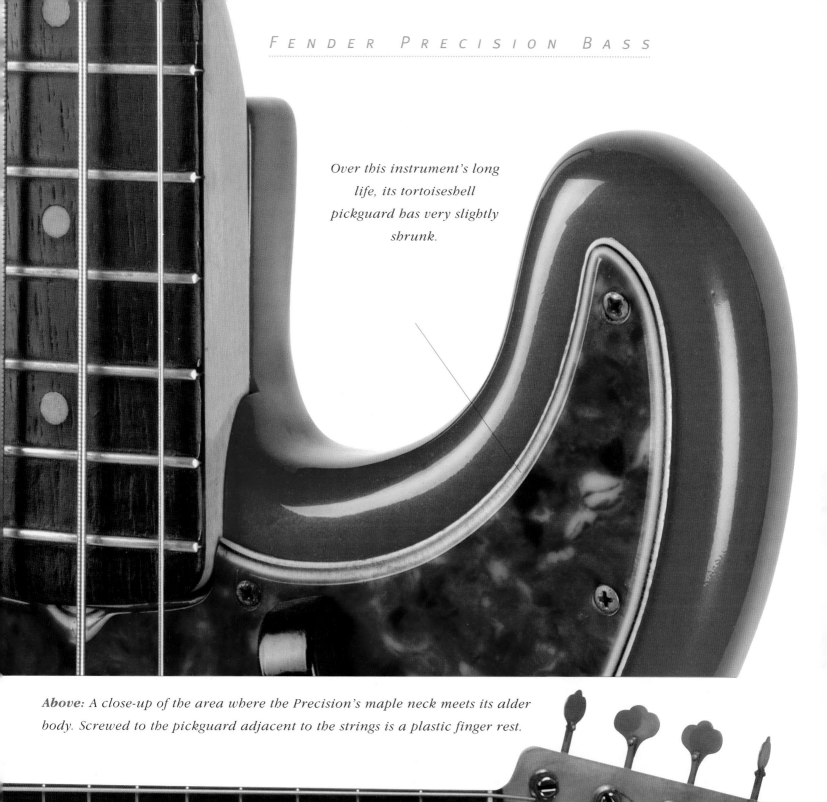

Over this instrument's long life, its tortoiseshell pickguard has very slightly shrunk.

Above: *A close-up of the area where the Precision's maple neck meets its alder body. Screwed to the pickguard adjacent to the strings is a plastic finger rest.*

the noisier instruments on the bandstand.

Leo Fender solved all three difficulties with his Precision bass guitar, launched in 1951. Its slim, solid body was far smaller and lighter than its "stand-up" cousin's; its single pickup supplied a clear, sustained sound from its strings; while its fretted neck guaranteed accurate intonation, and also made it easy for regular guitarists to "double" on the new instrument. The Precision quickly caught on, and soon, rival firms, including some that had initially dismissed Leo's instrument as a gimmick were eagerly designing their own electric basses.

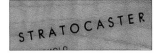

FENDER STRATOCASTER ("RELIC")

L EO FENDER'S STRATOCASTER appeared in 1954: his company's own publicity hailed it as "a revolutionary new instrument...years ahead in design [and] unequalled in performance," and it quickly took the guitar world by storm. Unlike its predecessor, the Telecaster, it sported a vibrato mechanism controlled by its pivoting bridge section, three pickups, a double cutaway, and a contoured body designed to be more comfortable to hold than the Tele's. (Interestingly, it was this latter feature that seemed to excite some contemporary commentators the most: in May 1954, **Music Trades** magazine observed that it "actually seems to make the guitar a part of the player...and must be seen and tried to be appreciated.")

Early Stratocasters are among the most collectible of all Fenders, and change hands at many times their original $249.50 price. For many enthusiasts, however, the deliberately aged "Relic" models first produced by the Fender Custom Shop in 1995 are pleasing and

Left: The recessed jack socket was another of the Stratocaster's innovative design features.

Below: This Relic Strat dates from 1996; like the original, its body is made from ash.

Screws and other hardware are as carefully "aged" as the guitar's body and neck.

Right: One of the pioneers of "aging" guitars is Vince Cunetto, a member of the original team that produced this and other "Relics" at Fender.

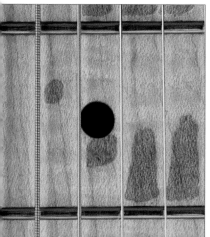

Left: These fake "wear spots" replicate the effects of decades of finger pressure and sweat on the Stratocaster's fingerboard.

desirable substitutes for one of these originals. The Relic seen here is a replica of the 1956 "custom-color" Strat with gold fittings used by singer and guitarist Mary Kaye—a major 50s and 60s star, whose trio enjoyed hits with songs such as "You Can't Be True Dear" and "Do You Believe In Dreams?"

Left: The Stratocaster's pickups and controls are all directly attached to its pickguard.

This is the 5-way pickup selector mentioned in the main text.

FENDER MARK KNOPFLER STRATOCASTER

GUITARISTS WERE SOON taking advantage of the Fender Stratocaster's capabilities—and occasionally using it in ways that surprised its creator. Its original pickup switch, for example, was a three-way device that "officially" enabled only one transducer to be selected at a time; however, by careful positioning, it was possible to activate two pickups (neck and center, or center and bridge) simultaneously, creating a characteristic, "out-of-phase" sound that would soon be widely exploited. It was not until 1977 (according to information from A.R. Duchossoir's exhaustive study of the Stratocaster) that the switch was replaced with a five-way component; in the meantime, players often resorted to using matchsticks to hold it in these intermediate settings.

Over the years, some performers have taken more extensive liberties with Leo Fender's design—changing pickups, adding electronics, and sometimes even fitting alternative vibrato units—but for others, the unaltered Stratocaster remains an unsurpassable tool. Among this category of contented musicians is Mark Knopfler, whose 1961 "Fiesta Red" model has featured on many of his classic recordings (including, most famously, Dire Straits' 1978/9 hit "Sultans of Swing"); he also continues to use it extensively onstage and in the studio. In 2003, Fender began producing replicas of Knopfler's Strat, one of which is shown here. Its woods and colors all match those of a '60s instrument, although it does have a 5-way pickup selector!

Below: The guitar's neck is maple, with a rosewood fretboard.

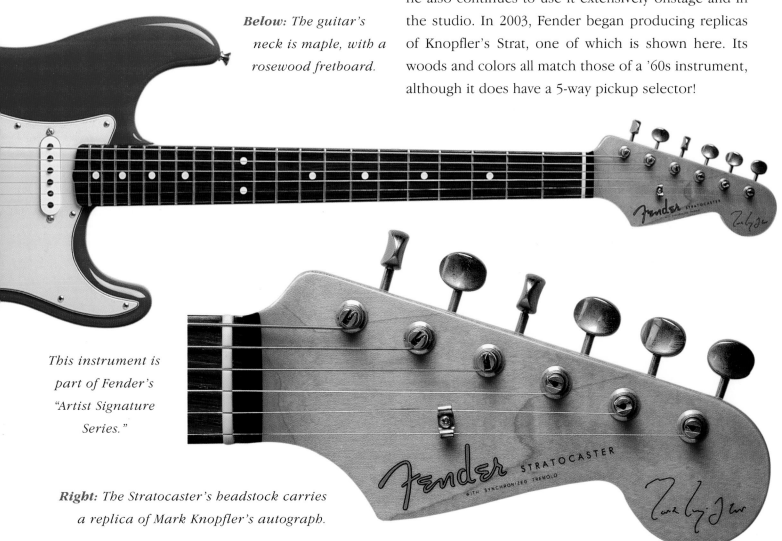

This instrument is part of Fender's "Artist Signature Series."

Right: *The Stratocaster's headstock carries a replica of Mark Knopfler's autograph.*

FENDER JAZZMASTER

WITHIN A FEW YEARS of launching the Stratocaster, Leo Fender was working on a major new electric guitar, the Jazzmaster. As its name suggested, this was aimed at the jazz fraternity rather than the rockers, country pickers and bluesmen that had favored the Telecaster and Strat, and it featured mellower sounding pickups, plus a switchable "rhythm circuit" for the neck transducer, allowing its volume and tone to be preset for playing backing chords. There was also a locking vibrato, and a body that was shaped to maximize comfort for seated players.

The guitar debuted in 1958 (though a prototype survives from the previous year), but failed to win over many jazz performers, and attracted a good deal of criticism for its unstable bridge, excessive weight, and odd shape: Fender plant manager Forrest White once likened it to a "pregnant duck"! Nevertheless, it has had many admirers, especially among "surf" guitarists and (later) punk and indie bands, and is recognized as a genuine, if quirky, Fender classic.

These two wheels set the volume and tone for the rhythm circuit controlled by the switch.

Above: *This Jazzmaster is a recently made one; the arm has been removed from its vibrato for our picture.*

Right: *The design of the guitar's headstock closely resembles that previously used for the Stratocaster.*

Below: *The strange, asymmetrical shape of the Jazzmaster's body was designed principally for the comfort of seated players, but did not improve its popularity with the jazz performers it was aimed at.*

Bottom: *The Fretless Precision has a curved rosewood fingerboard; the neck beneath it is made from hard rock maple.*

Above: *A 1970s Fender catalog described the Precision as "the most well-known and widely used electric bass in the world."*

removed the frets from his own standard Jazz model, and went on to feature it with the great jazz-rock band Weather Report, as well as on his own solo albums and session dates.

In 2006, Fender launched a new fretless Precision: it carries the signature of Tony Franklin, the English-born musician (famous for his work with Paul Rodgers and Jimmy Page in The Firm) who is also the company's Artist Relations Manager.

FENDER TELECASTER THINLINE

IN THE MID-TO-LATE 1960s, Fender and its CBS masters were hungry for novelty—and the increased profits that it could bring. Having already ventured into unfamiliar territory with its hollowbody Coronado range (see separate entry), the company now began experimenting with one of its staple products, the Telecaster. There had been concern that some players found the Tele too heavy, and in 1968, an attempt was made to solve this problem by routing out substantial sections of its body, adding an f-hole, and marketing the result as the Telecaster Thinline. Offered in a choice of "natural" finishes (mahogany or ash), the adapted Tele underwent a further modification in 1972, when its single-coil pickups were replaced with humbuckers designed by former Gibson staffer Seth Lover (these are fitted to the Thinline in our photos). The instrument was discontinued some six years later.

Right: The classic Fender pickup controls look rather different when surrounded by a glossy, smartly bound pickguard.

Below: The Thinline shown here dates from 1972, and has an ash body.

PHOTOGRAPHS COURTESY OF A PRIVATE COLLECTOR

Thanks to its carved out body, the Thinline is about 50% lighter than a standard Telecaster.

The classic Tele neck remains unaffected by the changes that created the Thinline.

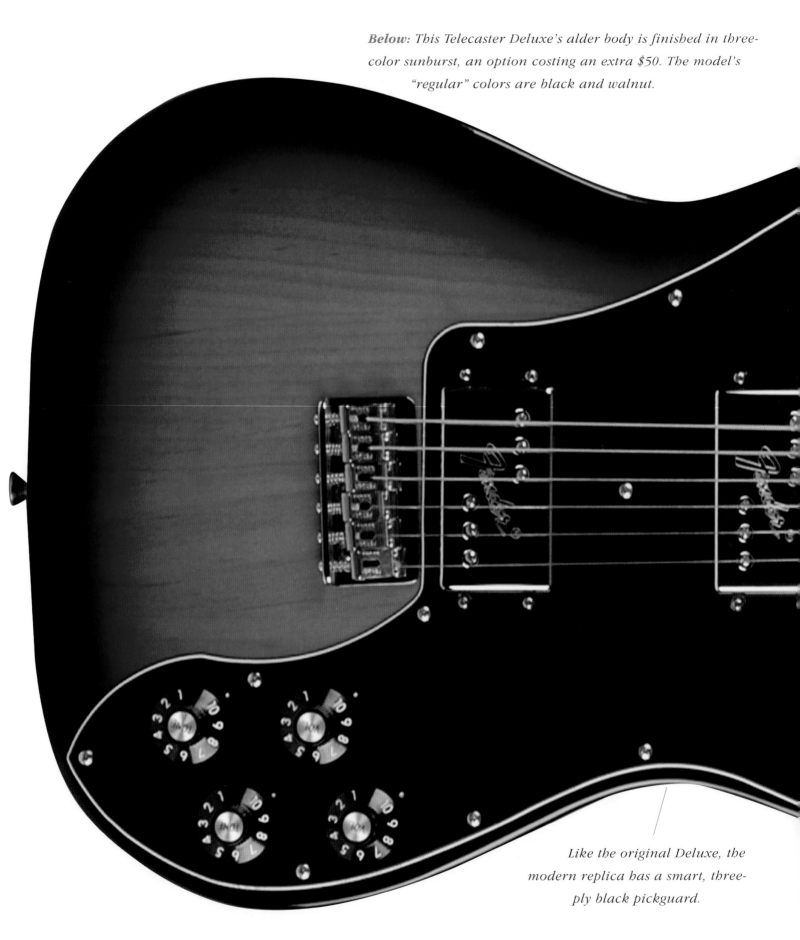

Below: This Telecaster Deluxe's alder body is finished in three-color sunburst, an option costing an extra $50. The model's "regular" colors are black and walnut.

Like the original Deluxe, the modern replica has a smart, three-ply black pickguard.

FENDER TELECASTER DELUXE

THE SETH LOVER "WIDE RANGE" humbucking pickups installed on the Thinline Telecaster (see previous pages) reappeared on two other early-70s Teles: a new version of the Custom, fitted with a neck-position humbucker; and the Deluxe, which boasted twin double-coil units, and debuted in 1972. Like the revamped Custom, the Deluxe had individual volume and tone knobs for its transducers, with a small pickup selector on its upper bass bout replacing the chunky, but eminently practical "lever-switch" designed by Leo Fender. However, it differed from its predecessor in several key respects: its maple neck incorporated a Stratocaster-style headstock instead of the regular, narrower Tele one; it had a more sophisticated, fully adjustable bridge; and it was, for a while, available with a vibrato.

The Deluxe was discontinued in 1981, but made a comeback in January 2004: a recently-made example is shown here. Though the reissue's specification is similar to its predecessor's, its pickups have been re-designed.

Above: The all-maple neck and fingerboard on the Tele Deluxe are authentic features derived from the 1972 model.

Bridge, pickup covers and other hardware on this instrument are chrome-plated.

FENDER TELECASTER, 1976

AMONG CONNOISSEURS of vintage guitars, Fenders made before 1965 are widely regarded as superior to those produced during the period in which CBS owned the company (1965-1985). This judgment fails to recognize the fine quality of many CBS-era instruments; the 1976 Telecaster in our photos, with its elegant sunburst finish, fast neck, and gutsy tone, is an excellent, highly collectible model. Nevertheless, it is a fair generalization that, to quote music historian Richard E. Smith, the firm's "older guitar[s] were not necessarily better, [but] most of the better guitars were old;" and by the mid-70s, ongoing problems at Fender's Fullerton, California headquarters were leading to an undeniable decline in standards.

Lack of investment, remote and sometimes rather misguided management, and stiff competition from Far Eastern manufacturers have all been cited as contributing factors to Fender's difficulties, and in 1981, CBS brought in a team of experienced music business executives (including Bill Schultz, who became president of Fender that year) in an attempt to sort matters out once and for all. Their arrival represented a turning point for the troubled company, and in 1985, Schultz headed the group that purchased it from CBS in a deal worth $12.5 million.

Bill Schultz went on to serve as Fender CEO for the

Below: This Tele's "Three-tone Sunburst" finish is still in pristine condition.

PHOTOGRAPHS COURTESY OF GUITAR JUNCTION, WORTHING

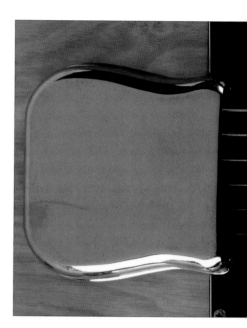

Left: The Fender "F" was registered as a trademark in 1967, but first used several years earlier..

Above: The Telecaster's bridge cover is often removed by players... and sometimes used as an ashtray!

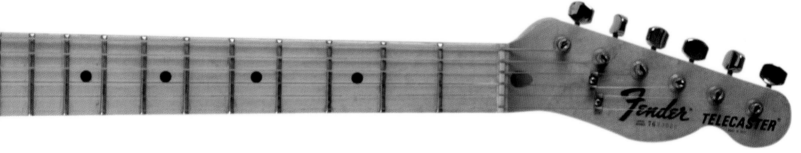

next two decades; during this period, the firm has prospered and expanded, establishing a new manufacturing base in Corona, California, as well as a corporate headquarters in Scottsdale, Arizona.

Left: The first two digits of this serial number are an abbreviated indication of its year of manufacture.

Above: A florid Sting signature graces the upper bass bout of the
Precision. The instrument was supplied in a stout flight case
carrying a sticker (presumably attached by a former owner) that
bears the words, "Play it? I can hardly carry it!"

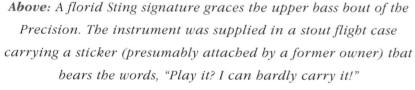

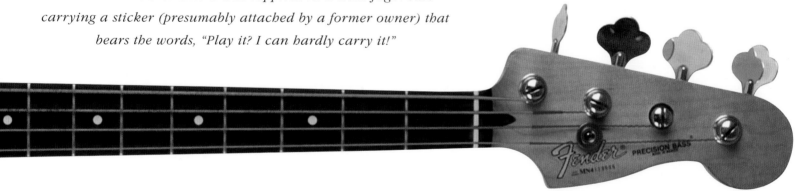

company's Artist series P-basses named in his honor. However, the model shown here is a humbler, Mexican-made Precision that Sting is known to have used only once—on a radio broadcast for the BBC (British Broadcasting Corporation) in 1994. After the show, he signed its body, and the bass was then offered as a prize in a listeners' competition. Eleven years, and several changes of ownership later, it found its way into a guitar store on the English South Coast, where we photographed it just a few days before it was purchased by an eager collector...for rather less than two million dollars!

FENDER CUSTOM SHOP JAGUAR STRAT

THIS FENDER CUSTOM SHOP Stratocaster dates from 1999, and is one of a limited edition of only 25 produced in partnership with Jaguar, Britain's world-famous sports car maker. The guitars are adorned with Jaguar logos, have a "British Racing Green" finish, and feature inlays and headstock facings crafted from walnut burl supplied by the automobile company's Coventry factory. Even their gig bags have a Jaguar connection: these were made out of the soft white leather used for the firm's car seats! They also boast deluxe Fender features, including Lace Sensor pickups and gold hardware.

The idea for the instruments came from the late Ivor Arbiter, managing director of the firm that distributed

Below: Unusally, this Strat's elegant pickguard is attached to its body without screws.

Right: *This "leaper" logo is Jaguar's most famous symbol.*

All the guitar's headstock embellishments are gold.

Fender products in the UK, and their creation was supervised by Jaguar's Director of Styling, Geoff Lawson. Sadly, Lawson died before the Strats appeared, but had previously told the UK's **Guitarist** magazine how much he had relished being involved in the development of this "very British take on the world's most famous guitar."

Right: *A very limited edition...the Jaguar Strat seen here was one of the very last to be produced.*

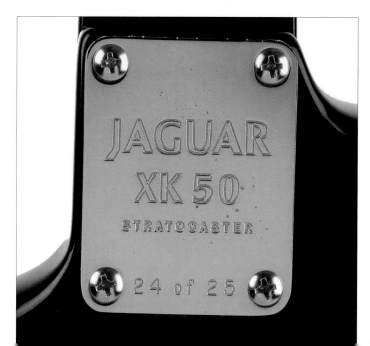

FENDER JAG-STANG

KURT COBAIN OF NIRVANA was a devotee of both Fender Mustangs and Jaguars, and longed for a single guitar that would combine their best features. In 1992, he commissioned Californian-based luthier Danny Ferrington (whose other clients include Ry Cooder) to build him a Mustang-influenced axe, which he went on to use mainly in the studio, and about a year later, he began discussions with Fender over the creation of what would become the Jag-Stang.

This curious guitar is, quite literally, a Jaguar-Mustang "fusion:" at an early stage in its development, Cobain cut up photographs of the two models, and stuck them together in the shape he wanted, with handwritten notes detailing neck dimensions, pickup types, and finishes. Larry Brooks of Fender's Custom Shop supervised the process of transforming these ideas into two finished instruments, one of which was featured on Nirvana tour dates in early 1994. Following the star's suicide in April that year, it was decided to

Above: The Jag-Stang's neck (front) pickup is a Stratocaster-type unit; Kurt Cobain had originally asked for one from a Fender Mustang in this position.

Below: The guitar's body is made from basswood.

PHOTOGRAPHS COURTESY OF NICK FREETH

Above: This chromed bridge/tailpiece incorporates a Fender
Dynamic vibrato, whose "whammy bar" has been removed.

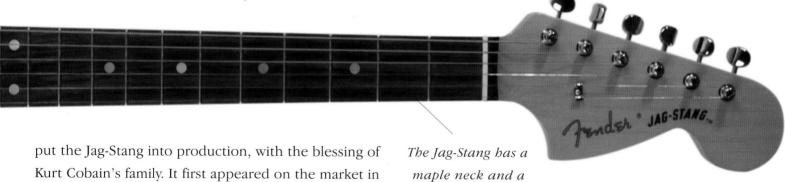

The Jag-Stang has a
maple neck and a
rosewood fretboard.

put the Jag-Stang into production, with the blessing of
Kurt Cobain's family. It first appeared on the market in
1995, was withdrawn in 2001, and has been
sporadically available since.

The Jag-Stang's odd-looking body divides opinion,
as does its idiosyncratic pickup configuration,
featuring a bridge humbucker, a single-coil neck unit,
and a switching set-up that allows them to be used
singly, or combined either in- or out-of-phase.
However, a substantial number of players have fallen
for its charm and versatility: they include the author,
whose Jag-Stang is pictured here.

FENDER SPLATTER STRATOCASTER

IN SUMMER 2003, Fender announced the introduction of a limited edition of Mexican-made Stratocasters with unusual, even bizarre finishes. These were applied to the instruments' bodies and pickguards, prior to their necks and electronics being installed, by rotating them on turntables while spraying them with a combination of colored paints; the resultant swirls, blobs and lines were later sealed into the wood when its finish was applied. The random nature of this operation meant that no two "paint jobs" were exactly the same, although the color mixes used in each case were, of course, pre-selected.

After the first "Splattercasters" (as they were quickly nicknamed) were displayed at that year's NAMM (National Association of Music Merchants) show, interest from dealers exceeded expectation, and consequently, an initial run of 300 was extended to 3,000, with the guitars selling at a recommended retail price of just over $570. While many purchasers now cherish their Splatter Stratocasters as collectors' items, the likelihood of these strange, though striking models ever becoming sought-after classics is doubtful.

Below: Beneath its "splatter" finish, this Stratocaster is a regular production instrument, with an alder body, maple neck, and rosewood fingerboard.

Strats were produced in red, blue, yellow, white and black splatter finishes.

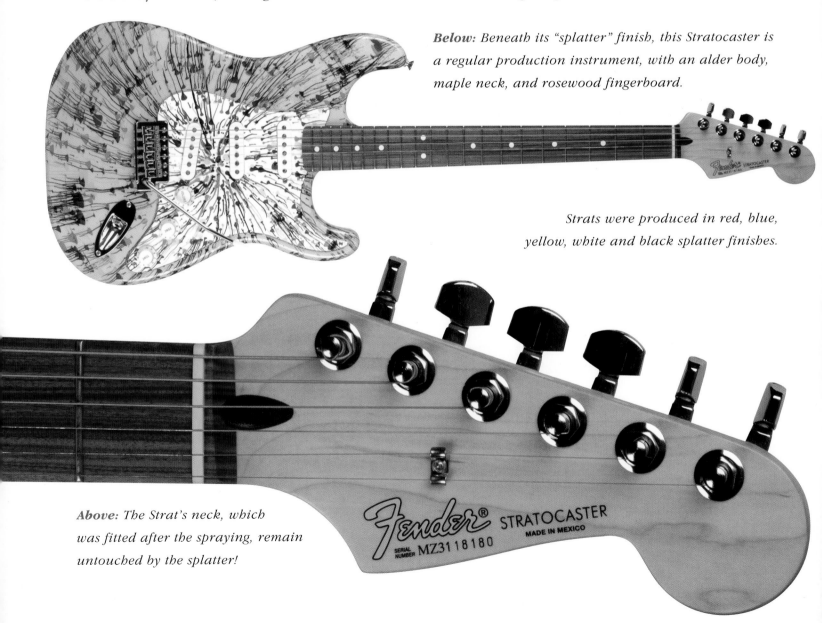

Above: The Strat's neck, which was fitted after the spraying, remain untouched by the splatter!

VOLUME

FERNANDES MONTEREY ELITE

THE TOKYO-BASED Fernandes company, founded in 1969, focused initially on building nylon-strung guitars for the domestic Japanese market. However, it went on to set up an American division in 1992, and has since become a major producer of electric instruments. Star names currently associated with these include Dave Kushner of Velvet Revolver, and

Robert Fripp and Adrian Belew of King Crimson, and in 2002, the firm pulled off an impressive marketing coup when it started making guitars carrying images of characters from George Lucas's *Star Wars* movies.

Fernandes' most famous technical innovation is the Sustainer, developed in the late 1980s, and now installed on many of its models—including the maple

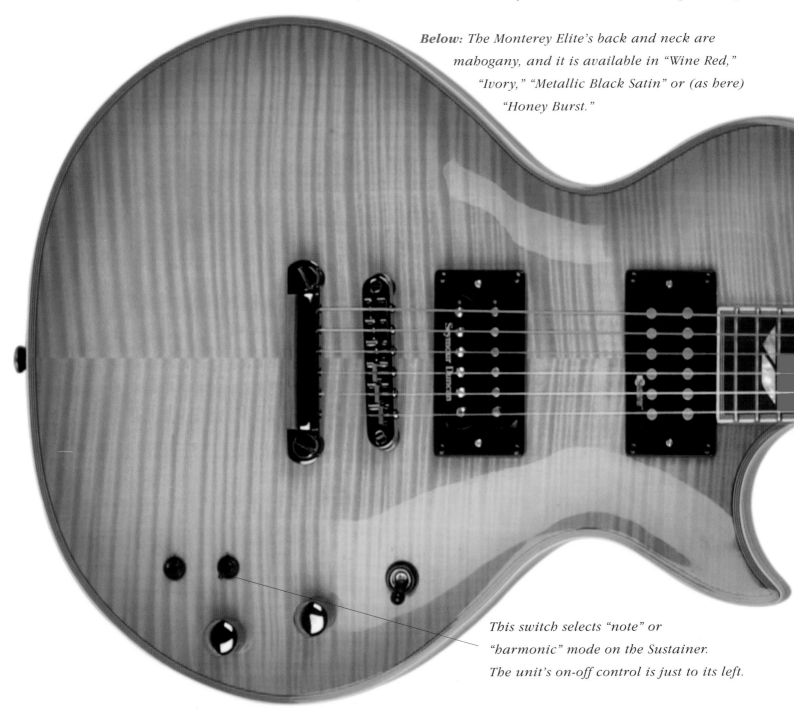

Below: The Monterey Elite's back and neck are mahogany, and it is available in "Wine Red," "Ivory," "Metallic Black Satin" or (as here) "Honey Burst."

This switch selects "note" or "harmonic" mode on the Sustainer. The unit's on-off control is just to its left.

This nut is made from graphite.

MONTEREY

FERNANDES
GUITARS

The Elite has a rosewood fretboard.

Sustainer™

Left: *A special transducer in the neck (front) position on the Monterey supplies the signals for the Sustainer circuitry on the Fernandes.*

topped, two-pickup Monterey Elite seen here. As its name suggests, this electronic device can generate indefinite sustain on notes or chords, and it also features a second, "harmonic" mode that usefully mimics the effects of feedback.

213

This deep cutaway
makes high
position playing
easy and
comfortable.

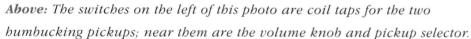

Above: *The switches on the left of this photo are coil taps for the two humbucking pickups; near them are the volume knob and pickup selector.*

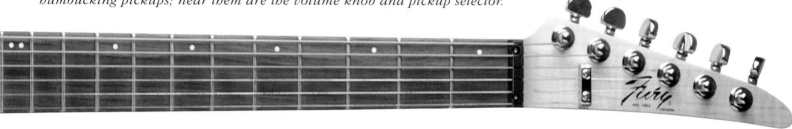

Though new technology has boosted and speeded up Fury's instrument production—its output now includes six regular models, including a bass, an electric 12-string, and a baritone guitar—Glenn McDougall's personal aims have changed little in over four decades. As he states on the company's website, he remains "committed to designing and manufacturing guitars that...produce pure, balanced tone [and] high output power...In short, guitars that are easy to play." The Bandit displays all these qualities: made from maple and available in three different pickup configurations (the instrument featured here is fitted with two humbuckers), it incorporates a high-mass truss-rod for optimum neck rigidity, as well as Fury's patented "Uninut" acrylic nut, designed to improve sustain and playing action.

FYLDE FALSTAFF

IN 1973, A YOUNG ENGLISHMAN, Roger Bucknall, who was experiencing growing demand for the guitars he made at nights and weekends while working for an electronics company, decided to go into business as a full-time luthier. His new company, Fylde Instruments, took its name from the Fylde Coast in northwestern England, and was initially based in St. Anne's, south of Blackpool in Lancashire, subsequently relocating a few miles inland to Kirkham. Its rich

sounding flat-tops were popular with British folk musicians, and also attracted overseas customers; however, what the firm's official history describes as "an awful combination of personal and economic circumstances" led to the closure of this first incarnation of Fylde in 1980.

Roger Bucknall was eventually able to re-establish himself as an instrument maker, and in 1996, he moved to Penrith, in the English Lake District, where he now

Below: The Falstaff is designed, in Roger Bucknall's words, "to provide a rich deep tone, with bright trebles and strong bass."

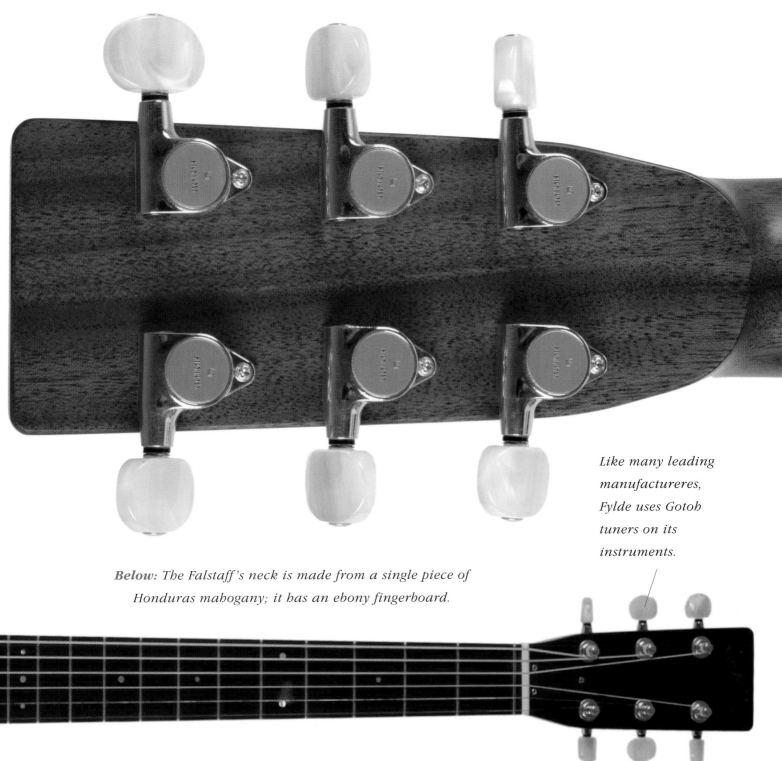

Like many leading manufactureres, Fylde uses Gotoh tuners on its instruments.

Below: *The Falstaff's neck is made from a single piece of Honduras mahogany; it has an ebony fingerboard.*

Right: *A view of the Falstaff's heel and upper back, showing its delicate inlays.*

produces a distinctive range of guitars, mandolins, bouzoukis and citterns. Almost all his creations have names associated with Shakespeare plays: the Falstaff shown here takes its inspiration from the "Fat Knight," Sir John Falstaff, who features in **Henry IV** and **The Merry Wives of Windsor**. Spruce topped, its back and sides are made from Indian rosewood, and it has a maximum body width of just under 16 inches.

G&L F-100

G&L STANDS FOR "GEORGE & LEO": the firm was set up in 1980 by Leo Fender and his long-standing friend and colleague George Fullerton. They had recently left Music Man (see separate entry), and were seeking a new outlet for Leo's latest guitar design innovations. G&L established itself in Fullerton, southern California, where the original Fender Electric Instrument Company had been based, and its first product was the F-100 solid-body, an example of which, dating from 1980, is shown here.

The F-100 came in a number of slightly different forms: the one in our photographs is a Series 1 F-100E model. Series I F-100s have a larger fingerboard radius (12 inch) than their Series II counterparts, and the "E" suffix denotes the presence of active electronics, powered by an onboard battery. The guitar is fitted with two humbucking pickups (plus a coil-tap switch that converts them to single-coil mode), and a vibrato whose operation is described in the caption below. The F-100 series remained in production at Fullerton until 1985.

The F-100E in our pictures is finished in "Translucent Red."

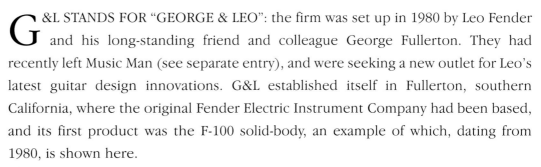

Left: *This vibrato pivots on two knife-edge fulcrum points. The tension of its operating arm can be adjusted to suit players' preferences.*

Above: *The F-100E has an ashwood body (mahogany and maple were also sometimes used) and a maple neck and fingerboard.*

G&L ASAT DELUXE

L EO FENDER WORKED AT G&L from 1980 until his death 11 years later. His co-founder George Fullerton still acts as a consultant to the firm, although its ownership and management have now passed to BBE Sound, a business run by Leo's friend and associate John McLaren. McLaren's son, Johnny, is currently G&L's Plant Manager, and he and his staff remain dedicated to the guitar-making goals that Leo Fender spent his life pursuing. Their achievements have been aptly summed up by Kebin Arhens, who wrote recently in *The Music Paper* that "G&L has perpetuated the art of fine instrument making...in the distinguished tradition of its founder."

Among the company's most successful guitars are the ASATs, originally introduced in 1986, and still in production. Their curious name can be explained in two different ways: ASAT may, perhaps, refer to the US Air Force's Anti-Satellite Missile (the F-100 described on the previous two pages also has possible military associations—F-100s were America's first supersonic fighter planes), but is more likely to be a reference to Leo Fender's own remark that the instrument was conceived as "a Strat and a Tele"! ASATs have been used by a substantial number of top players, from Peter Frampton and INXS's Andrew and Tim Farriss to the late Carl Perkins.

The ASAT model seen here is the Deluxe Semi-Hollow. It boasts a figured maple top and a mahogany body, and is fitted with two Seymour Duncan humbucking pickups, which (as on the F-100) can both be coil-tapped.

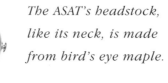

The ASAT's headstock, like its neck, is made from bird's eye maple.

Left: *The ASAT Deluxe Semi-Hollow is slightly reminiscent of one of Leo Fender's earlier designs, the Telecaster Thin Line, but has many innovative features.*

GIBSON L-5 "MASTER MODEL"

THE GIBSON MANDOLIN-GUITAR Manufacturing Company was founded in Kalamazoo, Michigan, in 1902. It was named for Orville Gibson (1856-1918), a talented and innovative luthier who produced the first-ever mandolins with carved, violin-type tops and backs, and was making large-bodied, steel-strung guitars with arched tops and oval soundholes by the start of the 20th century. "Orville-style" instruments dominated Gibson's early catalogs, but their creator held no executive post within the firm, serving instead as a consultant and a staff trainer. By 1911, however, he had moved away from Kalamazoo due to failing health, and he died seven years later.

In 1919, Gibson bosses recruited Lloyd Allayre Loar (1886-1943) as an "acoustic engineer." Loar quickly became a major force within the firm, and was responsible for the introduction, in 1922, of its F-5 archtop mandolin, which, for the first time, featured f-holes instead of a more traditionally shaped soundhole. The same year saw the launch of the ground-breaking L-5 "Master Model" guitar—the instrument now recognized as the starting point for almost all subsequent archtop acoustic designs. It shared the F-5's f-holes and carved top and back, and had a handsomely finished, 16-inch wide body whose powerful sonic projection was ideal for rhythm playing

Below: The L-5, finished in "Cremona Brown Sunburst," has a spruce top and maple back and sides.

GIBSON ES-295

Lighter-colored binding offsets the rich gold of the ES-295's body.

THE GIBSON ES-295 DEBUTED in 1952; the company's promotional literature, with justifiable pride, called it a "golden beauty" and "a 'royal' instrument," and asserted that "tone and action wise the ES-295 measures up to its outstanding appearance." Visually, the elegant new archtop matched Gibson's Les Paul solid-body, but in other ways, the ES-295 bore close resemblance to the ES-175 described on the previous pages, with the same overall dimensions, and sporting identical "florentine" cutaways and "parallelogram" fret markers. All three models featured P-90 single-coil pickups.

Unlike the Les Paul, the ES-295 never became a best-seller, and it was dropped from the Gibson range in 1958—but it has an enduring place in musical history as the guitar used by Elvis Presley sideman Scotty Moore on "The King's" 1954 sessions for Sun Records in Memphis, Tennessee that produced classic sides such as "That's All Right" and "Blue Moon of Kentucky".

Left: The ES-295's control knobs are gold-tinted to match its body's "royal" color scheme.

Above: The "flower" decoration on he ES-295's pickguard had been seen before on a Gibson lap steel.

GIBSON L-5 CES

GIBSON'S TWO "FLAGSHIP" pre-war archtop acoustics, the L-5 and Super 400, appeared as electrics in 1951; they kept their original names, but were given the suffix CES (Cutaway Electric Spanish). As befitted their elevated status within the company's product line—reflected in a movie-inspired 1952 Gibson ad proclaiming that the L-5 CES (shown here) "wins the starring roles in every important production"—they also, unlike many humbler models,

retained their all-solid wood construction. However, as A.R. Duchossoir explains in his book *Gibson Electrics: The Classic Years*, their tops were now built slightly thicker, and were more heavily braced, "in order to give more rigidity to the sounding board[s] and to inhibit [any] unwanted vibration" that might result from electric use. Unsurprisingly, both guitars were favored by leading jazzmen: the L-5 CES is especially associated with the great Wes Montgomery (1925-

Below: The L-5 CES has a solid spruce top, and solid maple back and sides.

PHOTOGRAPHS COURTESY OF A PRIVATE COLLECTOR

Left: *This handsome, mother-of-pearl inlaid headstock is complemented by Kluson machine heads with elegantly shaped buttons.*

Above: *Each of the six polepieces on the Alnico V pickup seen here is individually adjustable.*

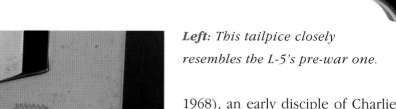

Left: *This tailpice closely resembles the L-5's pre-war one.*

1968), an early disciple of Charlie Christian who later enjoyed huge success as a both a soloist and leader.

Between 1951 and 1953, the L-5 CES was fitted with P-90 pickups; these were subsequently replaced with Alnico V transducers (which can be seen on the guitar in our pictures), and, later, by humbuckers.

GIBSON BYRDLAND

FOR SOME MUSICIANS, "full-depth" electric archtops like the L-5 CES and ES-175, which measured a substantial 3³/₈ inches from top to back, were a little too bulky for comfort—and when two leading Nashville-based players, Billy Byrd (1920-2001) and Hank Garland (1930-2004), were invited to discuss guitar design with a Gibson representative in early 1955, they suggested that the company should come up with what Garland later described to *Guitar Player* magazine as "an instrument like the L-5, but with a thin body and a bunch of other stuff."

This advice was duly conveyed to Kalamazoo, and the same year saw the launch of the appropriately named Gibson Byrdland, which, although based on the L-5 CES, but was just 2¹/₄ inches deep, and had a slightly shorter scale length and narrower neck than its predecessor. Ads in the music trade press described the Byrdland as "streamlined," and claimed, with some justice, that it "successfully combin[ed] the characteristics of solid body and conventional guitars." Gibson customers concurred, and the new model was quickly followed by other thinlines.

Below: The 1961 Byrdland in our photos boasts humbucking pickups. These were made standard on the model in 1958.

Right: This Byrdland has had its original tailpiece (which carried the model's name) replaced with a Bigsby vibrato unit.

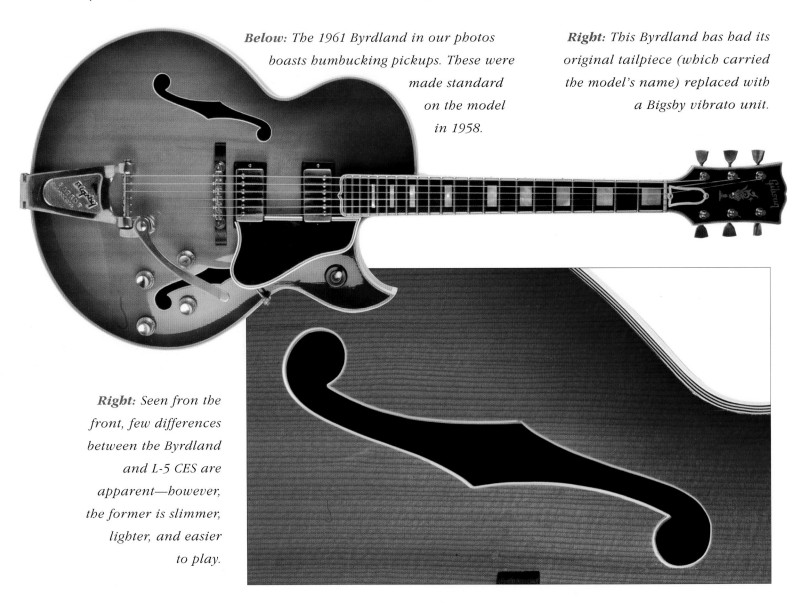

Right: Seen fron the front, few differences between the Byrdland and L-5 CES are apparent—however, the former is slimmer, lighter, and easier to play.

The ES-335 is 16 inches wide—a comfortably compact size for most players.

Below: Like the original 335s, this example has a "stop" or "stud" tailpiece, see overleaf for a model with alternative hardware.

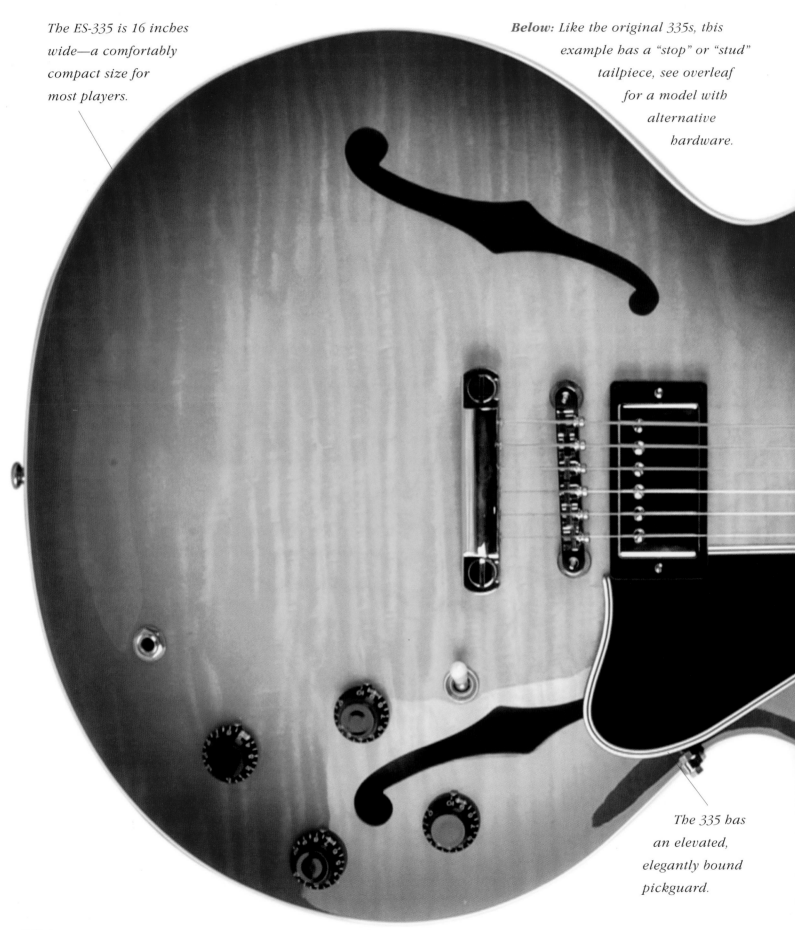

The 335 has an elevated, elegantly bound pickguard.

GIBSON ES-335

These mounting rings allow precise adjustment of pickup height.

GIBSON'S ES-335, introduced in spring 1958, had several immediately striking features, including a double cutaway (a first for the company), a thinline body (whose 1³/₄-inch depth matched that of the ES-225, launched three years previously), and a pair of "patent applied for" humbucking pickups, developed by staff engineer Seth Lover (1910-1997), and already seen on several earlier Gibson electrics. But the most revolutionary aspect of the 335's design was invisible from the outside: beneath its laminated maple top lay a wooden block that ran lengthways through the guitar, transforming what would otherwise have been a hollow-body into a "semi-solid;" the only empty cavities inside the 335 were its f-holed side-sections. The instrument's solid center drastically reduced feedback—a frequent bugbear for electric archtops when played at moderate to high volumes—while increasing sustain; and its stylish appearance and comparatively light weight (just over 7 pounds) made it an immediate success with players. The 335 has been in continuous production for well over 40 years.

Right: The headstock is mounted at a 17-degree angle to optimize the instrument's tone quality.

GIBSON ES-335 (2)

IN 1962, GIBSON MADE a purely cosmetic change to the ES-335, substituting block inlays for its "dot" fingerboard markers. A rather more significant alteration occurred some two years later, with the replacement of the model's "stop" or "stud" tailpiece with a trapeze-type unit. The 335 in our pictures dates from 1968, and has been owned since the late 1970s by the British jazz guitarist Charles Alexander, who purchased it after his previous Gibson, a stereo-equipped ES-345 (see next two pages), was stolen.

Like many jazz players, Charles regards the 335 as ideal for his needs, and feels that the sustain provided by its solid center block gives the Gibson ES-335 a "contemporary-sounding" tone more appropriate to his music than the rounder, more "retro" timbre that would be obtained from a hollow-body electric. However, he rarely uses the 335's bridge pickup, preferring the mellower sound of the neck transducer. Aside from some repair work—essential after over two decades of regular gigging!—recently undertaken by Tom Anfield (see separate entries), the instrument has never been modified in any way.

Below: 1960s Gibson ES-335s are now worth many times their original selling price.

These "Gibson-logo" pickup covers are another point of difference between original and later ES335s.

PHOTOGRAPHS COURTESY OF CHARLES ALEXANDER

Above: *Some players feel that the addition of a trapeze tailpiece to the 335 has some effect on the instrument's sound.*

GIBSON EB-2 BASS

THE GIBSON EB-2 first appeared in 1958; like the visually similar ES-335 guitar launched the same year, it contained an internal center block to improve sustain and reduce feedback. Initially fitted with a single-coil pickup, by 1959, it had acquired a humbucker, together with what a company catalog later described as "the sensational Gibson Bass-Baritone switch," a tone circuit giving an additional "edge" to the instrument's sound. The same feature was included on the Epiphone Rivoli, an EB-2 lookalike that also debuted in 1959. The EB-2 itself was dropped in 1961, but returned three years later, and 1966 saw the appearance of the 2-pickup version seen here. Both basses remained available until the early 1970s.

Below: One distinctive characteristic of the two-pickup EB-2 is the differing size of its two transducers: the bridge unit is a mini-humbucker, while the neck pickup is much larger.

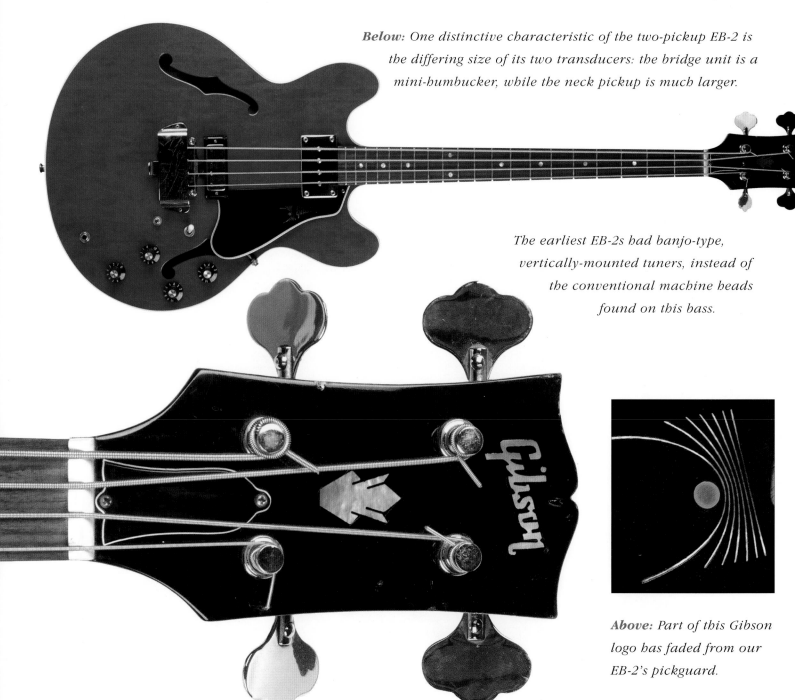

The earliest EB-2s had banjo-type, vertically-mounted tuners, instead of the conventional machine heads found on this bass.

Above: Part of this Gibson logo has faded from our EB-2's pickguard.

This button activates the EB-2's "Bass-Baritone" circuitry.

GIBSON ES-345TD

THE GIBSON ES-345TD was introduced in 1959. While similar in construction and appearance to the ES-335, it had two novel features: stereo wiring, and "Vari-tone" circuitry that, according to the company's publicity, "could produce *any* sound you've *ever* heard from *any* guitar."

Vari-tone settings are adjusted via a rotary knob mounted to the left of the instrument's volume and tone controls. This has six positions: the first of these defeats the Vari-tone, while the other five apply "notch filter"-type cuts to progressively lower frequencies (affecting the deepest notes most at position 6). Opinion has always been somewhat divided over the usefulness of Vari-tone, which lacks the more dramatic frequency shaping capacity of the active EQ circuits fitted to some modern guitars—although many players find it useful, and consider that positions 3 and 4 can make the ES-345's humbucking pickups sound a little like single-coil models.

The guitar's stereo capabilities were considerably

Below: The ES-345 has a laminated maple body and a semi-solid construction, like its ES-335 cousin.

PHOTOGRAPHS COURTESY OF CHANDLER GUITARS, KEW

The 345's Vari-tone switch normally
has a circular surround; it has been
lost from this instrument.

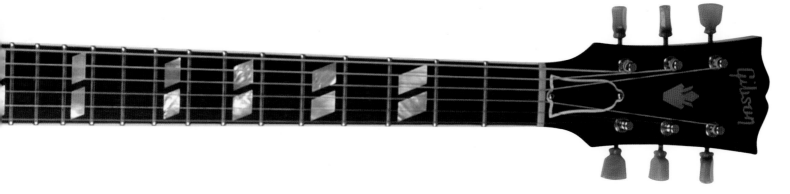

simpler than those adopted by Gretsch a few years earlier, which had involved a split between treble and bass strings. Gibson preferred to route each of the 345's pickups to individual channels; their signals could then be connected to separate amplifiers—or, preferably, to the company's own, recently introduced GA-88S stereo guitar amp, which was equipped with

two input sockets—via a "Y-type" connecting cord, terminating in a pair of jacks. Musicians with mono amps (the vast majority, both then and now) could use the 345 normally, but would not, of course, be able to enjoy the stereo effect.

The ES-345 remained in the Gibson catalog until 1982, but has subsequently been reissued.

GIBSON ES-355TD-SV

AS A LUXURY, top-of-the-line reworking of the ES-335, also featuring—in the version seen here—the stereo wiring and Vari-tone circuit found on the ES-345, the ES-355TD-SV (the suffixes stand for "Thinline Double-cutaway Stereo Vari-tone") has frequently inspired purple prose from copywriters. Soon after its launch in 1959, a Gibson catalog called it a "magnificent jazz guitar reflect[ing] all the beauty and skill of the guitar maker's art," while a later ad eulogized it as the embodiment of the "vibrant, vigorous, vital...spirit of

Below:"Cherry Red" was initially the only finish in which the ES-355 was available. Other colors were introduced later.

This vibrato unit is a Gibson Vibrola.

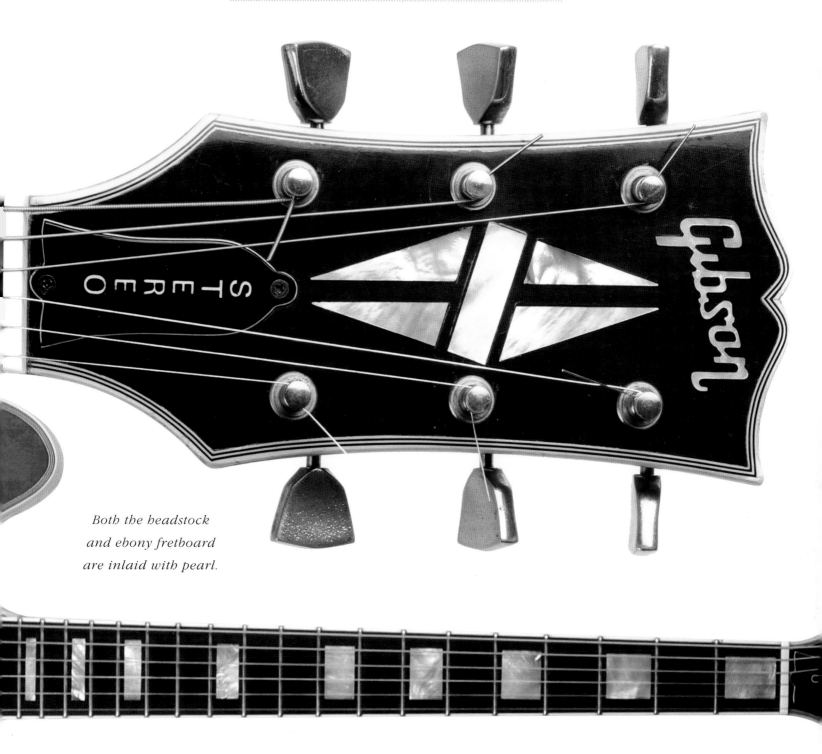

STEREO

*Both the headstock
and ebony fretboard
are inlaid with pearl.*

the electric guitar." It is indeed a handsome instrument, though players unimpressed with its ingenious onboard electronics must have been happy that, for a number of years, a mono, non-Vari-tone incarnation of it, named the ES-355TD, could be purchased for rather less money.

Both versions attracted eminent users: they included top Nashville session player Grady Martin who, as Thomas Goldsmith recalls in the book *Classic Guitars of the 50s and 60s*, had string benders fitted

to his 355 in order to create "steel-guitar-like pitch shifts." Jazzman Tony Mottola was another devotee—as was blues star B.B. King, who began using the ES-355 in the early 1960s (naming it, like all his instruments, Lucille), but subsequently switched to a version with a sealed top to prevent feedback: this was put into production as the Gibson "B.B. King Model" in 1980. The 355 itself was dropped in 1982, but has since made a number of comebacks, and is currently available as part of Gibson's "Limited Historic" series.

GIBSON ES-5 SWITCHMASTER, 1959

THE MAJOR SELLING POINT for the original Gibson ES-5, which debuted in 1949, was its unusual pickup configuration. Named "the instrument of a thousand voices" by the company's copywriters, it boasted three P-90s, each of which had its own volume knob; however, there was no selector switch for the transducers, and only a single, overall tone control, positioned on the instrument's upper treble bout. Opinion is divided over the efficacy of this arrangement—top player Ry Cooder has commented that he relishes the freedom it gives him to mix sounds—but during the late 40s and 50s, the ES-5's

Right: Like other Gibson archtops, the ES-5 has a "personalized" tailpiece.

Below: Humbucking pickups replaced P-90s on the Switchmaster in 1957.

PHOTOGRAPHS COURTESY OF A PRIVATE COLLECTOR

Above: The provision of a pickup selector on the ES-5 was widely welcomed.

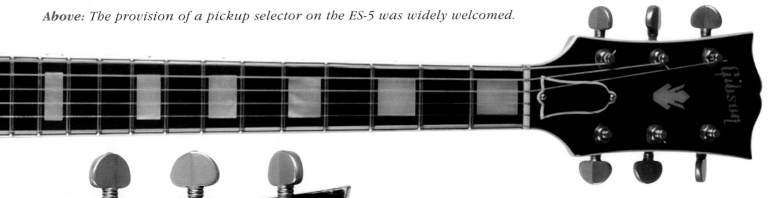

Left: The reverse side of the Switchmaster's headstock is painted black to match its front.

circuitry was widely criticized, and in 1955, Gibson altered it, adding a selector, providing individual tone controls for the pickups, and giving the model an additional name: the Switchmaster. An example of the revamped guitar dating from 1959 is shown here.

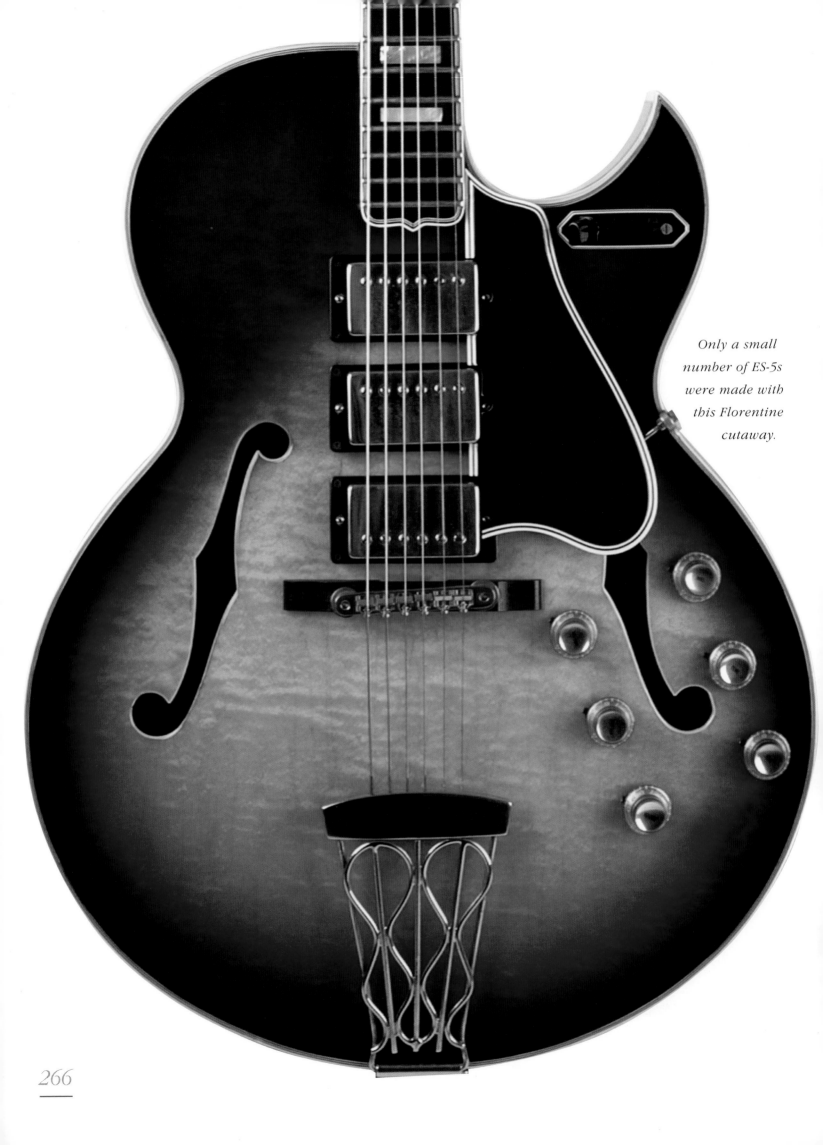

Only a small number of ES-5s were made with this Florentine cutaway.

GIBSON ES-5 SWITCHMASTER, 1961

IN HIS BOOK, *The History and Development of the American Guitar*, Ken Achard writes that the ES-5 "heralded the fifties and the start of a new generation of Gibson instruments." By the end of that decade, however, the instrument's future was less certain; thinlines and semi-solids were now the choice of many Gibson archtop users, and the bulky, though elegant Switchmaster was starting to look and sound dated. It had been given humbucking pickups in place of its P-90s in 1957, and it underwent a change in styling four years later, when it acquired a sharp, "Florentine" cutaway. However, by the time this alteration was made, the number of Switchmasters being produced was already beginning to dwindle, and the guitar was eventually discontinued in 1962.

The body of the 1961 Switchmaster shown on these pages conforms to the standard specifications for its year of manufacture, but its neck clearly does not match the comparatively plain, "regular" one found on our previous ES-5, and comes, instead, from an L-5...though it is not known when, or how, this substitution took place!

Below: Features such as its elaborate headstock binding and "flowerpot" logo reveal that this neck is from a Gibson L-5.

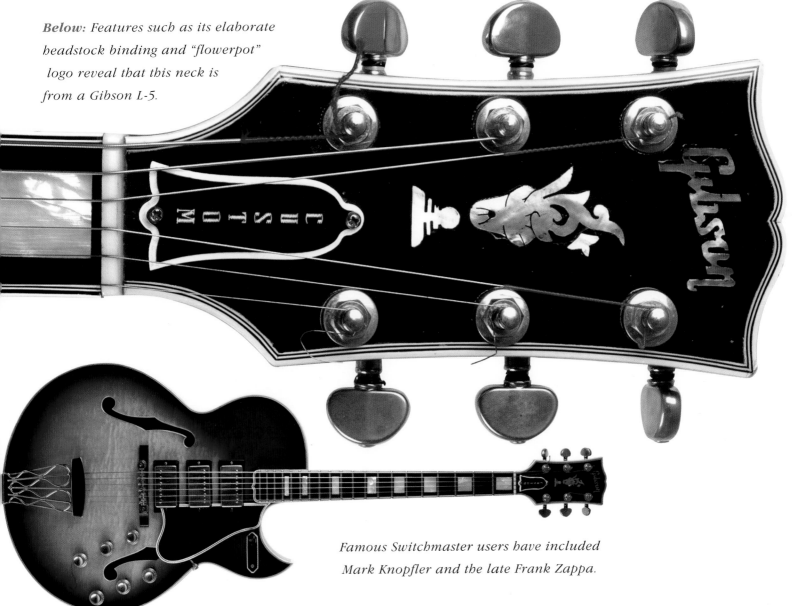

Famous Switchmaster users have included Mark Knopfler and the late Frank Zappa.

Below: The ES-120T has only a single, unbound f-hole.

Right: This view shows the position and depth of the ES-120T's pickup unit.

GIBSON ES-120T

This model's body is finished in "Cherry Sunburst."

D EMAND FOR THE "THINLINE" ELECTRIC ARCHTOPS introduced by Gibson in 1955 grew steadily over the following years, and in 1962, the company added a budget-price model to the series—the ES-120T, which sold at just under $150. It shared its body dimensions and some aspects of its styling with the ES-125T (the former "bottom-of-the range" thinline, which had appeared in 1956), but had one significant difference: on the 120T, the 125's P-90 transducer was replaced with a combined pickguard-and-pickup similar to the one found on Gibson's solid-body Melody Maker (see separate entry).

Because all the wiring and controls were mounted on a plastic plate, there was no need to install any electronics within the guitar's body; only routing was required to accommodate the pickup, reducing manufacturing costs to a minimum. While the unit had a considerable deadening effect on the guitar's $16\frac{1}{4}$-

inch wide maple laminate top, this mattered little on an instrument whose shallow, $1\frac{3}{4}$ inch depth had never been intended to provide very much acoustic sound. The 125T's back and sides were also made from plywood, and its single binding, lack of cutaway, and plain headstock (with a Gibson logo but no "crown" inlay) were further evidence of its lowly status within the thinline family.

Despite its simplicity, however, the ES-120T proved popular; its small size and light weight (a little over 5 pounds.) made it a favorite with younger players, and many users have commented favourably on its sweet yet powerful tone. The model survived in the Gibson catalog until 1970.

GIBSON L-5 CES, 1963

SOME GUITARS enjoy only a brief period in the limelight; but the Gibson L-5, whose original, acoustic version dates back to 1922 (see previous entries) is undoubtedly a hardy perennial. Unlike other classic archtops, its status and sales were largely untouched by the changes of taste and aesthetics that characterized the 1960s, and it was to retain an honored place in the Gibson catalog throughout the decade—and beyond.

The vintage model (seen here in its 1963 CES version) was not, however, entirely untouched by recent trends. By the late 1950s, its single-coil Alnico V pickups had given way to the Seth Lover-designed humbuckers fitted to other top-line Gibson electrics. Their addition made comparatively little visual difference to the instrument, but another new feature—the sharper, Florentine cutaway that replaced the soft Venetian one in about 1960—led to an additional cosmetic change: the shortening of the L-5's pickguard, whose top edge now reached only as far as the last of its 20 frets. On earlier cutaway L-5s, it had extended to the 19th fret or above.

These tuners, like the guitar's bridge and tailpiece, are gold-plated.

The L-5 CES has a spruce top, and maple back and sides.

GIBSON L-5, CUSTOM ORDER 1964

THE CONCEPT of a "custom shop" was still unknown to guitar makers and buyers in the early 1960s, largely because manufacturers—even major ones such as Gibson—were still able to accommodate special orders and modifications as part of their mainstream production process. The particular requirements of the unknown musician who commissioned this unusual L-5 would not have been difficult to accomplish: he simply wanted an instrument with a Venetian cutaway instead of the Florentine type then being given to standard models, and asked for a bar-type single coil pickup, like the one

Right: The L-5 sports elegant, cream-colored binding around its edges.

Below: The guitar retains its usual 17 inch width, and its regular features are largely unaffected by the customizing.

GIBSON LES PAUL CUSTOM

THE LES PAUL CUSTOM started out as an upgrade to Gibson's original Les Paul model. Introduced in 1954, it featured the adjustable "Tune-o-Matic" bridge invented by the company's Ted McCarty, and was fitted with two different types of single-coil pickup: a P-90 in the bridge position, and an Alnico V, named for the type of magnet used for its pole-pieces, near its neck. The Alnico transducer, developed by Gibson engineer Seth Lover, offered high output, but performed less well when—as frequently happened—players raised its height excessively. (Lover, quoted in A.R. Duchossoir's *Gibson Electrics: The Classic Years* (1994) explained that guitarists would "get sour notes from that pickup"

when it was brought too near the strings, adding, "They should have kept the magnets down the waist.") The other distinctive characteristics of the first Custom were its all-black finish (prompting the nickname "Black Beauty") and the low, wide profile of its frets, which made fast left-hand work easier and earned the instrument another soubriquet: "Fretless Wonder."

The all-black Custom's P-90 and Alnico pickups were subsequently replaced by three humbuckers, and by the early 1960s, the guitar had acquired a new, slimline shape, and was later renamed the SG Custom (see separate entry). Details of the Les Paul-style Custom's subsequent history can be found on pages 300-1, where a 1978 model is shown.

The "Black Beauty" seen here is an early model, preserved in near-perfect condition by its owner, a dedicated collector of vintage Gibsons.

Left: Gibson described the Les Paul Custom as "the ultimate in a solid body Electric Spanish guitar."

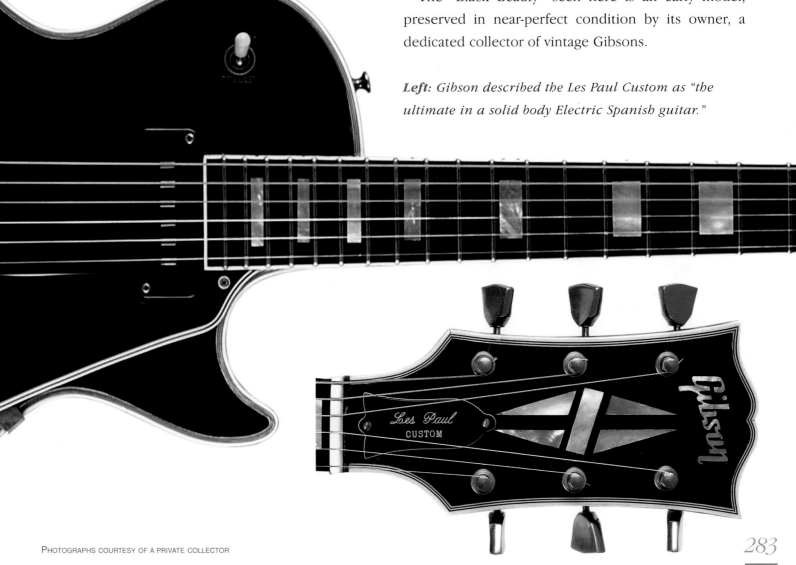

GIBSON LES PAUL STANDARD

IN 1957, both the gold-top and Custom Gibson Les Pauls acquired new pickups—the twin-coil, "humbucking" transducers developed a few years earlier by staffer Seth Lover (1910-1997). The rich timbre provided by these units has come to be widely regarded as the "classic Les Paul sound," although some players retain a preference for the P-90s and Alnicos fitted to earlier models.

The next important development in the Les Paul's history occurred the following year, when the original (non-Custom) instrument's gold finish was replaced with a sunburst look; to coincide with this change, the bosses at Kalamazoo decided to give the guitar a new name: the Les Paul Standard. Probably the most famous and highly revered of all the many different types of Les Paul, it was initially available for just three years, during which, according to figures quoted by guitar historian Tony Bacon, only about 1,700 were made. Partly as a result of their scarcity, 1958-60 Standards now have an almost mystical status among some musicians; but at the time of their production, they were not especially big sellers, and were eventually discontinued, along with the rest of the single-cutaway Pauls, to make way for Gibson's new SG-shaped solid-bodies.

Their disappearance was only temporary: a reissued Les Paul Standard debuted in 1968, but it sported a gold finish instead of a sunburst one, and its

Below: The Les Paul Standard's body is made from layers of maple and mahogany, with a maple top.

*Above: The cream-colored surrounds for its pickups
are one of the Standard's most distinctive features.*

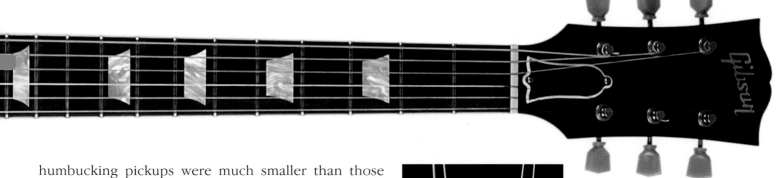

humbucking pickups were much smaller than those
found on its predecessor. It was followed by a variety of
other new models, but the 1958-style Standard with
full-size humbuckers did not return to regular
production at Gibson until 1976. It has since been a
fixture in the company's catalog, and a recently made
Standard is shown in our photographs.

*Left: Unlike some other
Les Pauls, the Standard
has no lettering on its
truss-rod cover.*

The single-pickup Melody Maker shown here dates from 1964; two-pickup versions were also available.

Below: The Melody Maker's body and neck are mahogany; it has a rosewood fingerboard.

Versions of this pickup were later used on Gibson's ES-120T and Epiphone's Olympic.

PHOTOGRAPHS COURTESY OF AMERICAN GUITAR CENTRE & BASSWORLD, TONBRIDGE

GIBSON MELODY MAKER

E AGER TO CAPTURE A SHARE of the market for less expensive electric guitars as well as premium models, Gibson launched a budget-priced Les Paul in 1954. Named the Junior, it sold for just $99.50, and was fitted with a single P-90 pickup; a 3/4-size version appeared two years later. 1959 saw the introduction of a new Gibson solid-body, also priced at $99.50. Christened the Melody Maker, it bore a strong resemblance to the single-cutaway Junior—although its body was slightly thinner than its predecessor's, while its headstock was narrower, and its pickup assembly was an all-in-one unit built into its pickguard.

By this time, Les Pauls were undergoing a gradual transformation into SGs; an intermediate stage in this process occurred in 1958 and 1959, when the Junior and TV models, and then the Special, appeared in rounded-horn double-cutaway versions. The Melody Maker acquired the same body shape—seen on the example in our photographs—in 1961, and underwent other minor changes before gaining a full SG styling in 1966.

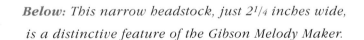

Below: This narrow headstock, just 2^1/4 inches wide, is a distinctive feature of the Gibson Melody Maker.

GIBSON FLYING V

BY THE MID-1950s, the success of the Fender Telecaster and Stratocaster—both products from a hitherto obscure firm with no real guitar-making track record—was having a corrosive effect on the reputation of other, longer-established manufacturers. Gibson, in particular, found itself the subject of unwelcome murmurings from its detractors to the effect that, as its retired boss Ted McCarty recalled during an interview published in Rittor Music's authoritative book *The Gibson* (1996) it "was a fuddy duddy old company without a new idea in years." To silence such comments, McCarty urgently needed to come up with some fresh, bold designs, and by 1957 he had devised body shapes for three radical-looking solid electrics, the Moderne, the Futura (soon to be renamed the Explorer) and the Flying V. The Moderne appeared in prototype, but was not

Above: This Flying V was made in 2002. While broadly similar to the original, it is made from mahogany, not korina, and has a number of other minor differences from the 1958 model.

Right: The Flying V's dramatic shape is perfect for rock star-style posing, but less than ideal for performers who prefer to play sitting down!

The 1958-style Flying V boasted a V-shaped tailpiece, not the "stop" unit seen here.

These tuning buttons match the 1958 model's.

Below: *Gibson described the Flying V in 1958 as a guitar that "would be a real asset to the combo musician with a flair for showmanship."*

On earlier Flying Vs, the "Gibson" logo was placed on the headstock; here, it has migrated to the truss rod cover.

actually marketed until the 1980s; however, the Flying V and the Explorer were unveiled to industry insiders at trade fairs in 1957, before going into production the following year.

These two so-called "modernistic guitars" were both made from West African korina wood, which, according to Gibson expert A.R. Duchossoir, had previously been used only for the firm's Hawaiian models. The assymetrical Explorer was certainly distinctive, but it was the Flying V, with its bold, arrow-like outline, that was to prove more appealing to customers in the long term—despite disappointing initial sales that led it to be temporarily dropped from the company's catalog only a year after its launch.

Above: The Custom boasts multi-ply binding around its headstock, gold-plated tuners manufactured by Grover, and pearl inlays.

Right: Gibson has traditionally named its neck (front) and bridge (back) pickups "rhythm" and "treble," and these terms are used on the legend for the Les Paul Custom's selector switch.

Rebel, still plays and cherishes his 1969 Custom.

Keen to capitalize on the instrument's enduring popularity, Gibson subsequently produced it in a range of different colors, and have gone on to mark the milestones in its long life with various "Special" models; the earliest of these, a 20th Anniversary instrument issued in 1974, had the distinction of being the firm's first-ever "birthday edition" guitar.

The "Natural," two-pickup Custom featured in our photographs dates from 1978.

GIBSON EDS-1275

THE GIBSON EDS-1275 6- and 12-string doubleneck electric debuted in 1958. Produced only to special order, it originally sported a hollow body, though this had no f-holes; but by 1962, it had been restyled as an SG-type solid. Early 1275s (or "Double 12s" as they soon became known) of both kinds had spaced pairs of volume and tone controls mounted close to each of their bridges; this arrangement was eventually abandoned in favor of the standard knob grouping seen on the 1989-vintage 1275 in our photos.

The company's 1962 catalog described the Double 12 as "a completely new and exciting instrument," and adventurous guitarists such as UK "prog-rockers" Steve Howe of Yes and Charlie Whitney of Family relished the opportunity it gave them to switch effortlessly between its necks—or, indeed, to use them simultaneously. The 1275's best-known exponent was Jimmy Page of Led Zeppelin, who invariably featured it onstage when playing "Stairway to Heaven." However, the guitar apparently failed to please another eminent musician,

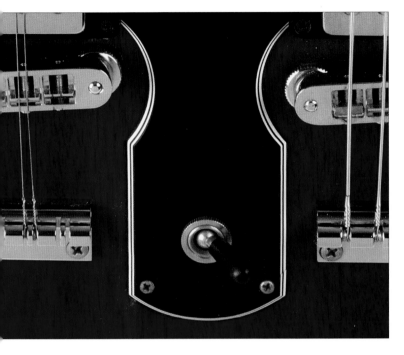

John McLaughlin of the Mahavishnu Orchestra, who tried it out in 1971, but quickly abandoned it in favor of a custom doubleneck made for him by luthier Rex Bogue. A later, more enthusiastic convert was Rush's Alex Lifeson, who began using the Double 12 in about 1977, and can still sometimes be spotted with one—notably on live performances of Rush's classic number "Xanadu," for which fellow band-member Geddy Lee dons a doubleneck Rickenbacker.

The EDS-1275's size and considerable weight may limit its appeal, and it was clearly never intended to sell in the same quantities as a Les Paul or an ES-335; nevertheless, it remains the world's only instantly recognizable doubleneck, and has a special place in the history of rock.

Above: This switch allows the player to select the pickups for just one of the two necks, or to combine them.

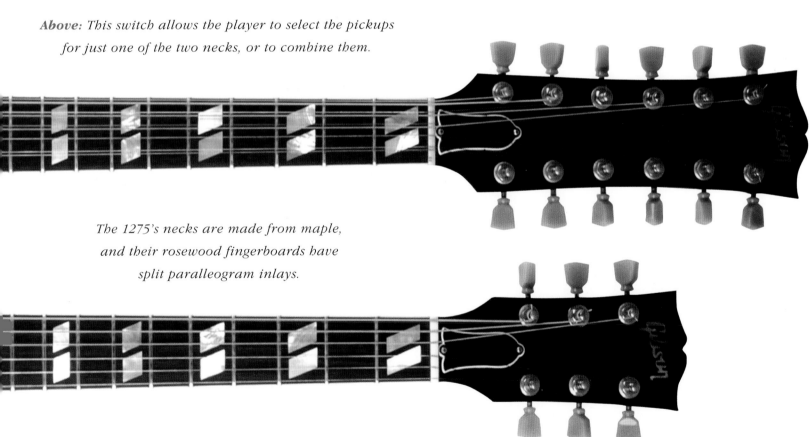

The 1275's necks are made from maple, and their rosewood fingerboards have split paralleogram inlays.

Left: To avoid a confusing proliferation of knobs, the 1275 has only overall volume and tone controls for the pickups on each of its necks.

CUSTOM
L-5

GIBSON L-5S

GIBSON'S FAMOUS L-5 MODEL had already been produced as an acoustic and electric archtop (see preceding pages), but in 1972 it appeared in a surprising new incarnation—as a solid. The L-5S, as it was termed, boasted an elegant maple body, a "Cherry Sunburst" finish (other color options were added later), and two low impedance pickups similar to the type previously used on certain late 1960s and early 70s Les Pauls. Impedance, sometimes referred to as Z, is a synonym for electrical resistance: the tendency of standard, high impedance guitar circuitry to pick up interference and unwanted noise often causes difficulties, especially in the recording studio, and low-Z pickups are much less prone to this problem. However, they also require additional electronics to allow them to work properly with regular, high-Z guitar amplifiers, and tend to produce weaker output signals. Such negative features severely limited the popularity of Gibson's low impedance transducers, and by 1974, they had been dropped from the L-5S in favor of conventional humbuckers. A year later, the guitar's tailpiece, which had been styled similarly to the one found on archtop L-5s, was replaced by a standard, "stop"-type component.

Below: The L-5S was eventually produced in three finishes: "Natural" (as here), and "Vintage" or "Cherry Sunburst."

Access to the L-5S's 22-fret neck is eased by its graceful cutaway.

Despite the "Custom" legend on its truss-rod cover, the L-5S was a regular, production instrument, albeit a top-of-the-line one. It was also one of the comparatively few models still being built at Gibson's original factory in Kalamazoo, Michigan; by the mid-1970s, the firm's owners, Norlin Industries (which had taken over from its previous parent company, CMI, in 1968), had shifted most other Gibson manufacturing to new premises located in Nashville, Tennessee.

The L-5S shown in our photographs was made in 1978, six years before the model was dropped from the Gibson range, and was previously the property of ex-Free, Bad Company (and latterly Queen) vocalist Paul Rodgers. Other major names known to be L-5S users include Paul Simon and jazzman Pat Martino, as well as Dave Davies of The Kinks.

Left: *This close-up reveals the fancy binding around the L-5S's ebony fingerboard—whose pointed end has been a feature of L-5 design since the 1920s.*

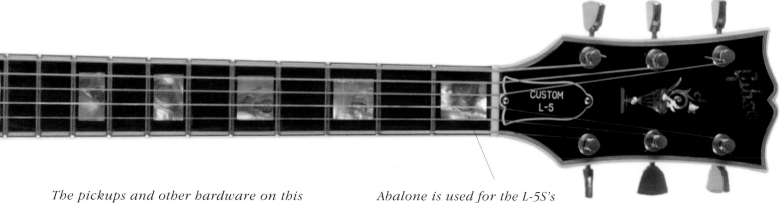

The pickups and other hardware on this guitar are gold-covered.

Abalone is used for the L-5S's fingerboard inlays and headstock decoration.

GIBSON LES PAUL BASS

THE FIRST Gibson Les Paul bass appeared in 1970. Like the Les Paul "Personal" 6-string guitar that debuted the previous year, it utilized low impedance circuitry, which offered greatly reduced background noise and an extended frequency response; company publicity claimed that the LP bass's "crisp, clear tones...[would] exceed [those] of any electric bass on the market to date." For most players, however, the undoubted benefits of low impedance instruments were outweighed by practical disadvantages, such as the need to use a transformer when plugging them into standard, high impedance amplifiers. Consequently, these models enjoyed only limited success—although the "Triumph" (as the original LP bass was relabeled in 1971), and a later, semi-hollow high impedance Les Paul bass named the "Signature," both remained in the catalog until 1979.

There were no more Les Paul basses until the 1990s, which saw the launch of a number of 4- and 5-stringers with bodies and looks inspired by the LP Standard and

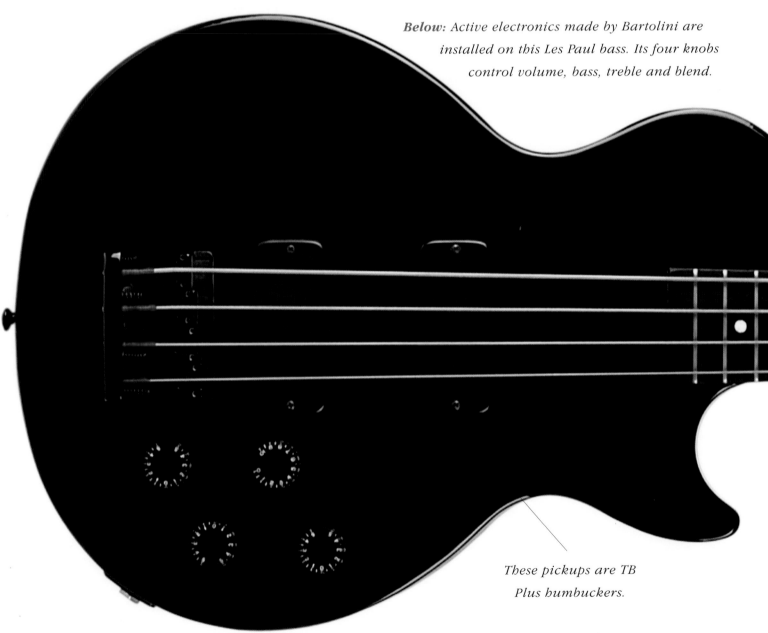

Below: Active electronics made by Bartolini are installed on this Les Paul bass. Its four knobs control volume, bass, treble and blend.

These pickups are TB Plus humbuckers.

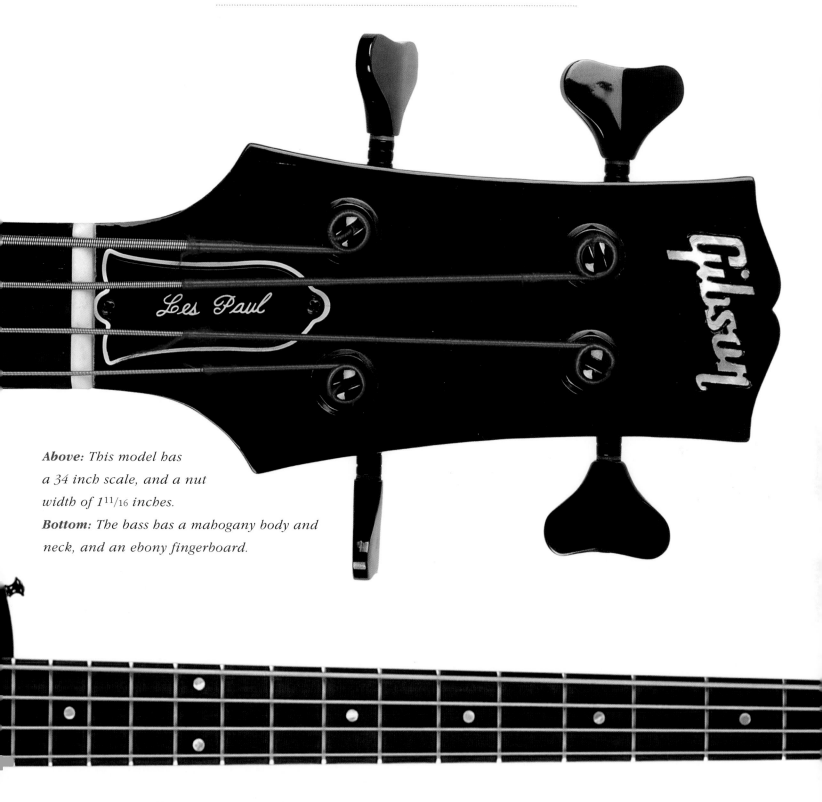

Above: This model has a 34 inch scale, and a nut width of 1¹¹/₁₆ inches.
Bottom: The bass has a mahogany body and neck, and an ebony fingerboard.

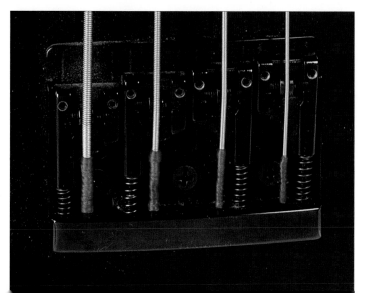

Special electric guitars. All had normal, high impedance pickups, and several boasted active electronics. The bass shown in our photos is a present-day descendant of these instruments: resembling a Les Paul Special, it is described by Gibson as combining "a classic look and solid performance with basic functionality." It is seen here in an "Ebony" finish, but is also available in "Classic White" and two other colors.

307

Grabbers were initially made in "Ebony" (as here) or "Red;" a natural-finish model appeared in 1976.

This sliding pickup is a humbucker.

GIBSON GRABBER BASS

Below: The Grabber has an alder body, and a maple neck and fingerboard.

IN 1973, GIBSON'S L9-S bass appeared—but, within a year, had been given a more memorable—not to say aggressive—new name, the Ripper. This was the start of a trend for Gibsons with a gutsy image: the next bass to come out of Kalamazoo was the Grabber, launched in 1974, and accompanied by a publicity campaign proclaiming that it "had not been hanging around for fifteen or twenty years," and was "not your standard bass in any way."

The Grabber was certainly "non-standard" for Gibson, as, unlike the company's previous basses, it had a bolt-on neck. Its other striking features included a pickup that players could slide up or down to alter the tone it produced, and a very distinctively pointed headstock that was replicated on the Maurader 6-string electric, which appeared the following year, in 1975.

The Grabber remained in Gibson's catalog until 1982.

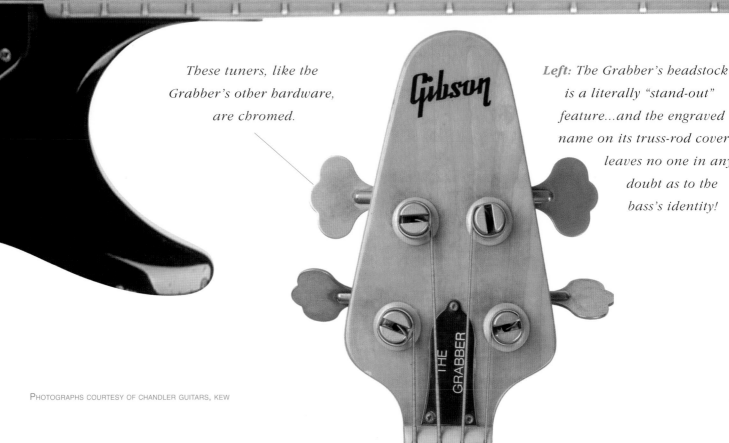

These tuners, like the Grabber's other hardware, are chromed.

Left: The Grabber's headstock is a literally "stand-out" feature...and the engraved name on its truss-rod cover leaves no one in any doubt as to the bass's identity!

GIBSON "THE PAUL"

IN THE LATE 1970s, Gibson unveiled its "Firebrand" series of electric guitars. This consisted of lower-cost, stripped-down versions of some of the company's most famous designs, and included a solid-body (!) imitation of the ES-335, as well as standard and deluxe reworkings of both the SG and Les Paul—which were differentiated from their full-price counterparts by the use of quote-marks around their names.

The standard "Paul" shown here dates from 1979. Its body is cut from a piece of mahogany, without the maple "crown" found on instruments such as the Les Paul Standard or Custom, and it has little in the way of visual refinement; even the "Gibson" logo is "burned" into the wood of its headstock instead of being inlaid.

Below: The dimensions of this guitar are almost identical to a genuine Les Paul—though its look and feel are very different.

Note the unusual placing of the pickup selector switch, which would normally be on the upper bass bout.

Below: The neck, like the body, is walnut; an ebony fingerboard is fitted.

The guitar's technical specification, in contrast, is surprisingly impressive: humbucking pickups and Grover machine heads are installed, and the owner of the store where this example was photographed comments that it has "very nice action, lovely sustain, and the usual range of Les Paul tones."

The regular "Paul" was available from 1978 until 1982; its deluxe cousin appeared in 1980, and survived until 1986. Neither has since been revived.

GIBSON LES PAUL (2002)

THE PROLIFERATION of Les Pauls in the current Gibson catalog provides a vast range of choices for players, whether their preference is for vintage-style models of the kind that Far Eastern manufacturers eagerly (and profitably) replicated during the years when the American originals were unavailable, or for striking new versions of the classic solid-body. The instrument shown here falls into the latter category. A Les Paul Standard Mahogany, dating from 2002, it lacks

Humbuckers supplied by the Santa Barbara, California-based Seymour Duncan company—which describes them as "built for aggressive playing styles," and "yield[ing] high output while retaining clarity."

Standard Mahogany guitars of this type are no longer produced by Gibson, and the example in our pictures is something of a rarity; the assistant in the store where it was photographed had not encountered one before, and eventually sold it to a collector.

Below: Mahogany, with a "Heritage Cherry" finish, is used for the Heritage Special's carved top and body; its neck is also made from mahogany, and has a rosewood fingerboard.

Right: This unusual Les Paul retains a regular headstock.

the maple top found on earlier Standards, and also departs from tradition by having three pickups instead of two. Despite being responsible, over the years, for the creation of a considerable number of classic transducer designs, Gibson occasionally turns to outside manufacturers for its electronics, and the units used on the Standard Mahogany are Distortion

Opposite page: This Les Paul boasts a trio of impressively powerful Seymour Duncan pickups.

GIBSON BLUESHAWK

The BluesHawk has a mahogany neck with a rosewood fingerboard.

GIBSON'S "HAWK" SERIES OF ELECTRIC GUITARS was born in 1993, when the solid-body, single cutaway Nighthawk made its debut. It attracted a considerable following (high-profile users included Joe Walsh of The Eagles), and three years later, the range was augmented by the BluesHawk—a thinline, hollow-body design fitted with two Gibson's "Blues 90" pickups. These incorporate a dummy coil to reduce noise and interference, and produce an impressive range of sounds, especially when used in conjunction with the NightHawk's Varitone tone selector. After being switched into circuit by pulling up the tone control, this can then adjusted, via a rotary knob below the pickup selector, to provide preset filter settings that thicken or brighten the BluesHawk's timbre.

Like its predecessor, the BluesHawk proved fairly popular with players, thanks in part to Gibson's shrewd marketing strategy. In 1998, the company offered a limited edition version of the guitar as a prize in the prestigious annual Chicago Bluesfest competition, and, during the 2000–1 hockey season, it awarded a BluesHawk to the best "air guitarist" spotted among the spectators at a Nashville Predators match. However, although such efforts undoubtedly boosted the instrument's profile, its success has never rivalled that of classic solid body Gibsons such as the Les Paul and SG.

These "Blues 90" pickups, in conjunction with the BluesHawk's Varitone circuitry, can offer eighteen distinct sound settings.

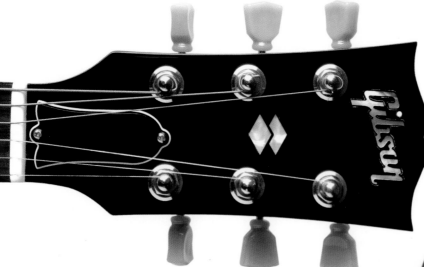

Right and above: *The BluesHawk's back and sides are made from poplar, and it has a maple top. "Diamond" inlays grace its both its headstock and fingerboard.*

PHOTOGRAPHS COURTESY OF PEACH, BLAKE END, BRAINTREE

…culminating in its recent reissue under the name of "Southern" rather than "Southerner" Jumbo!

Supplies of early SJs were limited due to wartime restrictions, but the new guitar quickly attracted a considerable following: prominent 1940s users included singer and political activist Woody Guthrie, who famously stuck a "This Machine Kills Fascists" label to the body of his Southerner. For a while, the headstock of all SJs carried a slogan of Gibson's own— "Only A Gibson Is Good Enough;" however, this was quickly removed in 1946 after the company's rival, Epiphone, launched an ad campaign based around the words "When Good Enough Isn't Good Enough."

During the 1950s, SJ sales grew, prompting Gibson to produce it in a new, natural-finish version; in 1956, this was given a separate identity as the "Country-Western," and details of it are provided overleaf. The Southerner itself remained in the catalog until the late 1970s, and is now available once more as the "Southern Jumbo:" a newly made example of it is featured here.

GIBSON SJN COUNTRY WESTERN

AS PREVIOUSLY EXPLAINED, Gibson "Country-Western" flat-tops were simply Southerner Jumbos with natural finishes. The Country-Western name was retained only until 1960, when it was altered to SJN (Southerner Jumbo Natural). This relatively unimportant change was followed by a more significant modification to both the SJN and the original sunburst-finish Southerner Jumbo, as their "traditional," non-adjustable bridges were replaced with units sporting a saddle that could be raised or lowered by two screws.

(The substitution was controversial: quite a number of players felt that the new bridges had an adverse effect on the instruments' tone, and by the end of the decade, Gibson had reverted to the earlier type.)

In 1962, the natural SJN received yet another new name, the SJN Country Western, and that year's Gibson catalog extolled the model's "deep resonance, powerful tone and deluxe appearance." However, the familiar, round-shouldered shape of the SJN and Southerner was about to disappear: a year later, the

Below: This 1964 SJN Country Western has a spruce top, and mahogany back and sides.

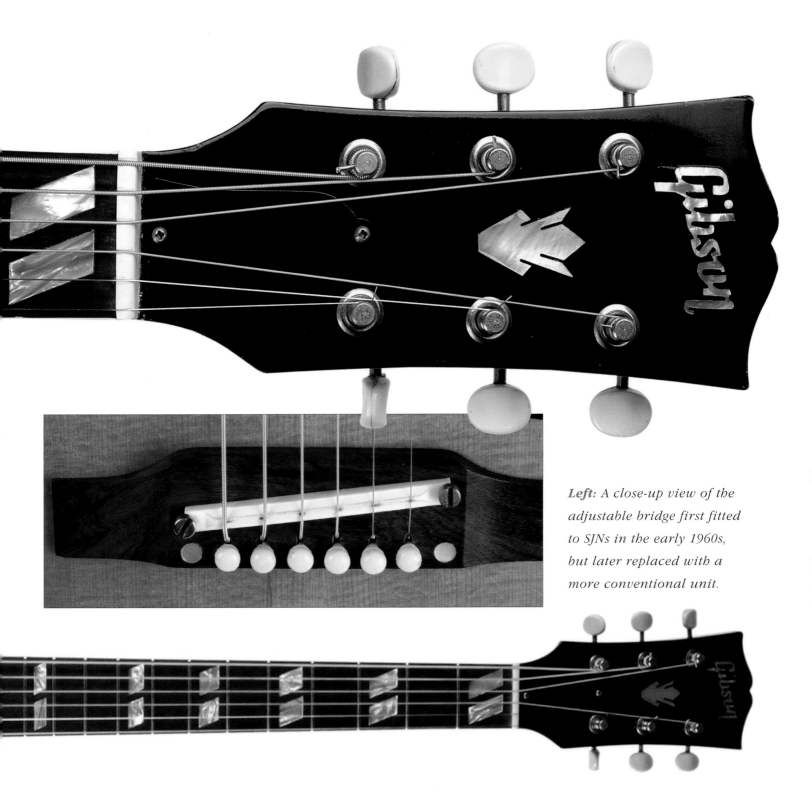

Left: A close-up view of the adjustable bridge first fitted to SJNs in the early 1960s, but later replaced with a more conventional unit.

guitars received new, squarer body stylings similar to those on the highly successful Hummingbird (see separate entry) and Dove flat-tops. The Country Western in our photos dates from 1964, and features the different outline, which the CW and Southerner both kept until they were discontinued in 1978.

Despite the drawbacks caused by its adjustable bridge, the "squared-off" SJN Country Western is a striking instrument, both sonically and visually. Among its many devotees is singer-songwriter Sheryl Crow, who bought one in the 1960s, and has used it onstage and in the studio for many years. In 2000, Gibson launched a "Sheryl Crow Signature Model" closely based on the star's guitar; more recently, the company has produced a "Country Western 1958 Reissue" that replicates the pre-1962 version of the acoustic.

J-45

GIBSON J-45

THE JAPANESE ATTACK on Pearl Harbor took place on December 8, 1941. The USA declared war on Japan the following day, and was soon devoting most of its industrial capacity to defence-related projects—a move that inevitably restricted the production of non-essential goods such as guitars. During the war years, Gibson saw the majority of its staff redeployed onto war work (music historians Eldon Whitford, David Vinopal and Dan Erlewine state that only 10% of its craftsmen were available to make instruments between

1942 to 1945), while shortages of wood and other materials led to inevitable variations in the specifications of the models that were actually built. With steel at a premium, some of these lacked truss-rods, while others had to be constructed with non-standard timbers and surplus parts.

America's first full year of conflict was scarcely an auspicious time to launch new flat-tops, but in summer 1942, the company's latest acoustics, the J-45 and the Southerner (featured on pages 330-1), began shipping

Below: The J-45 is no longer available in this square-shouldered form, but has been reissued in its original, rounder body shape.

PHOTOGRAPHS COURTESY OF GUITAR JUNCTION, WORTHING

from its Michigan headquarters. Both were 16 inches wide, round-shouldered, spruce-topped jumbos that initially carried an "Only A Gibson Is Good Enough" slogan on their headstocks—although the J-45, unlike the earliest, rosewood-bodied batch of Southerners, had a mahogany back and sides. Its appearance was somewhat spartan, but its gutsy tone quickly endeared it to customers, and, in spite of the uncertainties of wartime manufacturing, it went on to become a best seller.

Post-1945, the J-45 succeeded in retaining its status as a popular "workhorse" instrument, despite several changes in design. The most important of these occurred in 1969, when it acquired the square-shoulder body outline already sported by the Southerner and SJN. The J-45 in our photos dates from this time, and originally had a standard sunburst finish; however, in the 1970s, its then owner had this replaced with its current, "natural" coloring.

Below: *Rosewood is used for the J-45's 20-fret fingerboard, which has mother-of-pearl dot inlays.*

Left: *Though different in appearance to the adjustable bridge on the SJN Country Western (see previous pages), this unit operates similarly.*

GIBSON COUNTRY GENTLEMAN

AFTER THE INTRODUCTION of his nylon-strung acoustic by Gibson in 1982 (see previous pages), Chet Atkins went on to collaborate with the company on updated versions of two instruments bearing his name that had first been produced by Gretsch in the late 1950s. One of these was the Country Gentleman electric archtop, which appeared in its new

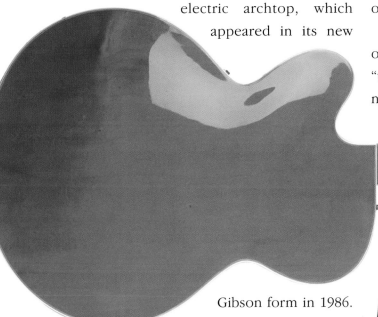

Gibson form in 1986. Gretsch Country Gentle-men made between 1957 and 1972 had boasted feedback-reducing sealed tops and fake, painted-on f-holes (a Gretsch-made Chet Atkins electric featuring these is shown later in this book), but for the Gibson model, this striking example of *trompe l'oeil* was

abandoned, and the guitar was given a Gibson 335-style solid center block to improve its performance at higher volume levels, and to boost sustain. Other changes included the replacement of Gretsch's "Filter'Tron" pickups with a pair of Gibson humbuckers, and the provision of a banjo-type armrest on the edge of the body.

This 2003 "CG" differs slightly from the 1986 original: block fretboard markers have replaced the "thumbprint" inlays seen on earlier Gentlemen, and a non-vibrato tailpiece has been fitted.

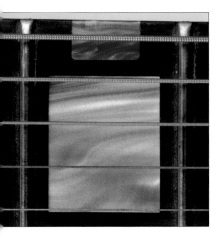

Left: A close-up of the distinctive double position markers on the instrument's ebony fingerboard.

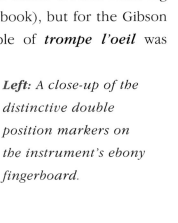

Right: The endorsee's name is inlaid on the guitar's truss-rod cover in "pearl holly."

DOBRO DM33 "HAWAIIAN"

The resonator cone on this Dobro measures 10¹/₂ inches.

IN 1993, GIBSON TOOK OVER the Original Musical Instruments (OMI) firm, which had been manufacturing Dobros since 1967 under the direction of the Dopyera family (see earlier Dobro entries). Today, OMI is part of Gibson's Original Acoustic Instrument division. This is based at the Gibson Bluegrass Showcase in the Opry Mills shopping mall near Nashville, Tennessee, where members of the public can watch models such as the DM33H Dobro featured in these photos (as well as Gibson banjos and mandolins) being constructed, assembled and finished; the 30,000 square foot venue also incorporates restaurant facilities and a concert venue.

The DM33 range comprises a number of identically specified, chrome-plated bell-brass guitars, etched or engraved with differing decorations; the "H" suffix on our Dobro indicates that it has a classic "Hawaiian" etching on its back. An extensive selection of other metal and wood-bodied acoustic and electric Dobros is also currently available from Gibson, including the popular, reasonably priced Hound Dog model; and as a result, the future of this classic resonator instrument, so often eclipsed by uncertainty, seems secure.

Above: A wooden neck, bearing the famous Dobro trademark on its headstock, is attached to the guitar's brass body.

Right: The "fan" pattern on the instrument's coverplate has been in use since the Dobro's earliest days.

Alternative designs available on the DM33s include "Sailboat" and "California Girl" etchings.

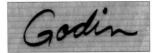

GODIN MULTIAC STEEL DUET

CANADIAN DESIGNER and musician Robert Godin has been the driving force behind a number of successful and innovative acoustic brands, such as Art & Lutherie and Norman (see separate entries). However, it is the product line bearing his own name, and established in 1987, which features his most cutting-edge instruments—electrics and electro-acoustics that combine traditional craftsmanship and high technology in ingenious ways.

Godin's Multiac series includes both nylon- and steel-strung models: the Multiac in our pictures is a Steel Duet. This has a mahogany body with two acoustic chambers, but is intended to be heard through an amplifier or a PA system, and incorporates two separate, but blendable transducers (hence the

Right: The Multiac's open headstock has a reassuringly traditional look.

Left: Like many more conventional acoustics, the Multiac Steel Duet has a spruce top, a mahogany neck and a rosewood fingerboard.

"Duet" in its name). The first of these is an "I-Beam" unit, which responds to vibrations from the underside of the guitar's top; the other sound source is a more conventional under-saddle pickup. Their signals are combined and adjusted via the controls to the left of the Multiac's strings, and then sent to two output sockets, mounted on the side of the guitar's body. The first of these is for a conventional jack, while the other accommodates a balanced XLR connector of the kind favored for professional recording and PA applications. In addition, the

XLR circuit is able to supply "phantom power" to the guitar's preamp, avoiding the need to rely on an internal battery.

Other Multiacs can also provide synthesizer access, as can the Godin xtSA shown overleaf.

These knobs and sliders adjust and blend the Multiac's pickups.

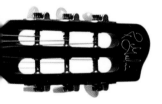

Right: *The Multiac is available in two types of natural finish: "semi-gloss" or "high-gloss."*

GODIN xtSA

THE GODIN xtSA offers players three separate "voices," which can be deployed separately or combined. Its "standard" electric guitar tones are produced via three magnetic pickups: a central single-coil unit, and two humbuckers at the neck and bridge positions. These are controlled by volume and tone knobs, as well as a 5-position switch that allows a variety of combinations, and provides coil-tapping. For realistic "acoustic guitar" sounds, the xtSA has transducers (designed and built by RMC of Berkeley, California) imbedded in each of its bridge saddles; their overall volume and EQ can be adjusted by means of the four sliders (volume, treble, midrange and bass) mounted on the instrument's upper bass bout. The xtSA's third output is a "hexaphonic" one, via which signals from each of the guitar's six strings can be used

Below: The xtSA's body is made from silver leaf maple and poplar; it has a mahogany neck and an ebony fingerboard.

PHOTOGRAPHS COURTESY OF PEACH, BLAKE END, BRAINTREE

Below: *A view of the single-coil center pickup, the bridge humbucker, and the transducer-equipped bridge that help to supply the xtSA's huge range of sounds.*

Above: *The xtSA is built in Berlin, New Hampshire, from parts supplied by Godin's headquarters in Quebec, Canada.*

to trigger a synthesizer and create an almost unlimited range of sounds. The synth output level can be turned up and down by the knob immediately below the magnetic pickup volume, while the guitar's output sockets allow its "pseudo-acoustic" and electric signals to be routed to separate amplifiers, and also provide a full synth interface.

As one user recently put it, "this guitar does everything but make the coffee!"

JAMES GOODALL JUMBO

JAMES GOODALL makes his acoustic guitars in the idyllic surroundings of Kailua-Kona, Hawaii. Born and raised in southern California, he was already a proficient and successful seascape painter prior to developing a fascination for guitar building in the early 1970s. He constructed his first-ever instrument using tools loaned by his father, a skilled woodworker, and the woods and other materials required for it were purchased with proceeds from one of Goodall's oil paintings. Over the following years, he continued to earn his living as an artist whilst pursuing his passion for lutherie, to which he eventually decided to devote himself full-time in 1978.

Goodall produces an extensive range of flat-top designs, from Parlor models to Dreadnoughts: like many of his creations, the superb KJ 2519 jumbo model seen here features locally-grown koa wood on its back and sides; its top is made from sitka spruce, and has maple bindings and abalone inlays. A built-in active pickup system is included.

Below: *The decorations around the KJ 2519's sound-hole are created with green heart abalone.*

Right: *Elliot Easton's signature appears on his guitar's pickguard. The edge of its bridge, set into the body to help provide stable intonation, can also be seen.*

Bottom: *The Duo Jet seen here is fitted with a Bigsby B7 vibrato; however, an alternative model is also available with a non-vibrato, "G-Stop" tailpiece.*

emerged with a Japanese-made line of instruments in 1989; and 11 years later, a Signature Jet model, endorsed by former Cars and Creedence Clearwater Revisted guitarist Elliot Easton, was announced. Like the original, it has a semi-hollow mahogany body, but its 25-inch scale is slightly longer than those on 50s and 60s Jets. Locking Sperzel machine heads are fitted to improve tuning stability, and the pickups are "Filter'Trons."

GRETSCH G6120 BRIAN SETZER

BRIAN SETZER shot to prominence in the 1980s with his trio, the Stray Cats, and, since 1992, has been serving up his distinctive brand of big band rockabilly with the Brian Setzer Orchestra. A longtime fan of Gretschs, he purchased a 1959 "6120 Nashville" electric in New York in 1999, and has used it extensively on stage ever since. Gretsch's "Artist Signature Model" range currently contains a pair of 6120s closely resembling this prized guitar. Named the G6120SSU and G6120SSL, these have identical specifications, but slightly different finishes; the SSL is seen here. Like the company's other Setzer-endorsed instruments, they feature pickups designed by TV Jones, who has worked on the star's personal guitar collection since the 1990s...as well as "white dice" control knobs like those on Setzer's own Gretsch!

Below: The bracing on this model matches that used on Brian Setzer's own 6120, providing (in Gretsch's words) "a more solid feel with tons of sustain."

A Bigsby vibrato like this one is a must for rockabilly!

Above: *The inclusion of these "dice" on the Setzer Gretsch may be inspired by a line mentioning them in his classic song "Drive Like Lightning (Crash Like Thunder)."*

Above: *The guitar bas a two-piece maple neck and an ebony fingerboard.*

GRETSCH SILVER FALCON

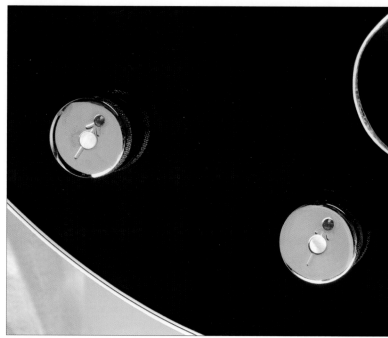

THE JAPANESE-MADE SILVER FALCON seen here is a direct descendant of the famous #6136 White Falcon—Gretsch's top-of-the-range model, introduced in 1955 at what was then the astronomical price of $600. Featuring gold-plated hardware, sparkly inlays and "wing"-decorated fret markers (later replaced by "thumbnail"-style ones), it was, even by Gretsch's less-than-restrained design standards, an extraordinarily glamorous guitar. At its launch, the company declared that it was intended as "an instrument for the artist-player whose calibre justifies and demands the utmost in striking beauty, luxurious styling, and peak tonal

Right: The Silver Falcon's stylish control knobs closely resemble those on late 1950s Gretsch electrics.

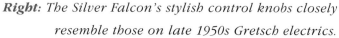

Below: The Silver Falcon has a 17-inch wide, 2¾-inch deep hollow body made from laminated maple.

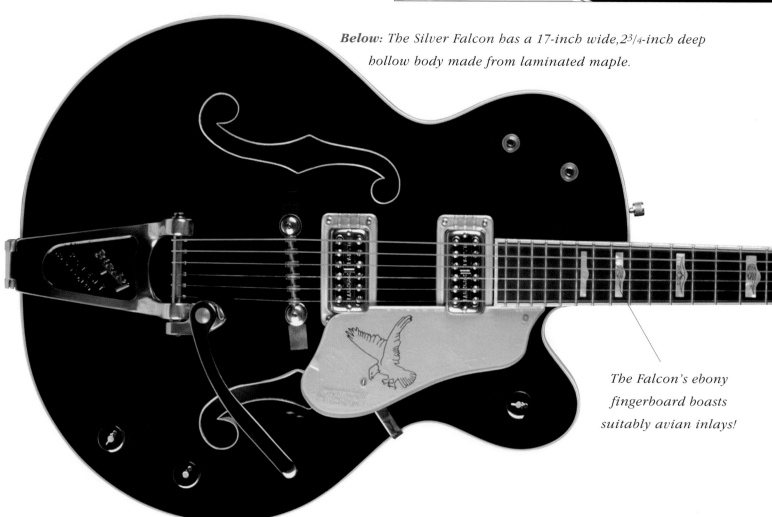

The Falcon's ebony fingerboard boasts suitably avian inlays!

PHOTOGRAPHS COURTESY OF AMERICAN GUITAR CENTRE & BASSWORLD, TONBRIDGE

performance, and who is willing to pay [for this]."

Over the next few years, the Falcon—whose name, according to Tony Bacon and Paul Day's **The Gretsch Book** (1996) may have been inspired by a World War II US services newspaper also called the **White Falcon**—was graced (or, perhaps, cursed) with a succession of specification changes and gimmicky add-ons. One beneficial upgrade was the substitution of "Filter'Tron" humbuckers for its original DeArmond pickups in 1957. Among the less successful innovations was the "Project-o-Sonic" option introduced in 1958. This provided a twin-channel effect that sent the output from the top three strings to one amplifier, and signals from their lower-pitched neighbors to another; an even more elaborate (and bewilderingly complex) "stereo" Falcon appeared in the mid-1960s.

The Falcon disappeared from regular production in the early 1980s, but was revived in 1990, and has subsequently been joined in the Gretsch catalog by Black and Silver Falcons (these made their debuts, respectively, in 1992 and 1995).

With its dual "Filter'Trons" and single-cutaway body (Falcons sported a double cutaway from 1962 to the early '70s), the "silver bird" in our pictures has many similarities to a late '50s White Falcon; and although its Bigsby vibrato is a slight anachronism (Bigsbys were not fitted as standard to Falcons until 1962), its construction and inlays all closely match those found on its distinguished forbear.

Above: The "sparkle" embellishments on the Falcon's "wings," Gretsch logo and truss-rod cover are not dissimilar to those seen on the company's drumkits!

GRIMSHAW 1960s SEMI-HOLLOW

EMILE GRIMSHAW (1880-1943) was a leading British banjoist and composer who set up an instrument-making firm, Emile Grimshaw & Son, in London, ten years before his death; it produced banjos and, subsequently, guitars, including a three-pickup semi-acoustic that was used (with a Rickenbacker truss-rod cover attached to it!) by Pete Townshend of The Who in the mid-1960s. The model seen here dates from approximately the same period, and, though sporting only two pickups, has the same outline and distinctive control panel as Townshend's. By the 1970s, the Grimshaw company was manufacturing copies of popular Gibson and Fender solid-bodies, but it had ceased operations by the end of that decade. Its acoustics and electrics are fondly remembered by many players, and one well-known UK luthier, Rosendean Guitars' Trevor Dean, bases the body shapes of his single-cutaway models on Grimshaws.

Below: This Grimshaw has a spruce top and maple back and sides; it carries the model designation "S.5 Custom."

This knob is a master volume control.

PHOTOGRAPHS COURTESY OF THE LONDON RESONATOR CENTRE

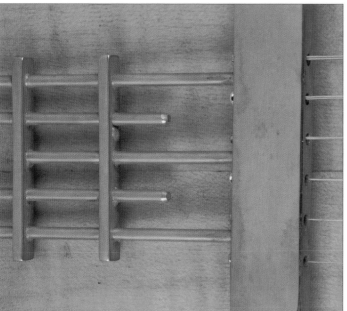

Above left: The guitar's body is in pristine condition.

Above right: These headstock decorations are similar to those on some Grimshaw banjos.

Left: On some Grimshaws, this elegant tailpiece was replaced with a Bigsby vibrato.

GUILD ARTIST AWARD ARCHTOP

THE GUILD COMPANY was founded in New York in 1952 by Polish-born store proprietor and musician Alfred Dronge (1911-1972) and his business partner George Mann, who had formerly worked for Epiphone (see separate entries). Mann's involvement with the new firm was relatively brief, but, as a result of Dronge's energy and enterprise, Guild soon managed to establish an extremely impressive reputation for its guitars, which were especially highly regarded by some of the Big Apple's leading jazz players.

In 1955, one of this elite group of musicians, Johnny Smith (who had achieved international recognition as a result of his recording of "Moonlight in Vermont" with saxophonist Stan Getz three years previously), agreed to collaborate with Dronge on the development of a Guild archtop, to be named the Johnny Smith Artist Award. The instrument appeared a year later, by which time the firm had relocated to Hoboken, New

Below: The Artist Award has a carved solid spruce top, maple back and sides, and a maple and walnut neck.

These inlays are mother-of-pearl; the same material is used for the headstock decoration.

Top: *The guitar has a 17-inch wide body, and is just over 3 inches deep.*

Jersey; however, due to a disagreement between Smith and Guild over its specification, the musician never actually used it in public or in the studio. It continued to bear his name until 1960, after which it became known simply as the Artist Award Model. It remained in production for decades, and is now regarded as a design classic. This example dates from the 1990s.

379

GUILD B-302F FRETLESS BASS

GUILD'S FIRST bass guitar, the solid-body Jet-Star, debuted in 1964; like nearly all the company's basses, it was closely modeled on an existing 6-string design—in this case, the Thunderbird electric that had appeared the previous year. Its single pickup was supplied by the Swedish Hagström guitar company, which was to provide transducers and bridges for all Guild basses until about 1972.

1965 saw the launch of the Starfire bass. It was quickly adopted by up-and-coming players such as Jack Casady of the Jefferson Airplane, and in an article for *Bass Player* magazine in 2005, Dave Pomeroy observes that the "beefy, resonant, and wonderfully dirty tone" Casady obtained from his customized Starfire paved the way for the bolder bass modifications subsequently undertaken by electronics experts such as Ron Wickersham of Alembic (see separate entries).

Guild continued to come up with distinctive basses throughout the late 1960s and 70s: the semi-solid, dual pickup M-85 was introduced in 1967 and recreated as a solid-body five years later; while in 1976 and 1977, the firm unveiled the B-301 and B-302. These were,

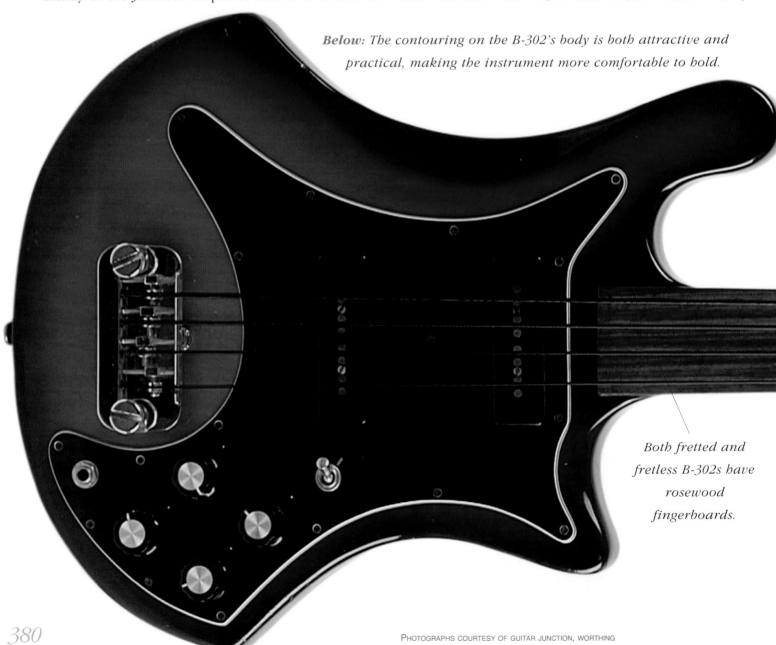

Below: The contouring on the B-302's body is both attractive and practical, making the instrument more comfortable to hold.

Both fretted and fretless B-302s have rosewood fingerboards.

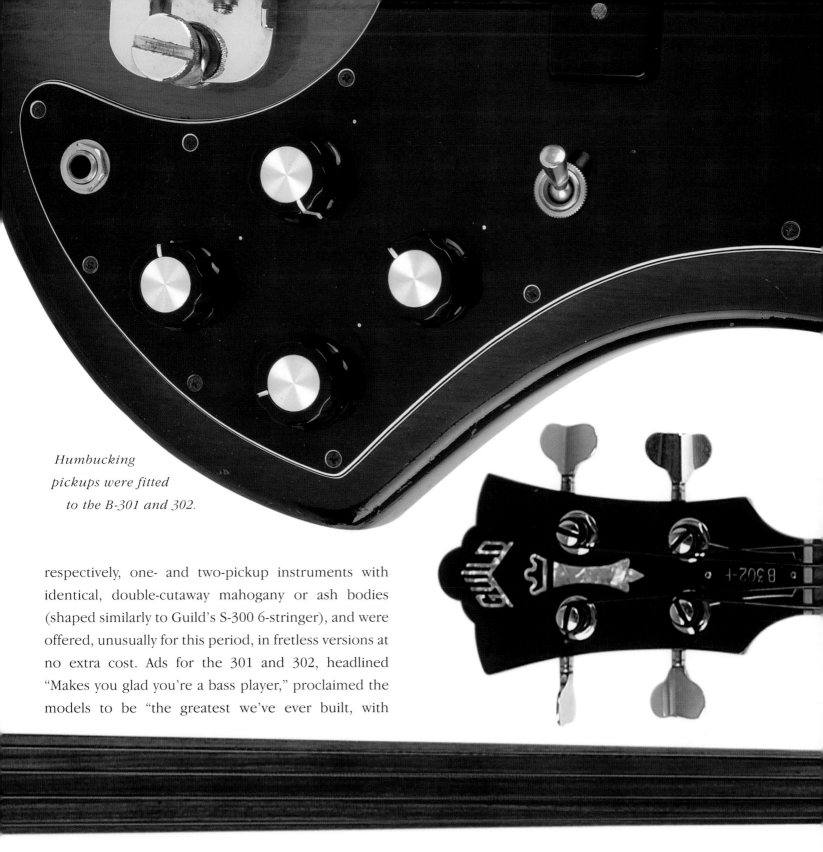

*Humbucking
pickups were fitted
to the B-301 and 302.*

respectively, one- and two-pickup instruments with identical, double-cutaway mahogany or ash bodies (shaped similarly to Guild's S-300 6-stringer), and were offered, unusually for this period, in fretless versions at no extra cost. Ads for the 301 and 302, headlined "Makes you glad you're a bass player," proclaimed the models to be "the greatest we've ever built, with

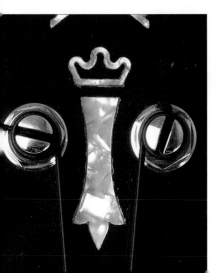

Left: According to Guild expert Hans Moust, this type of inlay is known as a "Chesterfield," as it resembles the logo on a Chesterfield cigarette packet.

everything you want for the way you play today," and with their long-scale fretboards, optional stereo wiring, and striking looks, they lived up to their publicity, and proved to be steady, though not spectacular sellers.

A fretless Guild B-302 dating from 1978 is shown in our photographs; the 301 and 302 were both discontinued in 1981.

GUILD D-40

GUILD BEGAN PRODUCING flat-top acoustics in 1954. Its early models had both prosaic catalog numbers and more evocative, Spanish-inspired names: hence the company's first three flat-tops, the F-30, F-40, and F-50, were also known, respectively, as the Aragon, Valencia and Navarre. The Aragon, described in a contemporary Guild brochure as "a quality leader among guitars," was just over 15 inches wide, and had a spruce top and maple back and sides (later changed to mahogany); the 16-inch Valencia and jumbo-sized Navarre were also maple-bodied, and, unlike the Aragon, were available in a choice of sunburst and blonde finishes. Two years later, the line was augmented by the Troubador F-20; smaller and cheaper than its sisters, it was intended, in Guild's words, for both "solo playing and ballad accompaniment." Further low-price flat-tops followed in 1958 and 59, when the all-mahogany Economy M-20 and Del Rio M-30 made their debuts.

The lack of any dreadnoughts in the Guild range was

Below: D-40s have spruce tops, with mahogany backs and sides. Their fingerboards and bridges are made from rosewood.

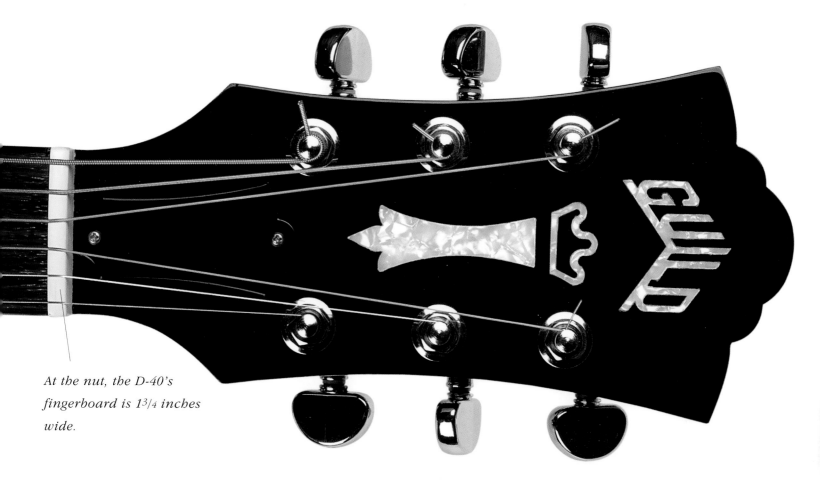

At the nut, the D-40's fingerboard is 1³/4 inches wide.

an obvious and puzzling deficiency that persisted throughout the company's first decade; according to Hans Moust's **Guild Guitar Book**, it was Alfred Dronge's son Mark who finally persuaded his father to introduce them. (Mark had joined the firm straight

Above: This D-40 is fitted with nickel-plated machine heads supplied by Grover.

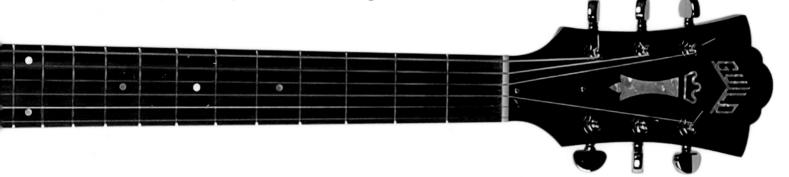

from college in 1960, and later became its sales manager.) Thanks to his efforts, the D-40 (seen here) and D-50 (featured on the next two pages) appeared in 1963. They proved to be a popular and cost-effective alternative to a Gibson or Martin, and, to quote Ken Achard's **History and Development of the American Guitar**, "laid the basis of a very successful line of...large square shaped [acoustics]."

Left: The reference to "Corona, California" on this label indicates that our D-40 was made after Guild's takeover by Fender in 1995.

The guitar's body is just over 3 inches deep.

This is a master volume control.

X-170

GUILD X-170

ALTHOUGH THE ORIGINAL X-175 Manhattan (see previous pages) was dropped from the Guild catalog in 1984 after two decades in production, the company soon introduced a substitute for it. Named the X-170 "Mini-Manhattan," it was slightly narrower and thinner than its distinguished predecessor, and, with its internal soundpost and more rigid, laminated maple top (the old Manhattan's had been made from spruce), was better able to resist feedback in noisy onstage conditions. The guitar was also given a glamorous new look, with gold plating on its pickups, machine heads, and "harp" tailpiece.

By now, Guild's instrument output had diversified considerably. A glance at one of its mid-1980s catalogs reveals old favorites such as the Artist Award and the Starfire rubbing shoulders with boldly styled solids—including, most strikingly, the angular, cut-out body X100 Blade Runner, designed by a third-party, David Andrews Guitar Research, and used by Eddie Ojeda of the heavy metal band Twisted Sister. Despite such courageous

innovations, however, times were not easy for the firm in the 1980s, a period that saw two changes of ownership, and various financial problems.

In 1995, Guild was purchased by Fender, a development that prompted one delighted long-time staffer to comment "We finally hit a home run." For a while, its guitars continued to be built at its Rhode Island factory, but this closed in August 2001, and Guild is now based alongside its parent in Corona, California.

Above: Sealed Grover Rotomatic tuners are fitted to the X-170, which also sports the classic Guild "Chesterfield" headstock inlay (see pages 380-1).

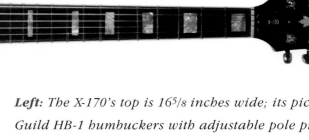

Left: The X-170's top is 16⅝ inches wide; its pickups are Guild HB-1 humbuckers with adjustable pole pieces.

This instrument was made in 1997; the X-170 was discontinued in 2002.

ARMIN HANIKA 6oPF CLASSICAL

HELMUT HANIKA SET UP the lutherie firm that bears his surname in 1953; it is located in Baiersdorf, in the south German state of Bavaria. Instrument making ran in the family: Helmut had originally been trained as a violin builder by his grandfather, Anton Mayer, and in due course, his own son, Armin Hanika, came to work alongside him at Baiersdorf. Armin obtained a master craftsman's diploma in 1987 (in Germany, this qualification is mandatory for anyone wishing to embark on a career as a luthier), and took over the business in 1994. He now produces his guitars, largely by hand, with a small team of employees, and frequently shares his skills with students at the "info-workshops" he holds in Germany and elsewhere.

Hanika guitars fall into four categories: "basic," "middle," "higher" ("oberklasse" in German), and "master;" the Baiersdorf plant also boasts a flourishing custom shop. Even its student instruments (unlike those of some competitors) are made from solid woods, which deliver a far better tone than plywood can provide, while more elaborate, master-grade models such as the 60PF shown here are designed for what the company terms "fastidious guitar virtuosos" seeking "unforgettable sound experiences." The 60PF has a spruce top, a back and sides of Indian rosewood, and an ebony fingerboard.

Above: Hanika guitars are available all over Europe and America, and are used by a wide cross-section of classical players.

Left: All Hanika "meisterklasse" guitars feature a characteristic "carved-out" upper headstock.

Right: This elegantly decorated rosette is a fine example of Hanika's painstaking workmanship.

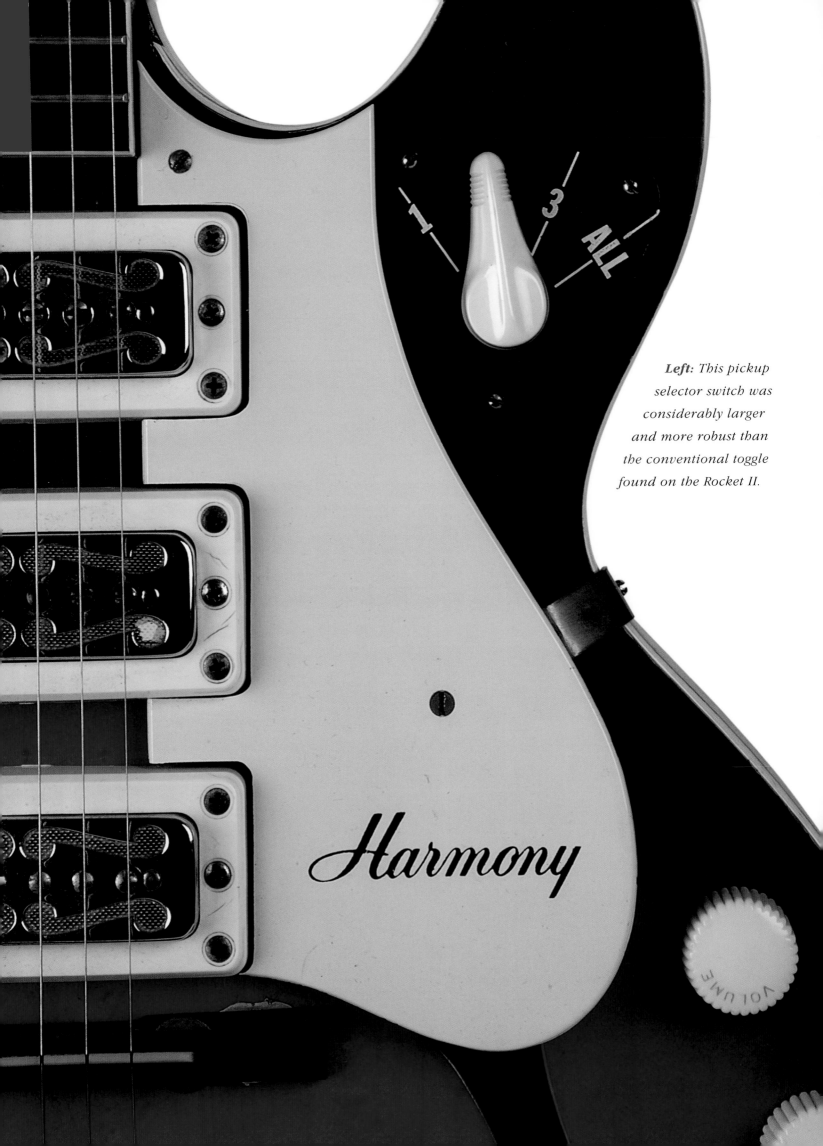

Left: *This pickup selector switch was considerably larger and more robust than the conventional toggle found on the Rocket II.*

HARMONY ROCKET III

HARMONY, FOUNDED IN CHICAGO in 1892, became a major supplier of inexpensive stringed instruments to retailers and catalog houses, including Sears, Roebuck & Company, which purchased it in 1916. A subsequent endorsement deal with vaudeville, movie and radio star Roy Smeck, who excelled on guitar, banjo and ukulele, brought Harmony even greater prosperity, and in the post-war era it skillfully adjusted its product range to match new musical trends by offering attractive, if basic, electrics alongside its longer-established lines.

The Harmony Rocket range of electric guitars debuted in 1958. The name seems to have been chosen in response to the "space-age" overtones of Fender's Stratocaster; significantly, other Harmonys launched during this period included the Stratotone Mercury and Stratotone Jupiter. The firm's 1960 catalog lists three Rockets, boasting (respectively) one, two and three pickups; all had single cutaways and ultra-thin bodies. This Rocket III dates from 1962; by the late 1960s, the Rocket models had been revamped, and double cutaways introduced.

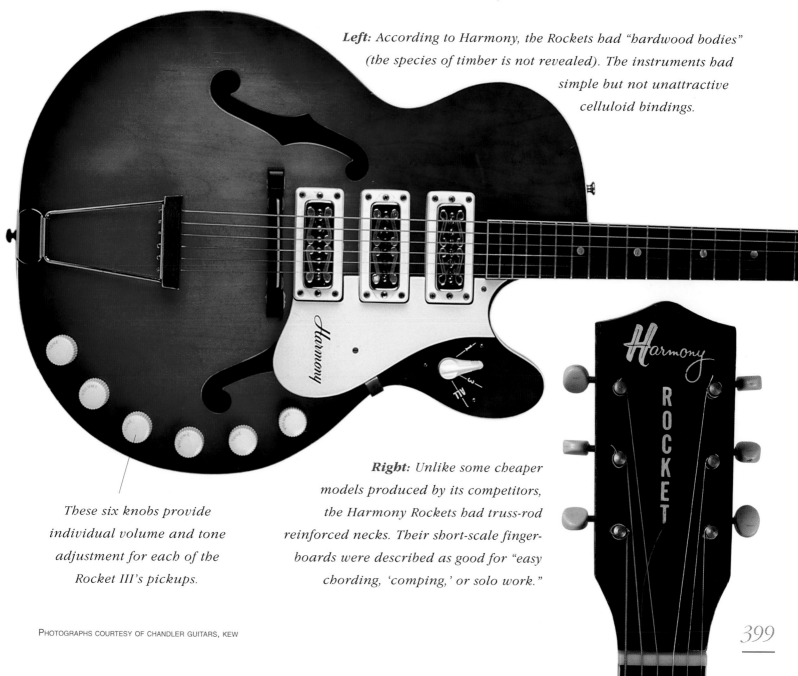

Left: According to Harmony, the Rockets had "hardwood bodies" (the species of timber is not revealed). The instruments had simple but not unattractive celluloid bindings.

These six knobs provide individual volume and tone adjustment for each of the Rocket III's pickups.

Right: Unlike some cheaper models produced by its competitors, the Harmony Rockets had truss-rod reinforced necks. Their short-scale fingerboards were described as good for "easy chording, 'comping,' or solo work."

Above: Like the original, this bass has paired, open-geared machine heads.

Above: The 500/1's spruce topped, maple-backed body is only 18 inches long, and 11 inches across at its widest point. It is just over 2 inches deep.

This zero fret removes some of the "ring" from openstrings, and helps the instrument stay in tune for longer.

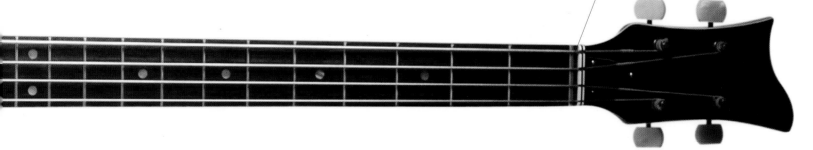

endorsement deal with Höfner, although for many years new 500/1s were sold with a label carrying his face and signature, plus a personal message wishing new purchasers "every success with this guitar."

The "Beatle bass" seen here is a modern, reissue instrument, produced by Höfner's factory in Hagenau, Germany. It retains all the distinctive features of the original 500/1, including a zero fret and somewhat quaint control panel, and despite its 50-year old design, still has considerable appeal to today's bassists.

HÖFNER 172 SOLID-BODY

BY THE EARLY 1960S, the traditional, violin-inspired appearance of Höfner's archtops was beginning to seem somewhat staid and dated, especially in comparison with the slim, solid-bodied electrics being produced by Fender in the USA. The German company responded by introducing solid guitars of its own: but confusingly, the names given to these (and Höfner's other products) by its British distributors, Selmer, were quite different from those used in other countries. Hence, the "Model 172" shown here, which was marketed in mainland Europe, would have been labeled a "Super Solid" in the United Kingdom. The 172 in our picture dates from about 1963, and, while it has only two pickups (other 172s

Below: The 172 has a bolted-on neck, whose "strip" fret markers replaced the dots seen on earlier models.

On later models, this basic bridge was upgraded to a fully adjustable one.

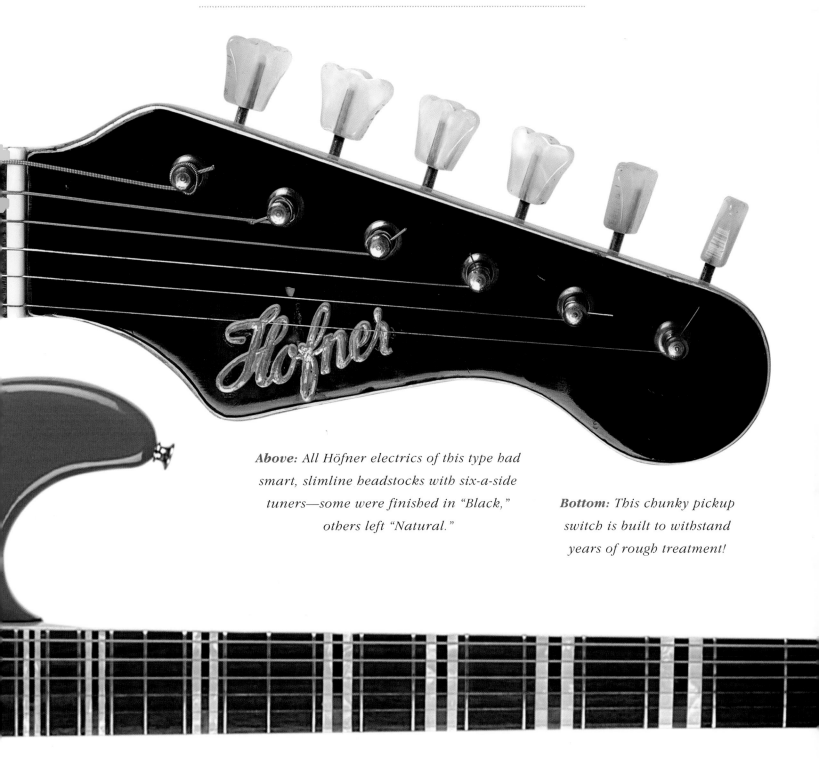

Above: *All Höfner electrics of this type had smart, slimline headstocks with six-a-side tuners—some were finished in "Black," others left "Natural."*

Bottom: *This chunky pickup switch is built to withstand years of rough treatment!*

had three), is clearly influenced by the Fender Stratocaster. Its controls are basic and its finish relatively plain; later Höfner solids were equipped with a plethora of additional circuits and switches, and, by 1968, a few were even sporting ostentatious colored vinyl body coverings! These instruments all sold well, though it is likely that many of their users would have preferred an American electric, had one been obtainable at an affordable price.

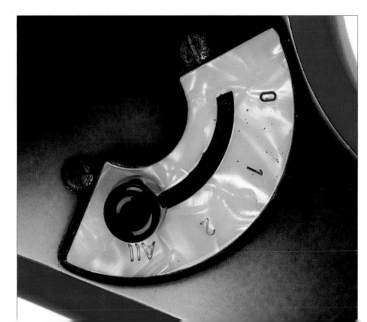

HÖFNER CHANCELLOR

HÖFNER MOVED TO its current headquarters in Hagenau, Bavaria, in 1997, and is now owned and run by a group of investors headed by its managing director, Klaus Scholler. The change in ownership, which occurred in 2005, appears to have boosted the firm's confidence, and helped to raise its profile. Its latest guitar designs are now widely available on both sides of the Atlantic, and have a pleasingly contemporary look, while remaining faithful to the company's distinguished traditions.

Höfner's success in blending past and present is exemplified by its current "flagship" archtop, the Chancellor, which appears in our photographs. Partly inspired by the highly acclaimed "Golden Höfner," a blonde 18-inch wide electric/acoustic made in limited quantities during the early 1960s, the new guitar, though an inch narrower than its predecessor, is made from the same fine woods (spruce for its top, maple for its back and sides) and sports similarly gold-plated hardware. However, its striking ebony pickguard and tailpiece are novel features, and it also boasts a modern, high performance "Diamond" humbucking pickup.

The Chancellor's 22-fret neck has an ebony fingerboard.

Only solid woods are used in this guitar's construction.

Below right: *The "Diamond" pickup's volume and tone controls are unobtrusively placed on the Chancellor's ebony pickguard.*

PHOTOGRAPHS COURTESY OF IVOR MAIRANTS MUSICENTRE, LONDON

Left: *The elegantly shaped ebony tailpiece matches the Chancellor's bridge and pickguard.*

Right: *Schaller tuners are fitted to this and most other Höfners.*

417

HÖFNER VERYTHIN STANDARD

THE VERYTHIN, like the Chancellor featured on the last two pages, has a recognizable Höfner "ancestor:" in this case, it is the company's "Verithin" (sic) model, which, when it debuted in 1960, was, somewhat debatably, hailed in contemporary catalogs as the "thinnest of all guitars."

A double cutaway, two-pickup design, the original Verithin bore some resemblance to the Gibson ES-335—as does its almost identically-named successor.

Verythins are currently available from Höfner in three versions: the Standard (seen here); the Classic, which has "cat's-eye" soundholes, and a "harpform" tailpiece of the kind found on the '60s Verithin; and the JS, a single-pickup reworking of the Verythin created for top American jazz player John Stowell. All have maple bodies (though the Classic sports a spruce top), and are designed, as Höfner puts it, to be "at home in just about any musical milieu."

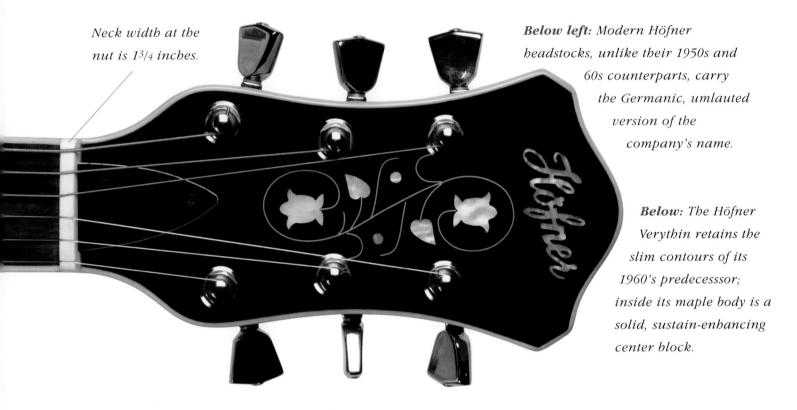

Neck width at the nut is 1³/4 inches.

Below left: Modern Höfner headstocks, unlike their 1950s and 60s counterparts, carry the Germanic, umlauted version of the company's name.

Below: The Höfner Verythin retains the slim contours of its 1960's predecesssor; inside its maple body is a solid, sustain-enhancing center block.

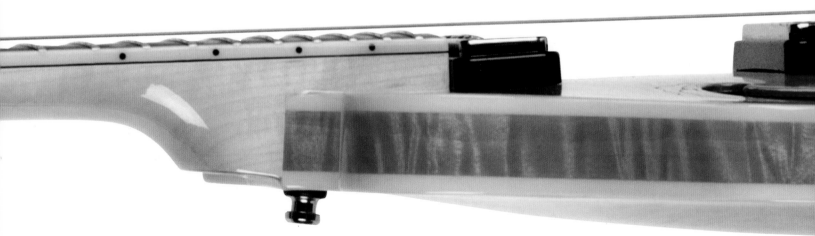

PHOTOGRAPHS COURTESY OF IVOR MAIRANTS MUSICENTRE, LONDON

Above: *Höfner 514 humbucking pickups are fitted to the Verythin.*

The upper and lower edges of the body are elegantly bound.

HOHNER B2A BASS

THE HOHNER COMPANY was founded by Matthias Hohner in Trossingen, south of the German city of Stuttgart, in 1857. Its first product was the harmonica, which had been invented (by a German clockmaker) in 1821, but never previously made in quantity. The little instrument proved to be an international best seller, and, within a few decades, Hohner had also established itself as one of Europe's leading accordion builders.

The firm has gone on to enjoy many more recent musical successes: in the 1960s, it developed the Pianet and Clavinet electric keyboards (the latter was featured memorably on Stevie Wonder's classic 1972 song "Superstition"), and in 1990, its American division became the first major manufacturer to license and produce its own version of Ned Steinberger's revolutionary headless bass guitar.

The Steinberger (whose full history is explored on pages 664-7) sprang from the notion that conventional basses, with their bulky headstocks, were uncomfortable to hold and poorly balanced. Ned Steinberger remedied these perceived problems by moving the tuners from the necks of his instruments to their bridge ends, and radically reshaping and lightening their bodies. He also constructed his guitars from epoxy resin, reinforced with graphite, but this aspect of his design remained the sole property of his own firm, the Steinberger Sound Corporation, and Hohner's headless models, including the B2A seen here, have always been made of wood.

Unlike the substantial quantities of shoddy "pirate"

Above: Steinberger Sound is now part of Gibson.

Below: The B2A has two humbucking pickups and active electronics.

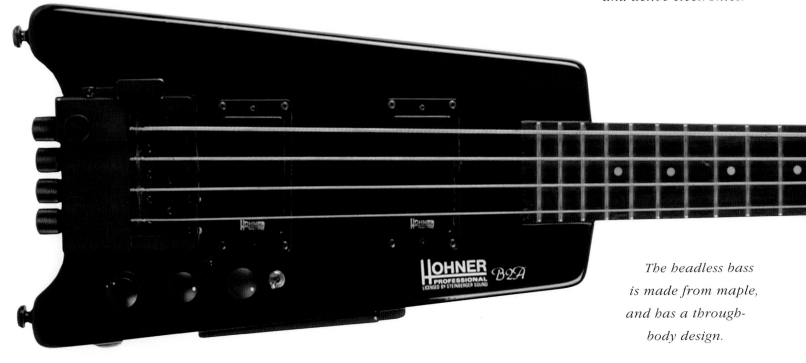

The headless bass is made from maple, and has a through-body design.

IBANEZ GB10 GEORGE BENSON

MANY YEARS BEFORE HE ACHIEVED success as a pop singer, George Benson (b.1943) had already been recognized as one of the finest jazz guitarists of his generation following the release of albums like *It's Uptown* (1965) and *Benson Burner* (1966). On these recordings, as well on his multi-million selling LP *Breezin'* (issued in 1976), Benson played archtop Gibsons such as an L-5 and a Johnny Smith model; however, instruments of this type, with their tendency to feed back at high sound levels, proved less suitable for his live appearances, and before long, he was in discussions with the Japanese Ibanez (Hoshino Gakki) company—whose US office was in Benson's home state of Pennsylvania —over the development of a new electric guitar, tailor-made to his requirements and bearing his name. The result was the Ibanez GB10, which was launched at the National Association of Music Merchants Association (NAMM) trade show in Chicago in 1977, and has remained in production for the best part of three decades.

Though a hollow-body like Benson's treasured Gibson semi-acoustics, the GB10's laminated spruce top is stiffer (and therefore far more resistant to feedback) than the solid woods favored by the Kalamazoo manufacturers, and its body depth is just over 2½ inches—a good half an inch shallower than either the L-5 or the Johnny Smith. As Benson has stated, these features cut down on potentially troublesome resonance, while providing a clarity and articulation that he considers unique.

Abalone is used for the decorative parallelogram on the neck markers.

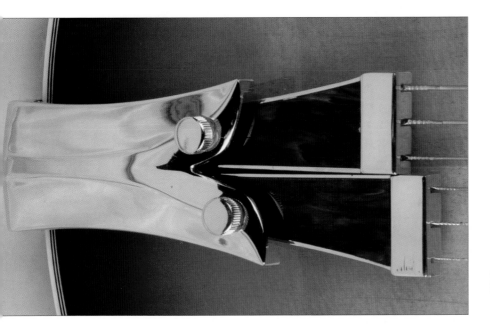

Above: *This handsome tailpiece (covered with gold like the rest of the GB10's hardware) features twin knobs that vary the tension of the upper and lower groups of strings.*

IBANEZ JSM100

JOHN SCOFIELD WAS BORN in Dayton, Ohio in 1951, but brought up in Connecticut; initially attracted to rock and blues, he began studying jazz guitar as a teenager. After attending Berklee College of Music in Boston, Massachusetts, he worked with major names such as vibes player Gary Burton and drummer Billy Cobham before joining Miles Davis's band in 1982. He spent three and a half years with the great trumpeter, and has gone on to distinguish himself as both a sideman and a leader, touring regularly with his own trio (whose other members are longtime collaborators bassist Steve Swallow and drummer Bill Stewart), and releasing albums that often traverse established musical boundaries—such as his tribute to Ray Charles, "That's What I Say" (2005).

Scofield has used Ibanez guitars since the early 1980s. For many years, his favorite instrument was the company's AS200, a double-cutaway, twin-pickup electric introduced in 1979, which, like Gibson's ES-335, contained an internal center block to boost

Below: Flamed maple is used for the JSM100's sunburst-finished body; its pickups are Ibanez Super 58s.

PHOTOGRAPHS COURTESY OF PEACH, BLAKE END, BRAINTREE

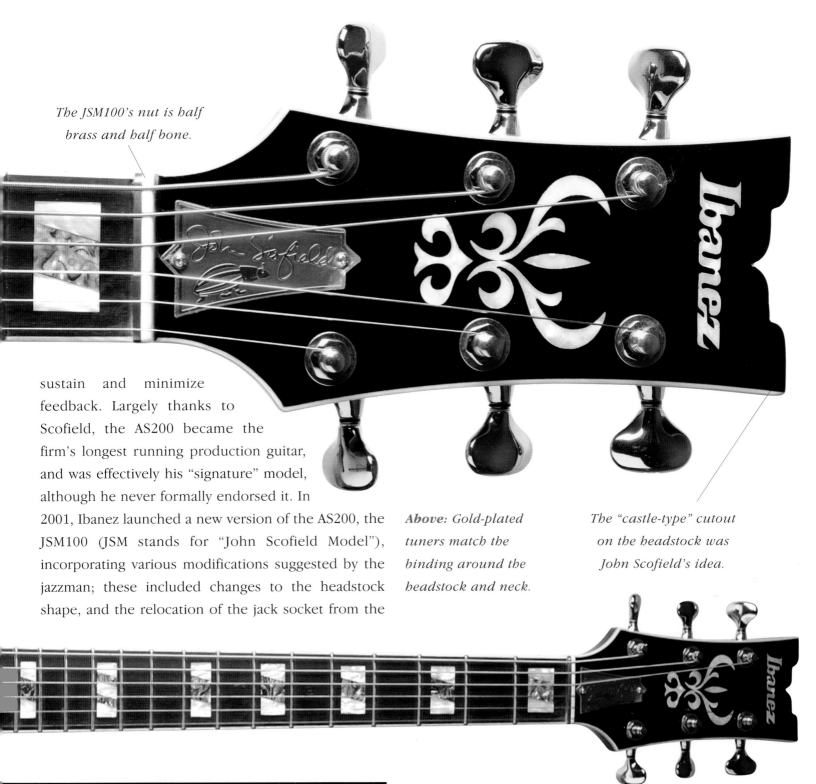

The JSM100's nut is half brass and half bone.

sustain and minimize feedback. Largely thanks to Scofield, the AS200 became the firm's longest running production guitar, and was effectively his "signature" model, although he never formally endorsed it. In 2001, Ibanez launched a new version of the AS200, the JSM100 (JSM stands for "John Scofield Model"), incorporating various modifications suggested by the jazzman; these included changes to the headstock shape, and the relocation of the jack socket from the

Above: *Gold-plated tuners match the binding around the headstock and neck.*

The "castle-type" cutout on the headstock was John Scofield's idea.

Above: *The Ibanez's ebony fingerboard is inlaid with abaone and pearl block markers; the neck itself is mahogany.*

top to the side of the guitar. Another significant difference between the AS200 and JSM100 lies in the design of the latter's "Prestige" neck, the first hand-finished one ever to be fitted to an Ibanez jazz guitar.

435

IBANEZ PM-100 PAT METHENY

PAT METHENY (b.1954) is a giant of contemporary jazz guitar, who first came to prominence as a member of vibes player Gary Burton's group in the mid-1970s; he has since enjoyed immense acclaim (and, unusually for a musician working in this genre, substantial record sales) for his work with his own ensembles. A Gibson ES-175 devotee for many years, Metheny began using a prototype electric developed in conjunction with Ibanez on his *Question and Answer* album in 1989. Seven years later, the company introduced its first Metheny signature model, the single-pickup PM-100, which he now plays regularly onstage and in the studio, and has praised both for its tonal richness and its durability. A two-pickup version, the PM-120, is also available.

Gold-plated hardware is used on the Ibanez Metheny guitars.

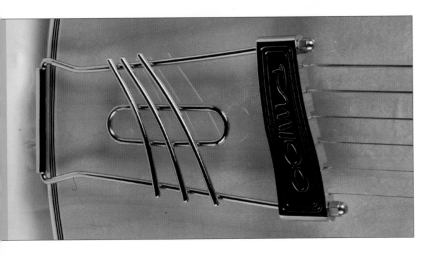

Above: *The traditional styling of the tailpiece reflects the subtle blend of old and new on this Ibanez.*

Right: *The guitar has an all-maple body, a double cutaway, and a "Super 58" humbucker.*

PHOTOGRAPHS COURTESY OF IVOR MAIRANTS MUSICENTRE, LONDON

The PM-100's mahogany neck joins its body at the 17th fret.

IBANEZ JEM555

GUITARIST STEVE VAI WAS BORN in 1960, and first came to prominence as a member of Frank Zappa's band in the early 1980s. He achieved wider fame through his work, later in the decade, with David Lee Roth and Whitesnake, and is now a major name in his own right, thanks to a string of best-selling albums and concert tours as a soloist and bandleader.

Unlike many virtuosos, Vai does not favor vintage instruments or "classic" Gibson and Fender designs; instead, he has developed his own "JEM" range of electrics with Ibanez. The first of these were the three JEM777s launched in 1987: described by the company as "unique in form and function," they incorporated DiMarzio pickups and ultra-fast necks, and also sported such distinctive features as a "monkey grip" handle hollowed out of their solid bodies. The JEM range has proved enduringly popular: the example shown here is the JEM555, which debuted in 1994.

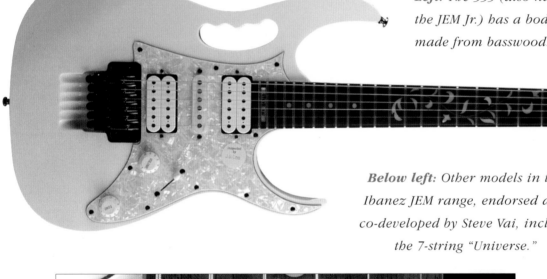

Left: The 555 (also named the JEM Jr.) has a body made from basswood.

Right: The famous "monkey grip" is found on all JEMs.

Below left: Other models in the Ibanez JEM range, endorsed and co-developed by Steve Vai, include the 7-string "Universe."

PHOTOGRAPHS COURTESY OF NEVADA MUSIC, PORTSMOUTH

JACKSON KVX10 KING V

WAYNE CHARVEL, a skilled guitar builder, customizer and parts maker who had been respraying and modifying both his own and his friends' instruments since the early 1960s, set up Charvel's Guitar Repair in southern California in 1974. His shop undertook refinishing work for Fender, while also catering to the individual needs of rock star clients such as The Who and Deep Purple. Another regular customer was Eddie Van Halen, then enjoying a growing reputation as a virtuoso guitarist, and later to become one of the very first high profile users of the Charvel company's "hot-rodded" solid-bodies.

In 1978, Wayne Charvel sold his business to a member of his staff, Grover Jackson, who continued to trade under the Charvel name, and to work with Van Halen and other major names. These included Ozzy Osbourne band member Randy Rhoads, to whose specification the firm built a "Flying V"-like electric in 1980. According to expert Robert Lane, Jackson was reluctant to use the Charvel logo on this wild-looking axe, and "simply signed his own last name on [its]

Opposite page, top: The KVX10 is fitted with two humbucking pickups designed by Seymour Duncan. Its body is made from alder, and its 24-fret fingerboard from rosewood.

Right: For several years, the King V was closely associated with Dave Mustaine of Megadeth.

Earlier V-shaped Jacksons had a more asymmetrical body outline than this King V

headstock"—thus creating the first-ever "Jackson"-branded model. The guitar quickly caught on with other musicians; subsequently marketed, in an altered form, as the "King V," it became one of the mainstays of the newly created Jackson line. Our photos show a current version of it, the KVX10.

DUNCAN DESIGNED

Jackson's headstock is instantly recognizable.

JACKSON DK2 DINKY

The guitar's rosewood fingerboard is inlaid with "shark-fin" position markers.

ONE OF JACKSON'S most popular design categories is the so-called "Superstrat." The firm has been making stripped-down, high performance double cutaway solids for musicians such as Eddie Van Halen since the late 1970s, but its first production "Superstrat," named the Soloist, was launched in 1983-4. It featured a "neck-through-body" configuration, rather than the Fender-type bolt-on neck favored by Van Halen. It was soon joined by the Dinky, a "bolt-on" Superstrat that was otherwise very similar to its "neck-thru" cousin, and both instruments are now recognized as Jackson classics.

The 2005 DK2 Dinky in our pictures remains faithful to the Superstrat tradition. Our instrument is finished in Transparent Black, but the company's custom department has long been renowned for its ability to produce "anything from life-like figures to off-the-wall, far-out abstract concoctions such as "Crimson Swirl" and "Eerie Dess."

Grover Jackson himself left Charvel/Jackson in 1989, three years after its acquisition by the Fort Worth, Texas-based International Music Corporation. Eight years later, IMC was purchased by the Japanese-based Akai Electric Company, which sold the guitar maker to Fender in 2002.

Below right: The DK2's headstock has a traditional "six-a-side" configuration inspired by the original Fender design of the early 1950s.

Right: A close-up of the strings-thru-body layout. The DK2 is also available with a Jackson JT580LP tremolo.

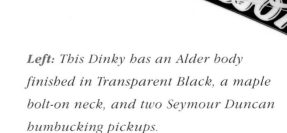

Left: This Dinky has an Alder body finished in Transparent Black, a maple bolt-on neck, and two Seymour Duncan humbucking pickups.

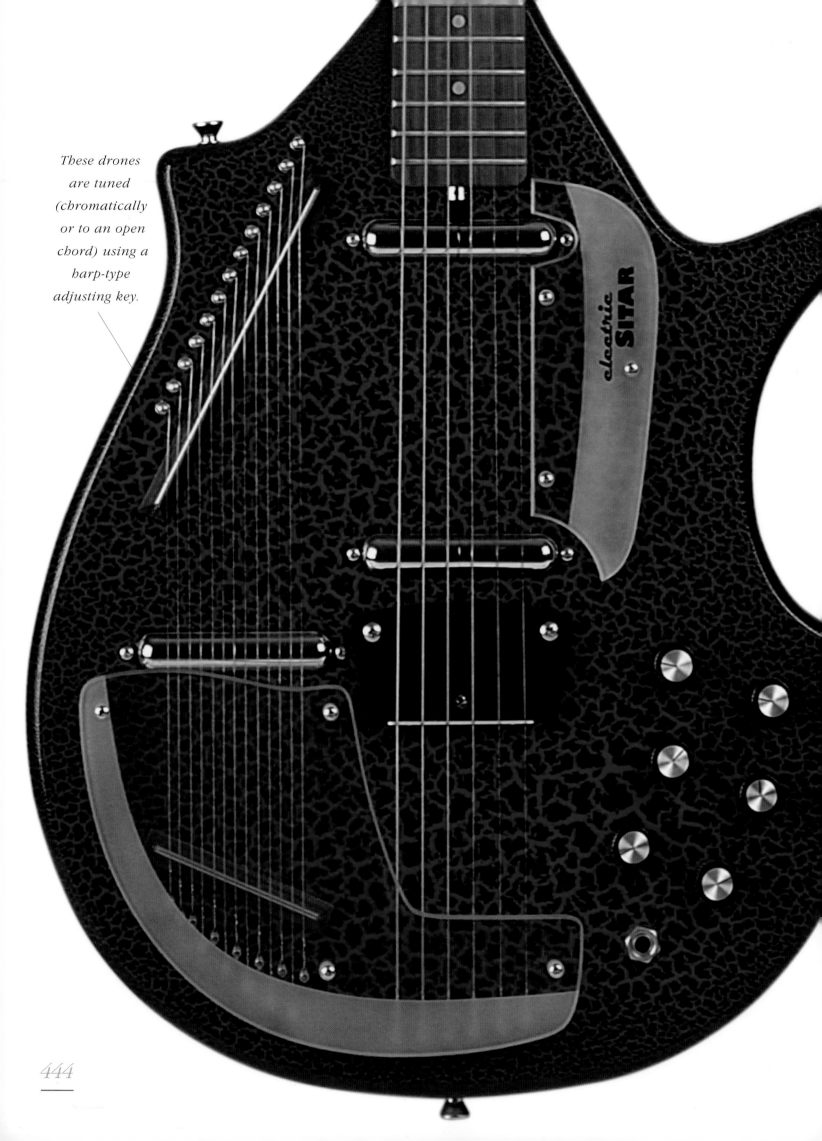

These drones
are tuned
(chromatically
or to an open
chord) using a
harp-type
adjusting key.

electric SITAR

JERRY JONES ELECTRIC SITAR

IN 1967, THE SHORT-LIVED Coral company introduced a curious instrument, designed by top American session guitarist Vinnie Bell in conjunction with former Danelectro boss Nathan Daniel. This was the "electric sitar," which owed its initial popularity to the craze for all things Indian that characterized the then-prevalent "flower power" movement. During the mid- to late sixties, real sitars were increasingly finding their way onto pop and rock records (George Harrison famously played one on the Beatles' *Sergeant Pepper's Lonely Hearts Club Band* LP), but Bell's hybrid electric model, which featured 13 sympathetic "drone" strings alongside its six fretted ones, also caught the mood of the times; Bell himself made an entire album, *Pop Goes the Electric Sitar*, to showcase it, and went on to use in on hits such as Freda Payne's chart-topping soul classic "Band of Gold," released in 1970.

By then, Coral's closure had put the electric sitar out of production; it remained a rare collectors' item for decades, but has recently been revived by Nathan Daniel devotee Jerry Jones, whose Nashville-based company makes three different versions of it. The model shown here is the Master, finished, like the Coral original, in "Red gator" ("Turquoise," "Cream" and "Black" are also available), and featuring three Daniel-style "lipstick" pickups: two for the guitar strings, and one for the drones.

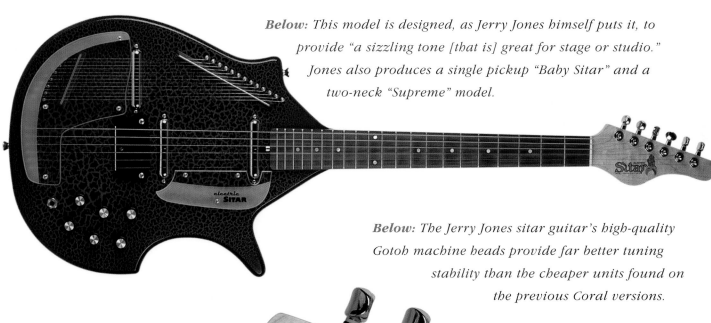

Below: This model is designed, as Jerry Jones himself puts it, to provide "a sizzling tone [that is] great for stage or studio." Jones also produces a single pickup "Baby Sitar" and a two-neck "Supreme" model.

Below: The Jerry Jones sitar guitar's high-quality Gotoh machine heads provide far better tuning stability than the cheaper units found on the previous Coral versions.

Left: The instrument's 13 drone strings pass over a rosewood "buzz bridge" (visible beneath the perspex cover) that produces sitar-like vibrations.

Left: *The Skyline Joe Osborn is available in a range of colors; this example has a "Lake Placid Blue" finish.*

Above: *The Osborn bass is produced in the less expensive, Korean version seen here, and also as a US made instrument. 4- and 5-string models are available.*

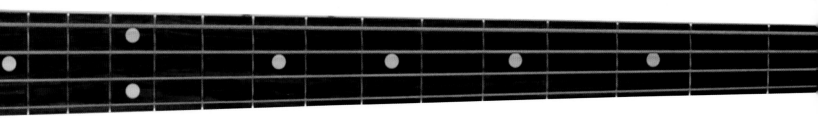

and the MGs and Blues Brothers stalwart Donald "Duck" Dunn, and Darryl Jones, who plays with the Rolling Stones. Today, Lakland (for which Hugh McFarland no longer works) has an enviable reputation. It remains based in Chicago's Goose Island, where all its high-end models are built; however, its mid-price Skyline basses are made in Korea, undergoing final assembly and adjustment in the USA.

The Lakland model shown here is a Skyline Joe Osborn. Osborn, one of the firm's "signature artists," is a celebrated session player who has recorded with a host of major names, from Simon and Garfunkel and Neil Young to The Carpenters. The instrument bearing his name resembles the Fender Jazz bass he has used for much of his career, but incorporates updated pickups and other contemporary touches.

LAKEWOOD M-32

MARTIN SEELIGER, a former apprentice of the distinguished luthier Manfred Pletz, established Lakewood Guitars in 1985 in the German town of Giessen, north of Frankfurt. Seeliger's existing knowledge of the musical instrument business—he had run a store selling guitars while completing his studies with Pletz—gave him a useful insight into the practicalities of his new venture, and when setting it

Premium series), as well as a special range of models named for the signs of the Zodiac; it also operates a thriving custom shop. The Lakewood seen here is a Deluxe M-32: M signifies a Grand Concert-size guitar, while the 32 suffix denotes an instrument with a spruce top and Indian rosewood back and sides. A version of the M-32 with a cutaway and a built-in pickup is also available.

Left: The guitar has a mahogany neck, and an ebony fingerboard and bridge.
Below: This open headstock is veneered with rosewood.

up, he was careful to attend to important details such as the choice of a suitable company name. As he revealed to Teja Gerken in a recent interview for **Acoustic Guitar** magazine, he settled on "Lakewood" after coming across Lakewood, Ohio in an atlas; "I thought [it] really sounded like a steel-string guitar," he told Gerken, "and [knew that] neither Americans nor Japanese would have any problems pronouncing it."

Today, Lakewood's customers include top US musicians such as Dave Matthews, as well as big names from Britain and Europe like Radiohead's Thom Yorke. The firm currently produces three main categories of acoustic (the Natural, Deluxe and

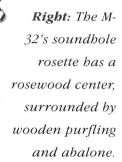

Right: The M-32's soundhole rosette has a rosewood center, surrounded by wooden purfling and abalone.

Below: *The Larrivée D10B has a 16-inch wide body, and is over 4 inches deep. Its bridge and fingerboard are ebony.*

The D10B's top is spruce, and its back and sides are made from Brazilian rosewood.

LARRIVÉE D10B

CANADIAN LUTHIER JEAN LARRIVÉE began his career in Toronto, where he initially focused on building classical guitars. He switched to flat-top making in 1971, and a year later, married Wendy Jones, who has been responsible for creating the abalone, pearl and imitation ivory inlays that are such a distinctive feature of his instruments. Larrivée Guitars continued to expand throughout the 1970s, eventually moving from Toronto to British Columbia. During a downturn in the market for high-quality acoustics in the 1980s the company briefly produced electrics, but subsequently reverted to full-time flat-top manufacture. Its production is now split between Vancouver and Southern California, where the firm, which is run by Jean, Wendy and their three children, established a base in 2001. Its designs are highly regarded by both customers and fellow luthiers: in an interview for this author's book *The Acoustic Guitar* (1999), Taylor Guitars co-founder Bob Taylor described Jean Larrivée as "one of my best guitar-building buddies." The Larrivée on these pages is a Dreadnought model made in 1999; its headstock is graced with Wendy Larrivée's "Dancing Woman" decoration.

Right: *The "Dancing Woman" is one of various custom inlays available on Larrivée guitars.*

LARRIVÉE D-09

THE ALPHABETICAL PREFIXES used in naming Larrivée guitars represent body types. "D" instruments, such as the D-10 featured on the last two pages, and the D-09 shown here, are obviously Dreadnoughts, and the company's range also includes "L" models (16 inch wide "Larrivée Bodies"), OMs (Orchestra Models—see Martin entries for the story of how this popular class developed), smaller, Parlor (P) flat-tops, and several other categories.

The numbers after the letters reveal the series— Larrivée's term for a group of guitars sharing the same woods, style of construction, and decorative features— to which an instrument belongs. "09" guitars, like the Dreadnought in our photos, are part of what is also known as the Rosewood Artist or Rosewood Select series. These have spruce tops, rosewood back and sides, mahogany necks, and ebony fingerboards and bridges. Larrivée sources its ebony from Africa, and its

Below: This model's lower bout measures 16 inches;
its binding is made from fine strips of maple.

The D-09 has a gloss finish body.

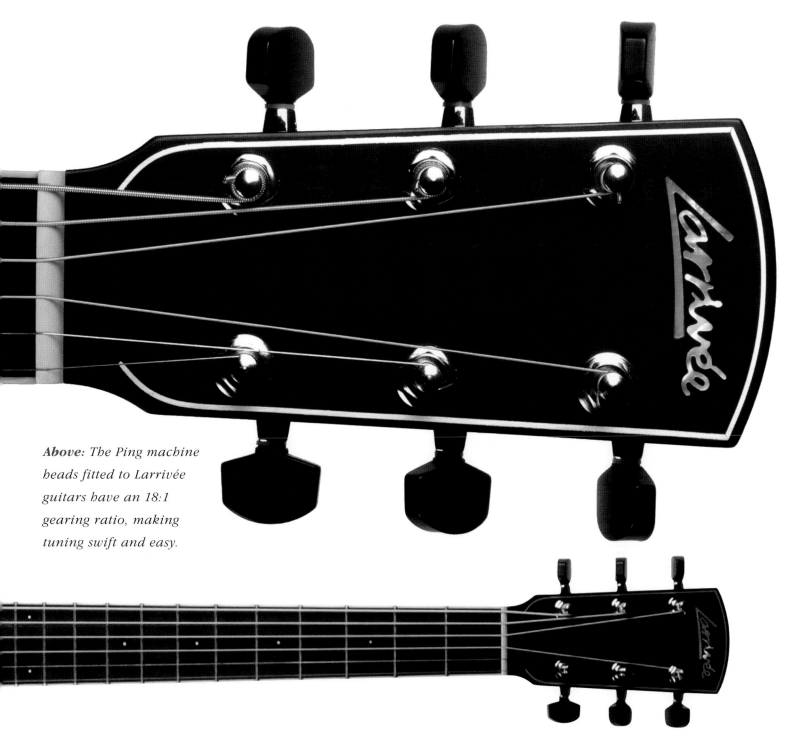

Above: The Ping machine heads fitted to Larrivée guitars have an 18:1 gearing ratio, making tuning swift and easy.

mahogany from South America, but the sitka spruce used for almost all its soundboards comes from its native British Columbia, where, as Jean Larrivée's son Matthew writes, the "rainy climate, coupled with mild never-too-hot temperatures, make perfect conditions" for this essential guitar-making wood to grow.

Left: Abalone rosette inlays are part of the specification for 09 series Larrivées.

LOWDEN F32

LOWDEN GUITARS ARE NAMED using letters and numbers that identify (respectively) their "style" and "model" types. Of the four standard body styles used by the company, two—the "Jazz" and "S"—are 14⁹/₁₆ inches across at their widest points. The other styles are larger: the Jumbo-type "O" is over 16 inches wide, while the "F,"

Left: The F32 is available in this "regular" version or (at extra cost) as a cutaway model.

an example of which is illustrated here, measures 15¹¹/₁₆ inches. Different models feature various combinations of woods and materials: a "32" such as this guitar normally has a sitka spruce top, Indian rosewood back and sides, and an ebony fingerboard.

Such information, of course, cannot convey the special qualities that attract so many fine players to Lowdens. One satisfied customer recently described his F32 as "beautiful, versatile and great sounding," and, with leading musicians such as Pierre Bensusan, Alex de Grassi, and Richard Thompson using their instruments, the firm, which recently celebrated its thirtieth anniversary, seems assured of a growing international reputation and a prosperous future.

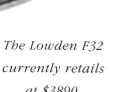

The Lowden F32 currently retails at $3890.

MADRIGAL DANIEL C

THE MADRIGAL LUTHERIE COMPANY is a family business, founded in 1949 and based in the town of Andújar, in the southern Spanish region of Andalusía. It produces classical guitars in three ranges: the most inexpensive of these, named "Conservatorio," contains high-quality student models, including some instruments with cutaways and built-in transducers. Madrigal's mid-price "Academia" guitars are all hand-made from solid (i.e. non-laminated) woods, while the premium "Concierto" category offers exceptionally high quality at competitive prices.

There are five currently available "Conciertos." All are named "Daniel" and differentiated with an alphabetical suffix, and the Daniel A model can also be purchased in a 10-string configuration of the type favored by the great classical guitarist Narciso Yepes (1927-1997). A Daniel C instrument is seen here: it has a spruce top, a rosewood back and sides, and a Honduras cedar neck with an ebony fingerboard.

Left: A central strip of ebony provides extra reinforcement for the Madrigal's neck.

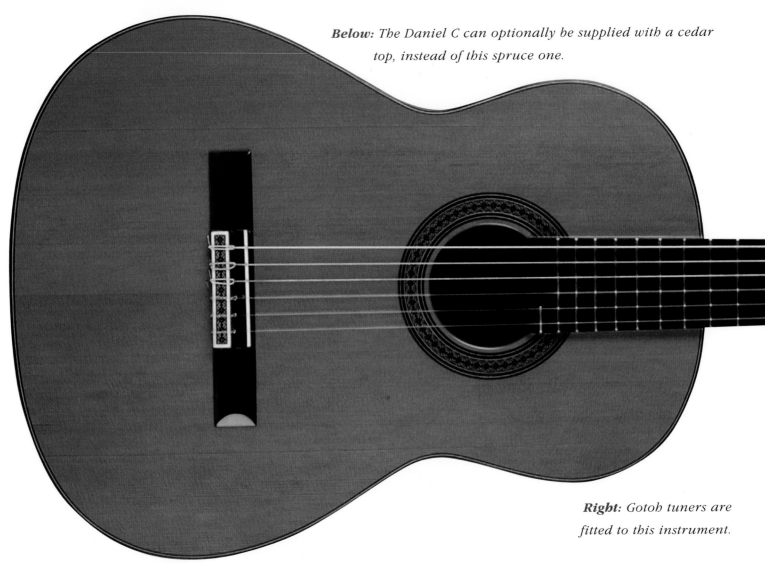

Below: The Daniel C can optionally be supplied with a cedar top, instead of this spruce one.

Right: Gotoh tuners are fitted to this instrument.

Above: *The top two strings are given an extra fret, extending the guitar's compass.*

All the Madrigal Concierto guitars share this unusual headstock shape.

ANDY MANSON CUSTOM 7-STRING

LUTHIER ANDY MANSON is based in Credition, in the English West Country, and has been designing, building and repairing fretted instruments for over thirty-five years. He specializes in exotic and unusual creations, such as the triple neck he made for Led Zeppelin bassist John Paul Jones; as Manson explains in his book *Talking Wood: A Guitar Maker's Diary* (1998), the idea for this came about after he saw Jones switching between mandolin, 6-string guitar, and 12-string guitar during a single song, and thought, "Pity you can't hang 'em all around your neck at once." When he presented the finished model to Jones, the star was delighted, and told Manson that he "couldn't wait to see [Zeppelin guitarist] Jimmy Page's face when I walk on stage with it." Other famous Manson clients include Ian Anderson and Martin Barre of Jethro Tull, Andy Summers, and Mike Oldfield.

The Manson guitar seen here is a 7-string Magpie I flat-top, custom built for British jazz guitarist Andy Robinson. Some years ago, this instrument was

Below: The Manson 7-string Magpie has a spruce top, and Indian rosewood back and sides.

The signal from this pickup can be combined with the guitar's bridge transducer.

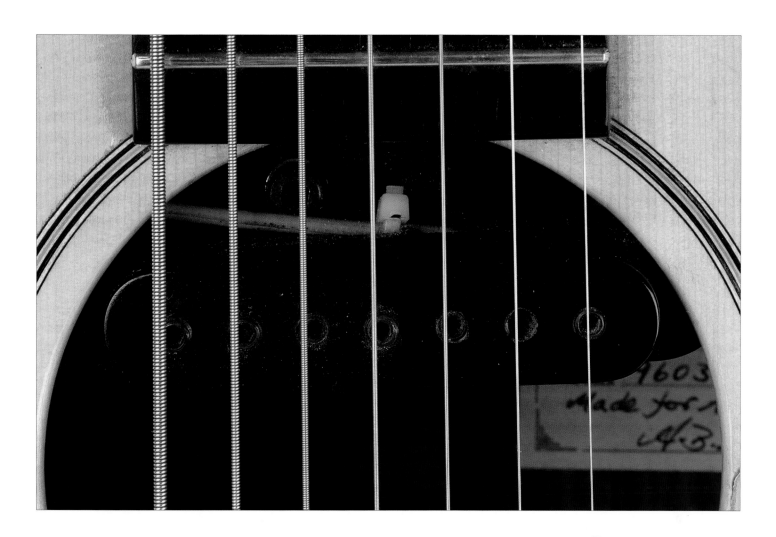

Right: Guitarists are always in danger of losing their flatpicks in the heat of a gig: this magnetized post is a safe place to keep a spare one!

featured in one of the author's previous books, *The Acoustic Guitar*: since then, it has been fitted with a soundhole pickup and some other additions by its owner, and has suffered a little inevitable wear and tear; however, it remains a fine example of Andy Manson's work. Andy's brother, Hugh Manson, is also a notable guitar maker, some of whose models can be seen on the following pages.

HUGH MANSON SOLID-BODY

LIKE HIS ACOUSTIC GUITAR-MAKING brother Andy (see previous pages), luthier Hugh Manson is based in the English West Country. His professional career began in the late 1970s (though he built his first-ever guitar at the age of only 14), and today, his small workshop, located near the city of Exeter, produces some of the United Kingdom's finest custom-built electric instruments. Among his long list of distinguished clients are Martin Barre of Jethro Tull, ex-Led Zeppelin bassist John Paul Jones (who has been known to take up to fifteen Hugh Manson instruments on tour with him), Kelly Jones of The Stereophonics, and Matt Bellamy of Muse, who owns no less than seven custom Mansons.

Hugh is famous for instruments that he himself rather modestly describes as "a little revolutionary;" these have included two-, three- and even four-necked models, custom-built lap steels, mandolas and electric sitars, as well as guitars and basses with special finishes and other unique touches. However, the example of his work shown here is somewhat more conventional, though equally distinguished. Made in 2003, it has a

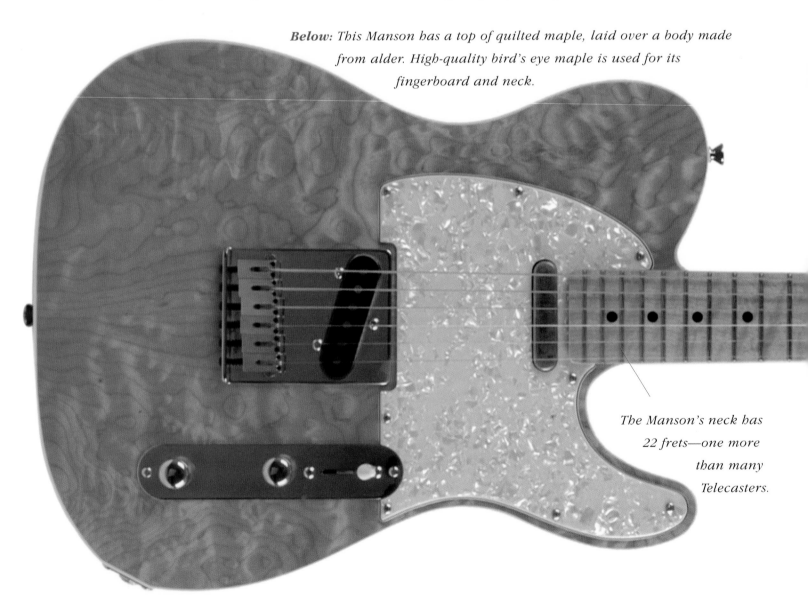

Below: This Manson has a top of quilted maple, laid over a body made from alder. High-quality bird's eye maple is used for its fingerboard and neck.

The Manson's neck has 22 frets—one more than many Telecasters.

Telecaster-style body and neck, but features superb tonewoods and high quality electronics (its pickups, like those on all Mansons, are wound to Hugh's exacting specifications) which combine to provide outstanding tone and overall playability. It was recently sold by a British guitar dealer for just over $2,600.

Above: A closeup showing the Manson's bound, pearloid pickguard and high performance neck pickup.

Bottom: These metal collars help to hold the strings' ball-ends in place at the back of the guitar's body.

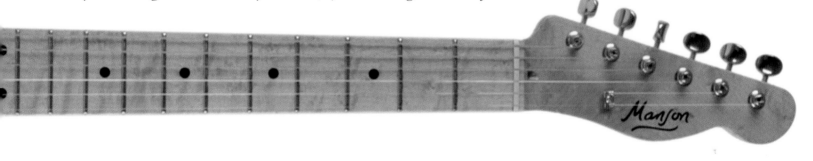

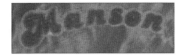

HUGH MANSON DOUBLE-NECK

AS A BUSY GUITAR MAKER who runs his own thriving music store in the English city of Exeter, and also spends a good deal of his time "on the road" as a "tech" (instrument technician) for one of his most famous customers, John Paul Jones, Hugh Manson thrives on variety, and chooses his lutherie projects with care. Talking to *Guitarist* magazine in March 2006, he commented that "I can afford to be fairly selective...[and] I generally prefer [building] the more creative stuff. It's much more rewarding than making another Telecaster-clone or a superstrat."

Over the years, Manson's output has, as he told this author in 1999, included almost "everything with frets or without frets on." One of his most striking guitars,

Left: The lower, fretted half of the bass is angled slightly downward to improve access to the unfretted section.

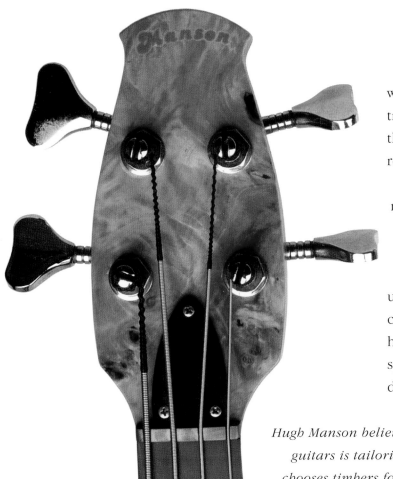

which was strengthened by two truss-rods, and it is a tribute to Manson's design skills that the instrument, though obviously large, was perfectly balanced and remarkably easy to play.

Compared to the 15-stringer, the Manson double-neck illustrated on these pages is (relatively!) conventional. It is based on the "Kestrel" body shape that he has used since his earliest days as a professional luthier, and features both fretted and unfretted 4-string bass guitar necks—a favorite combination for the many musicians who dislike having to switch between instruments to obtain the special qualities that each can offer. It is thought to date from the 1990s.

Hugh Manson believes that "the art of making electric guitars is tailoring the wood to the sound," and chooses timbers for his instrument with great care.

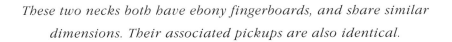

These two necks both have ebony fingerboards, and share similar dimensions. Their associated pickups are also identical.

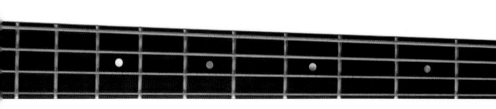

completed in the early 1990s, was a custom model sporting a total of fifteen strings, which could serve simultaneously as a 6-string bass and as a regular guitar with an extended upper register. All its strings were accommodated on a single, gradually widening neck,

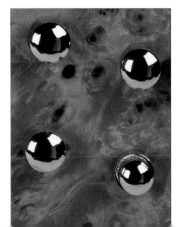

Left: Unlike some multi-necks, this Manson has strikingly simple controls.

C.F. MARTIN c. 1833

CHRISTIAN FRIEDRICH MARTIN (1796-1873) was a German-born guitar maker who studied his craft in Vienna with the distinguished luthier Johann Georg Stauffer (1778-1853). Martin's subsequent plans to set up in business for himself in his native Saxony foundered when he fell foul of the powerful guild system in operation there, and in 1833, he emigrated to America, establishing a music shop on New York's Hudson Street. In the city he sold and repaired guitars, and was soon building them as well: the instrument in our photographs is one of the earliest known Martins to have survived from this period.

According to classical guitar historian James Westbrook, the ledgers for C.F. Martin's New York shop contain no records of any purchase of woods or any other lutherie supplies prior to 1835. It therefore seems likely that the model seen here was constructed from materials shipped over from Europe, and this theory is borne out by the presence of the word "Wein"

Below: This tuner plate was probably part of a cache of supplies that accompanied C.F. Martin on his voyage from Europe to the New World.

The Martin's spruce top is decorated with ivory, abalone and awabi.

PHOTOGRAPHS COURTESY OF JAMES WESTBROOK

Above and Right: The neck angles on Stauffer-style guitars could be altered by means of a mechanism turned by a clock-type key.

Above: The instrument's ebony veneered neck is striped with ivory inlays.

(Vienna) on the nickel mounting plate for its tuners.

The guitar's overall design, and especially its scrolled headstock, is strongly reminiscent of a Stauffer, and its soundhole label proudly proclaims that "Frederick Martin from Vienna, Guitar and Violin Manufacturer," is his pupil. Martin did not begin to evolve a more individual style until well after his move, in 1839, from New York to Nazareth, Pennsylvania—a town with a substantial émigré German population, and the headquarters of the C.F. Martin company (which is still controlled by his descendants) to this day.

487

MARTIN 0-28K

IN NAZARETH, PENNSYLVANIA, C.F. Martin's guitar business flourished, though, as Walter Carter has commented in **The Martin Book** (Balafon, 1995), he was obliged to adapt his elaborate European designs "to a rougher-edged, simpler American society" by making them "plainer [and] more utilitarian." Gradually, Martins lost their scrolled headstocks and abalone body inlays, and started to acquire outlines closer to those of a 20th century flat-top instrument; while in the 1850s, the firm began applying X-bracing to its tops (Stauffer-style Martins had mostly horizontal strutting)—a key element of modern acoustic guitar construction, widely copied by other makers.

As Martin's catalog expanded over the following

Pyramid bridge embellishments like this are a distinctive feature on early Martin flat-tops.

Above: Rectangular, open headstocks such as this take standard, easily available tuners—unlike the 6-a-size peghead fitted to the Stauffer Martin on the previous two pages.

Abalone is used for these position markers.

The koa from which this instrument is made comes from Hawaii; musicians on the islands were among the earliest users of steel-strung guitars.

decades, it developed its now familiar system for naming instruments with a prefix denoting body size, followed by a code number identifying decorative style and woods. "0" sizes, such as the 1927 guitar seen here, are 13½ inches wide; and while a "Style 28" like this one would normally have a rosewood back and sides, the K suffix indicates that koa has been used. The 0-28K's steel strings were, at the time of its introduction, a comparative novelty: steel had only replaced gut as standard on Martins in 1922.

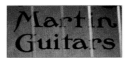

MARTIN OM-18GE

THE GROWING POPULARITY of steel-strung guitars, whose bright, powerful tone made them far more suitable for many kinds of onstage performance than their gut-strung counterparts, was not universally welcomed. Some players simply disliked the sound made by metal strings, while many banjoists feared that the louder new instruments would usurp their once dominant role in dance bands.

Perry Bechtel (1902-1982) belonged to the latter category of concerned musicians. A star banjoist and bandleader, he was being asked to play more and more guitar on shows and broadcasts. After failing to find one that satisfied him, he approached Martin in 1929, and asked the company to make him a flat-top that would retain such banjo-like characteristics as a narrower neck and better access to the upper frets. The outcome of his request was the "Orchestra Model" (OM)—the first-ever Martin to have 14 frets to the body (only 12 frets had been easily reachable on earlier guitars), and a solid, unslotted headstock.

Below: Adirondack spruce is used for the OM-18GE's top; its back and sides are mahogany, and it has a bridge made from ebony.

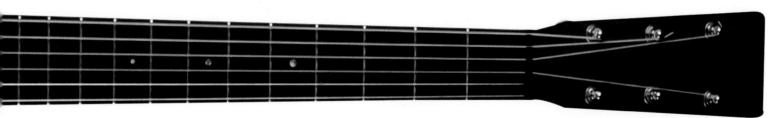

Above: OM fingerboards are 1³/4 inches wide at the nut; previous models measured 1⁷/8 inches.
Right: Banjo-type tuners like these were a distinctive features of the early OMs.

The OM went into full production in 1930; the example seen here is a recent replica of an OM-18 from this period, issued as part of Martin's "Golden Era" series.

Bottom: Early D-18s had 12 frets to the body; 14-fret models like the one here first appeared in 1934.

Above: The honey colored spruce top on this D-18 shows only slight signs of wear.

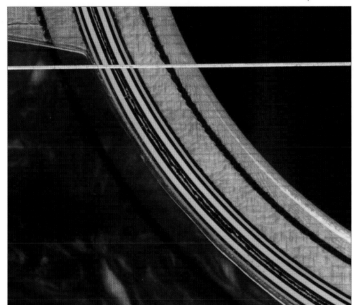

initial stood for "Dreadnought," a name borrowed from the British navy vessel HMS *Dreadnought*, one of the biggest battleships of its kind.

The first Style 18 (spruce top, and mahogany body) Martin Dreadnought, designated a D-18, appeared in 1931. It proved highly popular with musicians seeking powerful volume and booming bass, and has remained in the catalog ever since. The example seen in our photos dates from the early 1950s.

501

Like standard Style 28 models, the HD-28 has a spruce top and rosewood back and sides.

MARTIN HD-28

GUITARS PRODUCED in Martin's Style 28 incorporate an especially famous feature: the "herringbone" marquetry that embellishes their tops. First used in the 19th century, herringbone trim is made from strips of intricately cut wood, originally bought in from European suppliers, but later sourced domestically. The first Style 28 Dreadnoughts appeared in the early 1930s; they and other "28s" continued to include herringbone decoration until 1946, when it was dropped from the Style 28 specification because it had become so hard to obtain.

The lack of herringbone was a major disappointment to customers, and in 1976, Martin reintroduced it—not on Style 28 itself, but as a key feature of a new "Herringbone Dreadnought" category. The HD-28 was the first model to sport the revived trim, and has been a perennial best-seller.

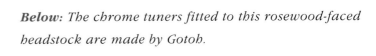

Below: The chrome tuners fitted to this rosewood-faced headstock are made by Gotoh.

The first C.F. Martin used herringbone trim on a number of his guitars.

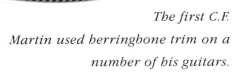

The OMC-16E's backstripe and binding contrast elegantly with its koa back.

MARTIN OMC-16E

LIKE THE 000C-16GTE shown on pages 498-9, this 21st century version of Martin's classic Orchestra Model features a high-specification Fishman preamp system, utilizing both a gooseneck-mounted microphone and a bridge-saddle pickup. The most striking difference between the two sets of electronics lies in the way they are installed and adjusted; while the 000-16 sports a conventional preamp panel on its side, the OM's remarkably unobtrusive "Ellipse" unit is positioned beneath the instrument's top, and its blend, volume, phase and microphone trim controls are all accessible via the soundhole.

The guitar itself is available with three different body woods. The example in our photographs has a back and sides of figured koa; maple and sapele are substituted for this on other OMC-16Es, although all the models have a sitka spruce top, and an ebony fingerboard and bridge.

Above right: This tiny microphone can be moved within the body to create the sound the player wants.
Above left: The Fishman's ingenious mounting conceals its presence from audiences.

Left: The guitar's soundhole rosette features a ring of abalone shell, surrounded with fiber.

CFM (MARTIN) EM-18

THE LATE 1970s were difficult times for acoustic guitar makers, as the cost of raw materials and labor rose, while the use of synthesizers and other—mostly Far Eastern-made—electronics continued to grow. Martin responded to these problems by attempting to break into the solid electric guitar market, and the company introduced its CFM range, with a fanfare of publicity, in 1979. The CFMs initially comprised two 6-stringers and a bass, and were glowingly described by Martin's promotional literature as "a new energy source...quality handcrafted instruments incorporating custom electronics and hardware as factory installed standard equipment." An additional guitar and bass appeared in 1981.

Despite giving the range a high-profile launch, Martin had a somewhat ambivalent attitude about it; significantly, it was decided not to use the full company name on the new guitars' headstocks, and, according to guitar expert Walter Carter's **Martin Book**, there was considerable disagreement within the firm over some aspects of the instruments' design. None of them sold especially well, but the model shown here, the EM-18, which featured twin humbucking pickups with coil-taps and phase reverse switches, did rather better than its sisters: official Martin figures published by the late Mike Longworth show that a total of 1,375 EM-18s were produced between 1979 and 1983, when all five CFM solid electrics were discontinued.

Left: The CFM range all sported contoured maple and walnut bodies, and mahogany necks with rosewood fingerboards.

Left: The EM-18's pickups are powerful, high quality humbuckers.
Right: The scrolled CFM headstock is reminiscent of 19th century Martin designs like the one on pages 486-7.

MARTIN ALTERNATIVE XT

MARTIN INTRODUCED the first-ever instrument in its "ALternative" range, the 00-size "X" model, in 2001. The capitalization of the L in its name is deliberate: AL is the scientific symbol for aluminum, and ALternatives all sport tops made from this ultra-light metal. Thanks to its exceptional strength, it requires much less internal bracing than a conventional wooden top, and many reviewers and players have commented favorably on the clear, responsive tone it produces on the X and its numerous successors—both when played acoustically, and when the guitars' built-in electronics are plugged in.

The Martin ALternative XT shown here debuted the following year. Constructed similarly to other models in the series (whose aluminum tops are combined with backs and sides made from high pressure laminates (HPL), and necks of Stratabond wood veneer), its most striking feature is its Bigsby vibrato—a heavy-duty unit that would be impossible to install on a conventional acoustic without dire structural consequences! The XT also boasts a DiMarzio Fast Track 2 pickup, which can be used in both humbucking and single-coil modes.

Below: The XT's aluminum top is decorated in what Martin terms a "graffiti pattern."

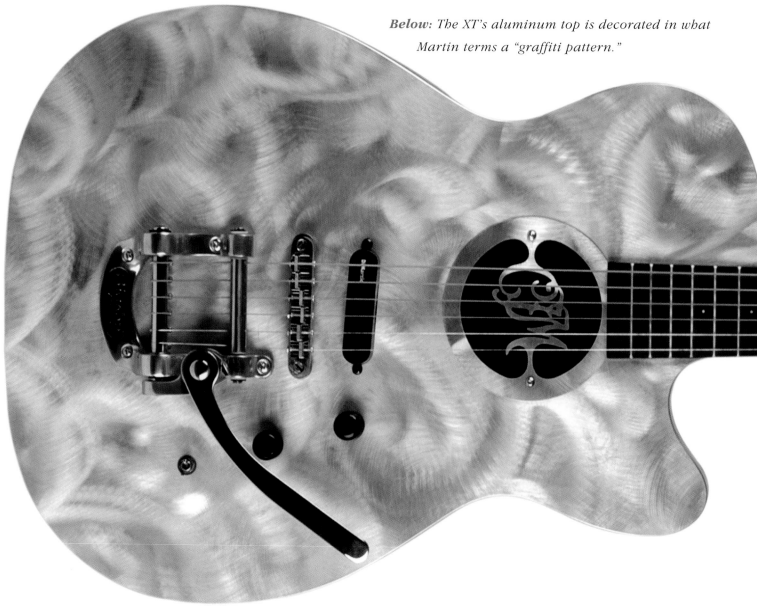

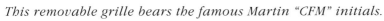

This removable grille bears the famous Martin "CFM" initials.

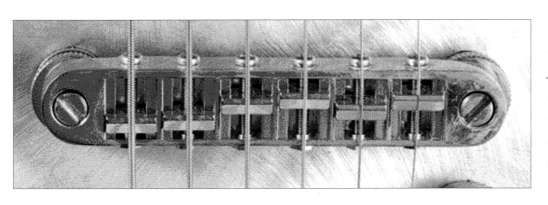

Above: *The XT's black fingerboard.is made from Micarta, a synthetic ebony substitute.*
Left: *A "Tune-O-Matic"-type bridge like this is not often seen on a Martin!*

MARTIN CF-1 ARCHTOP

DALE UNGER (b. 1954) grew up in the area around the C.F. Martin guitar company's headquarters in Nazareth, Pennsylvania. As a budding luthier, he was profoundly influenced by the firm's dedicated and painstaking approach to flat-top design; however, he chose to specialize in building archtop guitars. In the 1990s he went on to study and develop his craft with one of the greatest living makers of such instruments, Robert Benedetto—a New Yorker who was then based in the little Pennsylvanian town of East Stroudsburg.

After three years' work with Benedetto, Dale Unger set up American Archtop Guitars in 1995, and started producing his own models, some of which were built using Benedetto's patterns and molds (though Unger tended to use laminated tops instead of the solid woods found on Benedetto archtops). The next stage of Unger's career began in 2001, when he approached Martin with a proposal for a new range of f-hole guitars

Below: The CF-1 has a 3-inch deep body, with a 3-ply spruce/obeche/spruce top; its back and sides are made from maple.

Below: The label inside the CF-1's f-hole is signed by Dale Under and Christian Frederick Martin IV, Martin's Chairman and CEO

Above: The CF-1 and CF-2 represent Martin's first venture into archtop guitar production since the 1960s.

This "American Archtop" logo was co-designed by Dale Unger and Martin's Dick Boak.

that would, as he put it in an article written for the company's **Sounding Board** newsletter, "blend Martin's extraordinary craftsmanship and process with my particular archtop designs." The idea found favor with Martin's bosses, and two Unger/Martin instruments, the CF-1 (seen here) and the thinline CF-2, were launched in 2004. Both are made from premium tonewoods, and are fitted with Seymour Duncan pickups.

Above: *The dog in Robert Armstrong's picture seems to be howling along to the tune being picked by the cowboy guitarist!*

Right: *Stratabond, a laminate containing resin, is used for the Cowboy III's neck.*

The guitar's fingerboard is fashioned from black Micarta, instead of wood.

subsequent Martin/Armstrong instruments: the Cowboy II debuted in 2001, and the Cowboy III (shown here) a year later. Like its predecessors, the III boasts artwork full of subtle touches and allusions that will delight Martin aficionados. The guitar being played by the figure on the instrument's lower bout is unmistakably one of the company's OM-28s, while the character on the bucking bronco in the corral behind him is Martin CEO Chris Martin IV! Robert Armstrong's picture has been applied to the Cowboy III's top using a high pressure decorative laminating (HPL) technique that ensures vivid colors as well as high scratch resistance.

Only 750 Martin Cowboy IIIs were produced, but the range has continued in recent years with the Cowboy IV and the Hawaiian X.

MARTIN "FELIX" LIMITED EDITION

THE CARTOON CHARACTER Felix The Cat made his debut in a movie short in 1919; it was produced by the New York-based Pat Sullivan studio, and Felix himself was created and originally drawn by Otto Messmer, who directed the picture. Other film appearances helped to establish Felix as a star, and in 1928 he was used as a testcard image for RCA's pioneering television transmissions; he also featured in newspaper cartoon strips and comics, acquiring a restyled look when Joe Oriolo took over the

production of "Felix" artwork from Messmer.

The lovable feline has proved perennially popular in a variety of different media, and in 2004, it was announced that Joe Oriolo's son Don (who collaborated with his father on Felix projects for many years, and has been exclusively responsible for them since Joe's death in 1985) had teamed up with the Martin company to produce a "Felix" guitar. The limited edition instrument (only 756 were produced, one of which is seen here) has a travel-size body made

Below: Micarta, also seen on the Martin Cowboy guitar, is used for this model's fingerboard.

Don Oriolo has helped bring Felix
to a new generation of fans.

*Above: Martin's publicity describes this instrument
as "the ideal guitar for very hip cats!"*

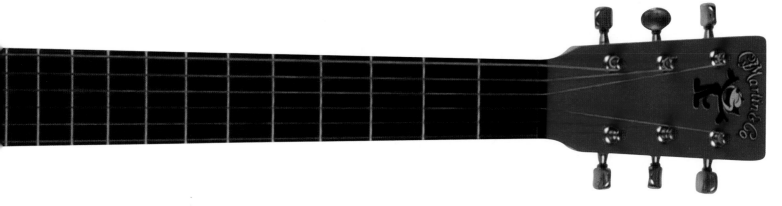

from high pressure laminates. Its back and sides are black, and its spruce-braced top is adorned with multiple Felix heads, as well as a "Felix The Cat" logo and Don Oriolo's signature. A miniature, full-length Felix appears on the headstock.

Unsurprisingly, this first Felix guitar quickly sold out, and in 2006, a second limited-run model appeared. Based, like the original, on a Little Martin acoustic, it boasts a new set of graphics, created by Don Oriolo and his colleague Jen Henning, on its top: these show more than one hundred miniature Felix figures—just one of whom is clutching a plectrum! Among the additional goodies supplied with the guitar are a comic book, and a "laughing Felix" flatpick.

A total of 625 "Felix IIs" has been made, and they have proved every bit as popular as their predecessors.

MARTIN BACKPACKER

THE MARTIN BACKPACKER'S uniquely compact design allows it to be taken to places that would be strictly out of bounds to regular-sized acoustics. Since the first of these endearing little guitars—built for Martin in Mexico, and based on an instrument originally created by luthier Robert McNally—rolled off the production line in 1991, they have been seen and heard in a string of exotic locations, from the South Pole to the Mount Everest Base Camp in Tibet. Backpackers have also been carried onboard the US Space Shuttle *Columbia*, and are said to be a particular favorite among airline staff: some years ago, Martin's *Sounding Board* magazine published a picture of a pilot strumming one while perched inside the engine cowling of a DC-10!

Despite its small size, the Backpacker's 24-inch scale length and standard fingerboard width make it easy to play; the only serious concession to portability lies in the design of its body, which, because of its narrow dimensions, requires a strap to keep it in position whether the user is sitting or standing. The lack of a truss-rod (as extra-light strings are fitted, the Backpacker does not need one) helps to reduce weight, and a built-in bridge transducer enables owners to plug the guitar into any amplifiers, PA systems or tape machines they may encounter on their travels. While the steel-strung Backpacker remains the best seller of the range, a "classical" model has also proved successful, and recently, Martin has introduced Backpacker mandolins and ukuleles.

Below: Despite its size, the Backpacker has a clear, well-balanced tone— thanks in part to the solid spruce used for its top.

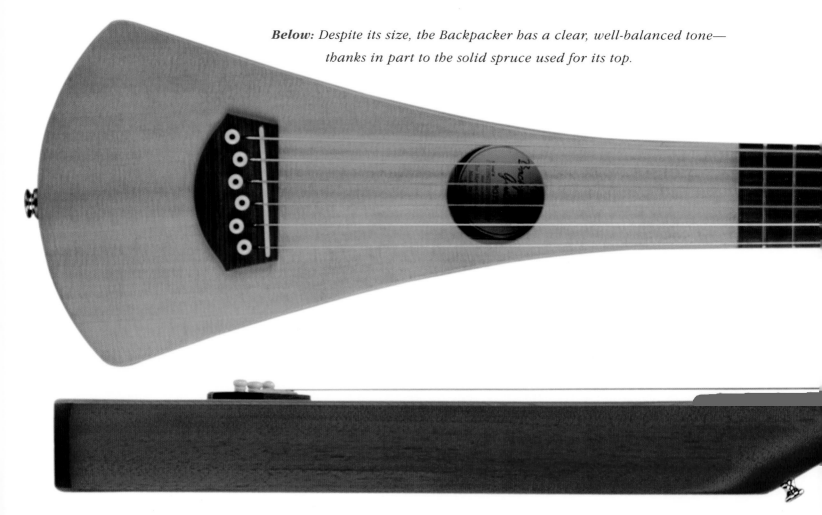

Above: *Miniature chrome tuners are fitted to the Backpacker's headstock.*

Below: *Thanks to the Backpacker's unusual shape, all fifteen of its frets are easily accessible.*

This nut is made from Corian, a solid material developed by DuPont.

TOM MATES ACOUSTIC

TOM MATES is a British guitar maker and repairer who is probably most famous for building a bass as a gift for Dave Pegg of the leading UK folk-rock group Fairport Convention. The timber from which that instrument was carved had formed part of the bar at one of London's favorite smaller music venues, the Half Moon pub in Putney, and had been thrown away during building work there. As Pegg later told Reinhard Groll in an interview posted on the *Fairport List* website, singer-songwriter Ralph McTell, who was passing the pub, "bought the wood from out of a rubbish skip [nearby]. He got Tom Mates to make a bass, and he and the Fairports bought it for me for my 50th birthday." Mates' other distinguished clients include ex-Pentangle guitarist John Renbourn.

The Mates model seen here is a flat-top customized

Tom Mates's current workshop is on the South Bank of the Thames in London, close to Tower Bridge.

These brass bridge pins have been added by the guitar's owner to boost its sustain.

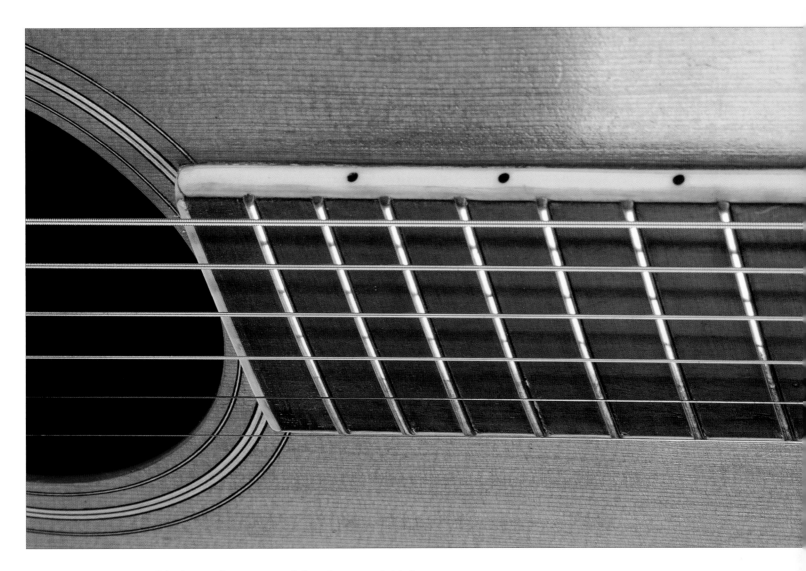

Above and below: Ebony is used for the Mates' 20-fret fingerboard, which has 12 frets to the body.

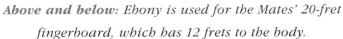

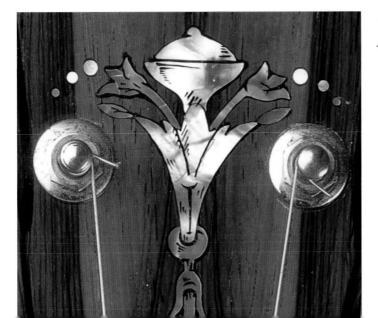

Left: An elegant abalone inlay embellishes the Mates flat-top's headstock. The neck itself has been refretted, and also reshaped to make it slightly thinner.

by Tom Anfield, who has stripped away its original thick lacquer finish, and made a number of other, more minor alterations to it. The instrument has a cedar top, a back and sides of Brazilian rosewood, and a mahogany neck.

MATON EBG808

MATON, AUSTRALIA'S ONLY sizeable guitar producer, is based in the Box Hill area of the city of Melbourne. The firm was established by musician, craftsman and teacher Bill May, who set up an instrument-making and repair shop in the garage of his home in the Melbourne suburbs in the mid-1940s. He christened the fledging business "Maton" (a blend of his own surname and the word "tone"). With the assistance of his cabinetmaker brother Reg, who began collaborating with him in 1946, he was able to open the first Maton factory at a former soap works in nearby Canterbury by the end of the decade.

Over the next 40 years, Maton's product range and reputation grew steadily; it relocated to larger premises in 1989, and moved into its current Box Hill headquarters—where its highly acclaimed acoustic and electric guitars are made using a combination of state-of-the-art Computer Numeric Control (CNC) technology and traditional craft skills—in December 2002. Sadly, Bill May himself did not live to see this latest expansion; he died in 1993, but the company remains a family-run concern, with Bill's daughter

Below: Maton's "Bluegrass" models have narrower bodies than Dreadnoughts or Jumbos, and are favored by fingerstyle players.

Right: The EBG808 has a "satin" finish, and herringbone trim around its soundhole.

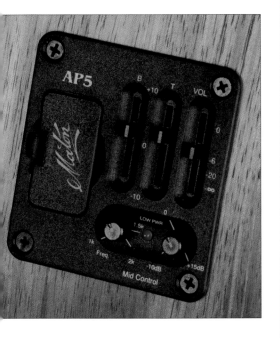

Above: This AP5 pickups gives players precise control over the guitar's amplified sound.

Linda and her husband Neville Kitchen at the helm.

In an international market dominated by American luthiers, Maton has had to struggle to gain the recognition it deserves, but superb instruments such as the EBG808 shown here are attracting increasing numbers of customers. Like all the company's "Bluegrass" (BG) series of flat-tops, it has a 14⁴/₁₀-inch wide body, and features a combination of traditional and Australian tonewoods: on this 808, cedar is used for the top, but the back and sides are made from blackwood (grown in Maton's home state of Victoria), and the neck is Queensland maple. Rosewood is used for the fingerboard and bridge, and the instrument includes a Maton-designed AP5 pickup system.

MATON EM100C MESSIAH

AUSTRALIAN MANUFACTURER Maton's top-of-the-line acoustic guitar is the Dreadnought-sized Messiah. (Dreadnoughts are large flat-tops favored by players seeking the ultimate in tonal richness and power; the classification was first used by Martin in the 1930s.) Just under 16 inches wide and approximately $4^9/_{10}$-inch deep, it is available in a number of different versions, and as a 6- or 12-string. The model seen here has a top made from AAA-grade sitka spruce, selected for its exceptional stiffness, as well as its evenness of coloring and texture. The guitar's back and sides are crafted from Indian rosewood, and for its neck, Maton has chosen a single piece of maple grown in the rainforests of Northern Queensland. Its cutaway is in the shallow, "Venetian" style, and, like the EBG808 shown on the previous pages, it boasts an AP5 pickup with a "sweepable" mid-range.

Top players are full of praise for the Messiah: Australian guitarist Brett Garsed comments that after he was lent one by the Maton bosses for a concert tour, "they almost had to hold me at gunpoint to give it back!" while singer-songwriter Pat Drummond summed up his sorrow following the recent theft of his Messiah in three words: "The angels wept."

Left: The binding around the Messiah's top comprises two layers: the outer one is rosewood, and the inner one features a herringbone pattern.

Below: The characteristic Maton "keyhole" headstock is faced with a rosewood veneer.

The guitar's nut is approximately $1^1/_{15}$ inches wide.

BRIAN MAY SIGNATURE

UNLIKE MANY LEADING rock guitarists, Brian May, who made his name with Queen in the 1970s and 80s, and was recently voted one of the world's top five players, has stayed largely faithful to a single instrument throughout his long and distinguished career. Even more unusually, he designed and built his favorite "Red Special" electric himself, with a little initial assistance from his father. The guitar dates from 1964: it was made with wood from a Victorian fireplace, and, in its earliest form, featured movable pickups for extra tonal versatility. Though it has undergone many subsequent modifications, the Red Special's essential character and appearance (its distinctive color comes from the fence varnish used on the body timber!) have remained largely unchanged, and it has been heard on decades of hit records as well as during memorable live performances—including May's unforgettable rendition of the British National Anthem from the roof of London's Buckingham Palace on the occasion of Her Majesty the Queen's Golden Jubilee in 2002!

The first official replica of the Red Special was produced as a limited edition by Guild in 1984. The

Below: This instrument is signed by Laurie Wisefield, one of the original guitarists in the UK stage show We Will Rock You, *based around Queen songs.*

The guitar has an ebony fingerboard with 24 frets, and a maple neck.

These knobs are master volume and tone controls.

Each of the three pickups has a dedicated on-off switch, and, below it, a phase switch, allowing the creation of a wide variety of sounds.

same company introduced a second Brian May model nine years later, but it was not until 2001 that a less expensive version appeared. This was the Brian May Signature, launched by Burns London (see separate Burns entries) in 2001. The original Red Special boasts 1960s-vintage Burns Tri-Sonic pickups, and the three transducers on the copy are closely modeled on these, while their associated controls (see caption) are identical to those on May's own instrument. Other aspects of the Special have also been carefully reproduced (though a basswood body has been substituted for the "fireplace" timbers), and the model has proved hugely popular with Brian May's legions of guitar-playing admirers. London's House of Guitars has now taken over its distribution from Burns.

WE WILL ROCK YOU!

MAYA C-132S

GUITARS CARRYING THE "MAYA" (and sometimes "El Maya") labels were made in the Japanese city of Kobe, about 200 miles west of Tokyo. The C-132S Grand Concert classic seen in our photographs dates from the mid-1970s, and is part of a series of acoustics, also including Dreadnoughts and other steel-strung models, that were notable both for their high quality and reasonable prices. They sold well domestically, and were also exported to Europe and America. Later, Maya seems to have focused on producing electric guitars closely based on popular US designs: its 1980s catalogs show instruments resembling Gibson Les Pauls, Fender Telecasters and Stratocasters, plus a variety of other highly derivative solid-bodies, semi-acoustics and basses. Little more is known about the firm, whose factory was destroyed during the devastating earthquake that struck Kobe in January 1995.

Maya used rosewood for the C-132S's back and sides; on another contemporary model, this is replaced with jacaranda.

Unlike some cheaper Far Eastern classics, the Maya has a solid spruce top.

Left: *Gold-plated tuners top the instrument's reinforced mahogany neck.*

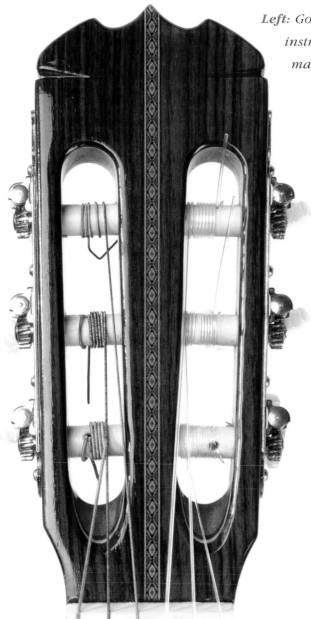

MOON RD3

SCOTSMAN JIMMY MOON combines instrument making with a busy schedule as a musician, playing bass with his popular bluegrass band, the Moonshiners. He founded Moon Guitars at his home on the Isle of Arran, off the Scottish west coast, in 1979, and, thanks to growing demand for his talents as a luthier, was obliged to relocate to the mainland city of Glasgow six years later.

With this move came a shift from acoustic to electric guitar design and construction, as Jimmy Moon found a ready market for his work among major bands such as Texas, Simple Minds, and Big Country However, the 1990s saw him return to making the flat-tops and acoustic mandolins that are now Moon Guitars' best sellers, although he still undertakes commissions for custom electrics. Moon's fame has spread widely in the last few years, boosted by favorable reviews for his latest models in British music magazines, and plaudits from international stars like Bryan Adams—who now uses a Moon RD3 dreadnought acoustic like the one seen here as his main onstage guitar.

The RD3, intended, in Moon's words, to be "ideal for

Below: The Moon RD3's body sports a white binding and a "natural gloss" finish.

PHOTOGRAPHS COURTESY OF IVOR MAIRANTS MUSICENTRE, LONDON

These tuners are made by Grover.

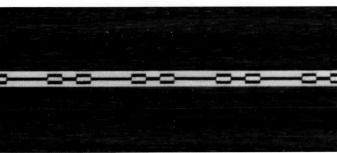

flatpickers and strummers everywhere," has a AAA-quality Alaskan sitka spruce top, back and sides of Indian rosewood, and an ebony fingerboard, bridge, and headstock facing.

Left and above: *The RD3 has a mosaic center "stripe" running down its back.*

MORGAN CONCERT C

This one-piece mahogany neck has an ebony fingerboard.

The Concert C's body is 16 inches wide.

DAVID IANNONE is one of Canada's most highly regarded luthiers. He learned his craft in the early 1980s as an apprentice of Jean Larrivée (see separate entries), and went on to found Morgan Guitars in Vancouver, British Columbia, in 1986. Iannone's firm (which should not be confused with Glen Morgan Guitars of Sklatook, Oklahoma) was named for his first-born child, and currently produces a range of superb acoustics whose famous users include leading Canadian singer-songwriter Sarah McLachlan.

The Morgan seen here is the Concert C, a Florentine-cutaway version of the company's "regular" Concert guitar, which can also be supplied with a soft (Venetian) cutaway body. Various wood options are available on these and all other David Iannone instruments; the model in our photographs sports a sitka spruce top, and koa back and sides.

Opposite page: *Colored binding forms an elegant contrast with the highly figured koa wood used on the guitar's back.*

PHOTOGRAPHS COURTESY OF THE LONDON RESONATOR CENTRE

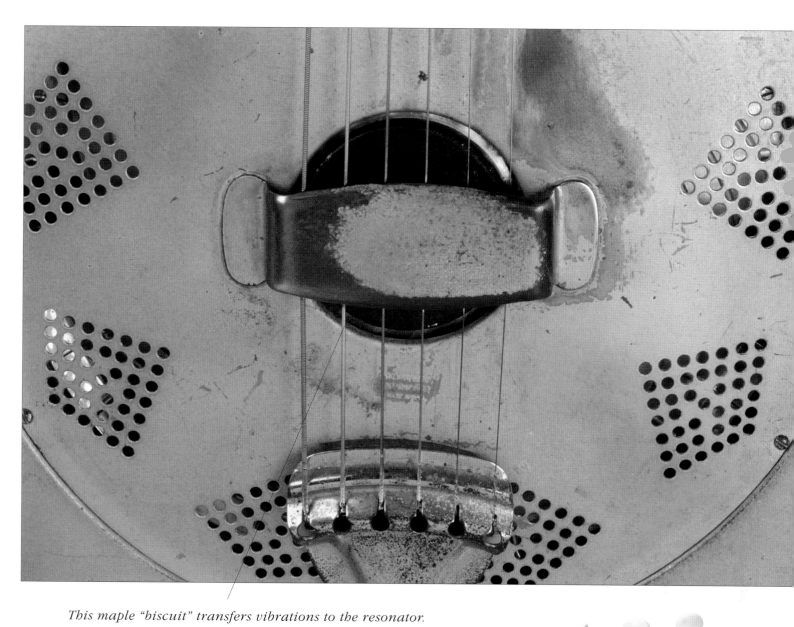

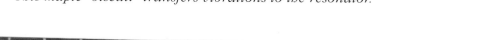

This maple "biscuit" transfers vibrations to the resonator.

Above and left: *National guitars were produced with both "Spanish" (as seen here) and "Hawaiian" necks, and also appeared in a bewildering variety of specifications and decorative styles.*

NATIONAL TRIOLIAN

JOHN DOPYERA was the technical genius responsible for National's innovative resonator instruments: he held the patents for the tri-cone system that had brought the company its initial success, and was also responsible for developing its single-cone counterpart. A reserved, ascetic figure (who, according to Bob Brozman's definitive history of National, published in 1993, consumed carrot juice and bananas at work while many of his colleagues quaffed illicit alcohol), he soon found himself at odds with the forceful, headstrong George Beauchamp, the firm's General Manager; and

in 1929, their already strained relations broke down completely when Beauchamp sought to claim the credit for inventing the single-cone resonator.

Beauchamp's actions led to Dopyera's abrupt resignation from National, and his establishment, shortly afterwards, of the Dobro company (see separate entries), which went on to produce single-cone resonators of its own. Beauchamp, meanwhile, applied for a patent on the National single-cone, and provoked a $2 million lawsuit with Dobro after he alleged that its new instruments infringed his and

Below: Metal Triolians debuted in 1929; the model quickly became a best-seller for National.

Bottom: Later Triolians had necks with 14 frets to the body, permitting easier access to higher notes.

Above: The steel used to make Triolians was slightly heavier than that found on Duolians.

National's intellectual property rights. This increasingly acrimonious dispute formed the background to the launch of National's Triolian steel-body, single-resonator guitar, an example of which is shown here. Differences between the models are largely cosmetic: unlike the plainer Duolian, the Triolian was produced with painted finishes, the most basic of which is our instrument's "two-tone walnut" coloring.

NATIONAL ROSITA

THOUGH NATIONAL remained financially buoyant in the early 1930s, the company was in considerable turmoil. The principal cause of this was the legal action initiated by John Dopyera and his colleagues (including several of his brothers) at Dobro, who alleged that their rival resonator-making business had been damaged by false statements made by National's General Manager, George Beauchamp. As Bob Brozman reveals in his history of the company, Beauchamp had indeed been visiting instrument dealers and claiming, quite baselessly, that "Dobro [guitars] infringed on National patents and that National had won a lawsuit with Dobro." His behavior eventually undermined his standing at National, and in 1931, he was sacked from his post there.

The dispute with Dobro dragged on for two more years before being settled out of court. Its resolution led to a rapprochement between National and the Dopyera family, who acquired a substantial financial stake in the company, and in July 1935 Dobro and National merged, with John Dopyera's brother Emil becoming the National Dobro Corporation's General

Below: This Rosita dates from 1936, the year in which National began its move from LA to Chicago.

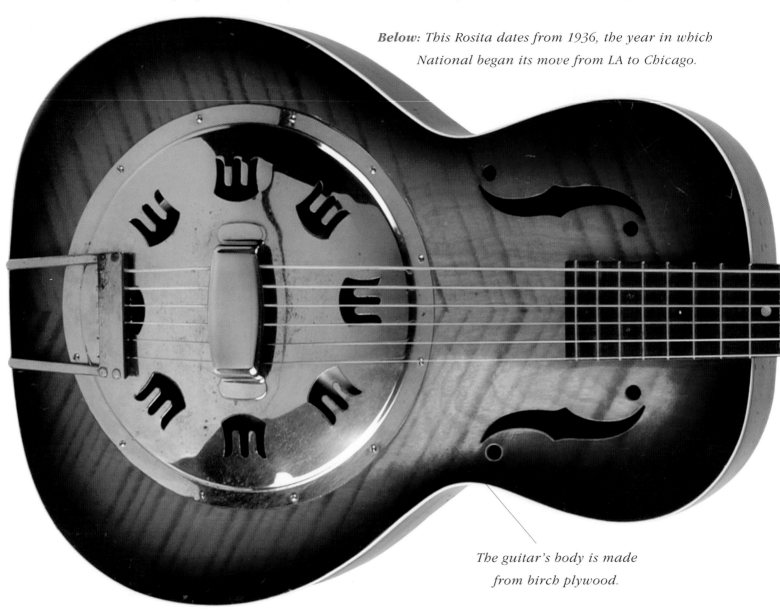

The guitar's body is made from birch plywood.

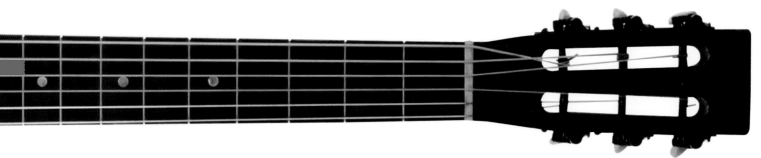

Above: The Rosita's resonator cover is decorated very differently to those on earlier Nationals.

Left: This V-shaped neck profile is a favorite with many players.

Manager. Under this new regime, National continued, for a while, to make both metal- and wood-body resonator instruments, including the elegant Rosita model illustrated here. However their sales were being increasingly eroded by the rise in demand for electrics, and it was in the latter area that the company chose to stake its future. By the start of World War II, its production of tri-cones and single-cones had ceased.

NORMAN B₂₀J

ROBERT GODIN IS RESPONSIBLE for a number of highly successful Canadian guitar brands (see individual entries for Art & Lutherie on pages 42-3 and Godin on pages 354-7). However, the longest established of his instrument making companies is Norman Guitars, founded in 1972 in the village of La Patrie, Quebec, and initially based in premises acquired from a local woodworker and luthier, Norman Boucher, whom Godin had met the previous year while on a hunting vacation in the area. The new firm quickly earned itself an impressive reputation for quality and value, and today, its La Patrie headquarters is equipped with the latest and best in guitar building technology.

Norman produces an extensive range of acoustics;

Right: The B20J's sound-hole decoration is simple but effective.

with the exception of the cheapest, the B15, all are fitted with solid spruce or cedar tops. At the heart of its range is the B20, which is available as both a standard and high-gloss finish dreadnought, and in various other sizes and configurations. The model seen in our photographs, a jumbo version of the B20, was introduced in 2005. Like other Normans, it has a back and sides of cherry laminate, a mahogany neck, a rosewood fingerboard, and a nut made from Tusq. It can be ordered with a built-in Fishman piezo bridge transducer and battery-powered preamp.

Left: Norman places particular emphasis on the quality of its lacquer finishes, which are designed to promote maximum vibration in the tops of its acoustic guitars.

These tuners have high-ratio gearing.

OAHU LAP STEEL

IN THE 1890s, A YOUNG HAWAIIAN, Joseph Kekuku, pioneered a method of producing notes from the strings of his guitar by pressing and sliding a flat steel implement (such as a bar or a knife blade) against them. To accomplish this most effectively, Kekuku and his successors placed their guitars flat on their laps, raising the height of the strings relative to the neck to prevent unwanted contact with the fingerboard, and retuning from the standard EADGBE to chordal settings like "open G" (DGDGBD). Doing so flattened, and therefore slightly loosened, several of the strings,

Right: With no pickguard to protect it, the Tonemaster's body bears the scars of long years' vigorous playing!

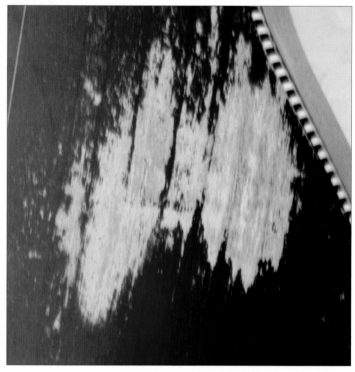

Below: The Oahu's headstock is finished in mock tortoiseshell, and bears a silkscreened logo.

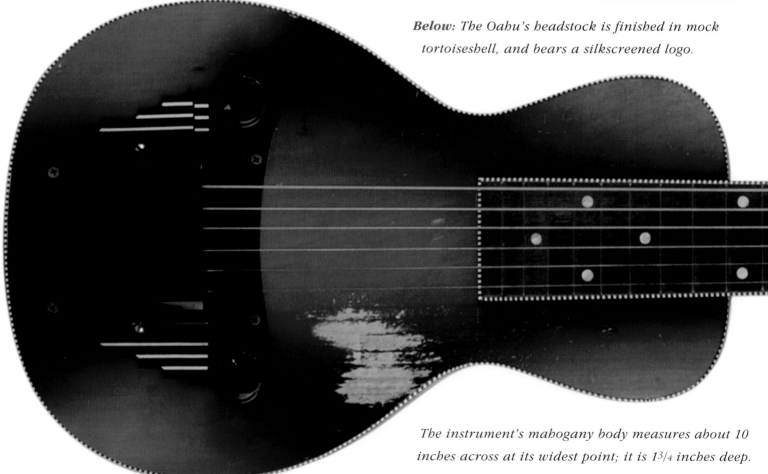

The instrument's mahogany body measures about 10 inches across at its widest point; it is 1³/4 inches deep.

and the term "slack key guitar" was coined to describe this form of Hawaiian-style playing.

Appearances by guitarists from Hawaii at the 1915 Panana Pacific Exposition in San Francisco helped to popularize the islands' music (and other aspects of their culture), and soon, a craze for all things Hawaiian had taken hold throughout America. This proved to be long lasting, and US manufacturers responded by flooding the market with "lap steel" guitars for slack-key playing. In 1931, Ro-Pat-In, the Californian firm that later developed into Rickenbacker, launched its famous "Frying Pan"—a solid-body lap steel that was the world's first mass-produced electric guitar. Others followed Ro-Pat-In's lead, and by the mid-1930s, the

Above left: *This shot shows the extra distance between strings and neck needed for slide playing.*

Above right: *There is a hint of Art Deco in the design of the Tonemaster's pickup cover.*

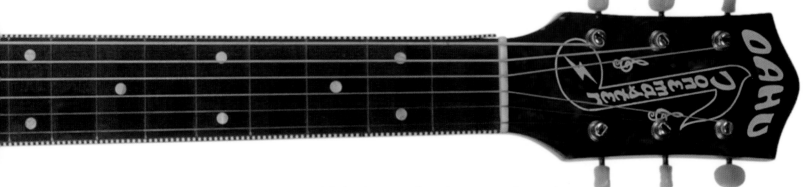

Oahu Publishing Company, originally established in Flint, Michigan, but now based in Cleveland, Ohio, was selling electric lap steels (as well as standard guitars and ukuleles) built for them by third-party makers. The late 1940s Tonemaster lap steel shown here is the work of Oahu's principal electric guitar supplier, Valco of Chicago (formerly National). A relatively inexpensive, workhorse model, it would have been ideal for beginners, who could also purchase an extensive range of tutor books, sheet music and tablature from Oahu. Tonemasters like this one currently change hands at approximately $400.

Below: This Balladeer has a solid spruce top, and a "mid-depth" Lycrachord bowl; other Ovations offer "contour," "deep" or "super-shallow" bowl-backs..

This model is Ovation's biggest-selling American-built guitar.

OVATION SPECIAL BALLADEER

Ovation's headquarters is in New Hartford, Connecticut.

MOST LUTHIERS ARE ADAMANT that wood is the only suitable material for the finest acoustics. The Kaman Music Corporation is one of the very few manufacturers to challenge this view: its Ovation guitars have (in most cases) wooden tops, but bowl-shaped backs made from the fiber/resin formulation Lyrachord. Charles H. Kaman studied the science of vibration while working in the aviation industry, and began applying his knowledge to guitar building in the mid-1960s. Concluding that round-back instruments performed better than flat-back ones, he used Lyrachord to increase their sonic projection, and his designs, introduced in 1967, were soon selling well. Later models with pickups proved even more successful, and many players have come to regard Ovations as the ideal "plugged-in" flat-tops for onstage use—though Kaman's approach remains controversial. Our photographs show a recently made Ovation "Special Balladeer;" the Balladeer was the company's first-ever guitar, and has been available, in various forms, for almost four decades.

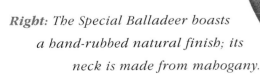

Right: The Special Balladeer boasts a hand-rubbed natural finish; its neck is made from mahogany.

OVATION BALLADEER (NYLON-STRUNG)

CHARLES H. KAMAN'S guitars were named Ovations by jazzman Charlie Byrd (1925-1999), who, after seeing an early model, commented that "it deserved an ovation." Byrd was keen to try one of the revolutionary, Lyrachord-backed acoustics for himself: however, he preferred classicals for his Latin-influenced music (including the best-selling *Jazz Samba* LP, released a few years previously, on which he had partnered saxophonist Stan Getz), and the steel-strung Ovation was not suited to his technique. Kaman quickly solved the problem by developing a nylon-strung version: this debuted in September 1967, and Charlie Byrd went on to adopt "classical-style" Ovations as his main instruments—using them both for solo projects, and when appearing alongside fellow jazz greats Barney Kessel and Herb Ellis in the "Great Guitars" trio, formed in 1973.

Unlike more traditional classicals,

nylon-strung Ovations (a 1970s example is seen here) are easily amplifiable and comparatively robust—qualities that render them particularly attractive to busy touring musicians. Over the years, they have become especially popular with folk and country players, but also have a place in rock: Eddie Van Halen famously featured one on "Spanish Fly," a brief solo track from the *Van Halen II* album (1979).

Right: This 1970s Ovation nylon-strung has a built-in pickup whose concentric volume and tone controls are mounted opposite its neck; these have been resited on more recent models
Far right: The Ovation's open headstock and wide neck are classically influenced, though a reinforcing truss-rod (never found on standard classics) is fitted.

PHOTOGRAPHS COURTESY OF PEACH, BLAKE END, BRAINTREE

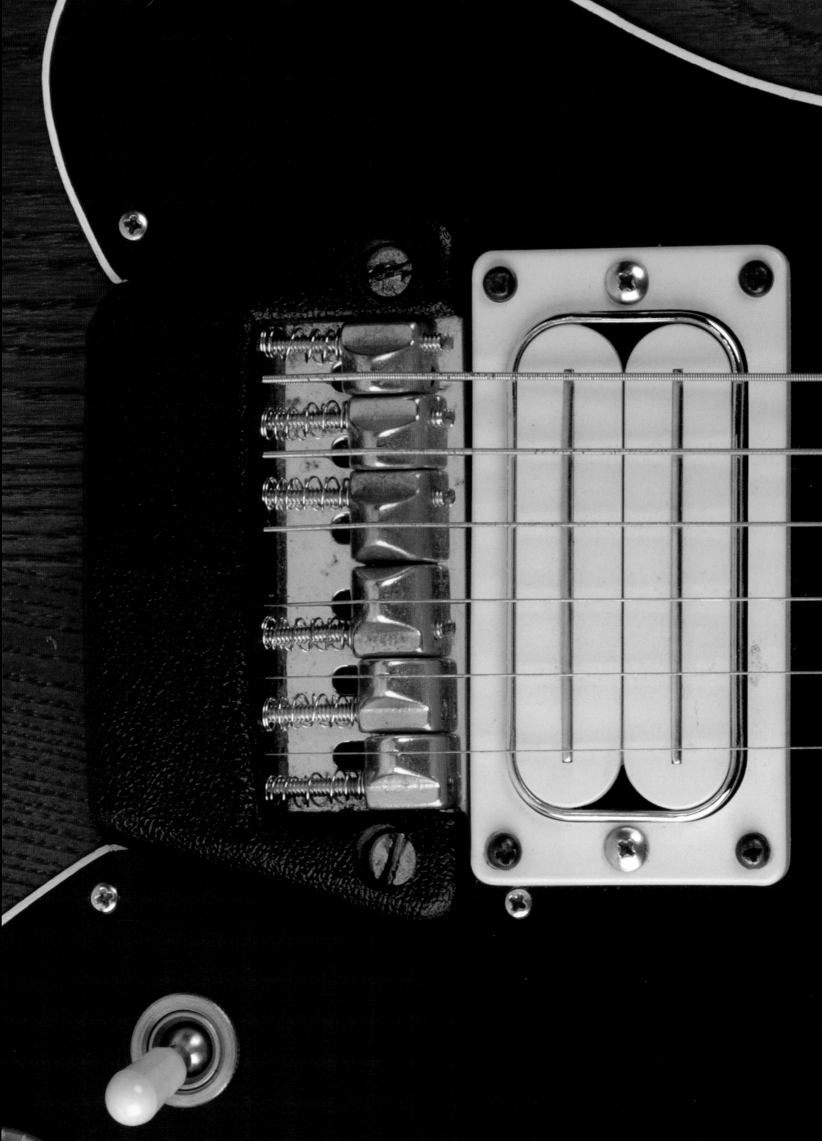

OVATION VIPER

OVATION ENTERED the conventional electric guitar market in 1968 with its "Electric Storm" range. This comprised seven semi-hollow models, including a 12-string and two basses, all of which were given appropriately "meteorological" names (Thunderhead, Tornado, Hurricane, Typoon). Various additions and changes were made to the line over the next few years, but the instruments were not especially successful, and were eventually dropped.

The company's second generation of electrics was solid-bodied. The Breadwinner and Deacon, launched, respectively, in 1972 and 73, shared a curious, asymmetrical shape, but the Preacher and Viper, dating from 1975, were more conventional-looking. The former sported a double cutaway and stereo circuitry, while the latter (shown here) was a simpler, single-cutaway design. It also had single-coil pickups, which have been replaced with twin-coil units on the instrument in our photos. None of these guitars ever attained the same popularity as Ovation's acoustics, although the Viper and Deacon were the longest lived of the group, remaining in production until the 1980s.

Below: On its 1970s electrics, Ovation chose to retain the "3-a-side" headstock shape already familar to users of its acoustic models.

Above: Unusually, the Viper's maple neck is both glued and bolted to its body.

OVATION ADAMAS II 1681-8

OVATION WAS NOT CONTENT to rest on its laurels following the introduction of its innovative acoustics in the mid-1960s. Having replaced wood with Lyrachord on the backs of its guitars, it now turned its attention to the formulation of their tops, and began experimenting with the use of graphite fiber for them. In 1976, after several years of painstaking research, the company unveiled its first Adamas acoustic, whose top comprised three layers: two ultra-thin slices of carbon graphite, and a center made from a slightly wider section of birch. As Ken Achard writes in his book *The History and Development of the American Guitar* (Musical New Services, 1979), the carbon top was "about one third the thickness of a conventional spruce top...and many times stronger." There was no standard soundhole; instead, a total of twenty-two smaller apertures were positioned on the instrument's upper bouts. The model's sound, carefully tailored by the scientists and luthiers who created what Ovation called its "fibronic graphite soundboard," was praised

Below: The Adamas's bridge, fingerboard and headstock veneer are all made from walnut.

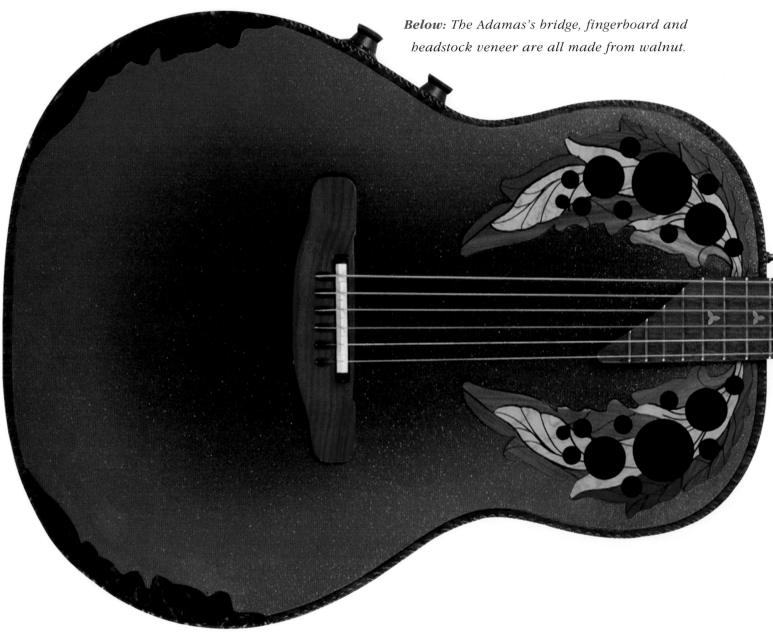

Above: *The "leaf epaulets" around these mini-soundholes were produced using maple veneer.*

Bottom: *These volume and tone knobs are undoubtedly elegant, but more modern Adamas guitars have more comprehensive controls.*

by many (though not all) previously skeptical players, and Adamas flat-tops are now well established in the pantheon of high-end guitars.

The Adamas in our photographs is a top of the range 1681-8, dating from 1982. It has a blue-tinted top, a stereo pickup with individual piezo transducers for each string, and a five-piece neck made from mahogany and laminated maple.

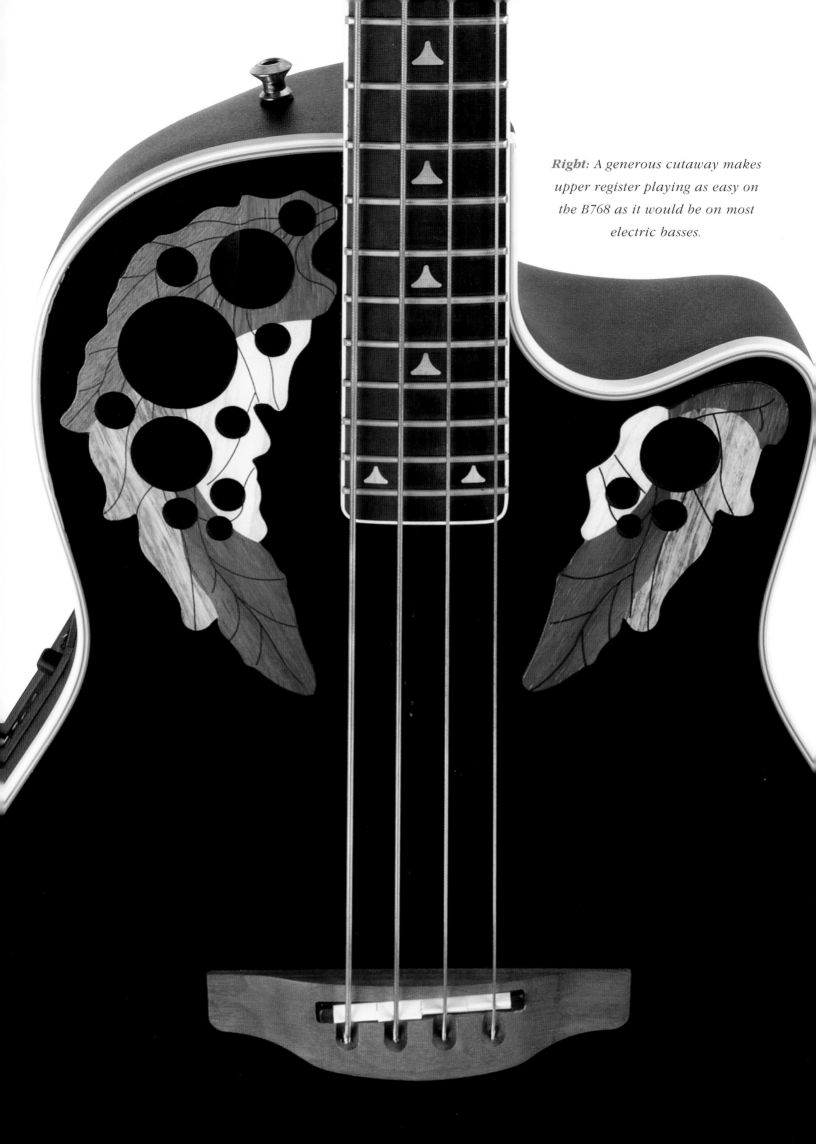

Right: A generous cutaway makes upper register playing as easy on the B768 as it would be on most electric basses.

OVATION B768 ELITE BASS

THE FIRST OVATION BASSES were electrics. Its 1968 catalog announced the introduction of two "Typoon" slimline models with, respectively, one and two pickups, which were part of the company's "Electric Storm" range—and proclaimed to be "[as] wild as the winds for which they [were] named"!

Today, the firm's basses all have acoustic bodies: the B768 model shown here is part of its "Elite" series, whose offset, miniature multi-soundholes, with their leafy "epaulets," resemble those found on Ovation Adamas guitars (see separate entry). However, unlike Adamas models, Elites have 100% wood tops made from either cedar or, in the case of the B768, spruce. A deep bowl is fitted to this bass, and its "plugged-in" sound is supplied via an OP24+ pre-amplifier with 3-band equalization (featuring a "tuneable" midband) and a rumble-reducing "pre-shape" circuit.

The B768 has now been discontinued; its successor, the B778, has a similar appearance, but boasts a "tru-balance" transducer and a more sophisticated OP40 preamp that, according to Ovation, "leaves other systems back in the 20th century."

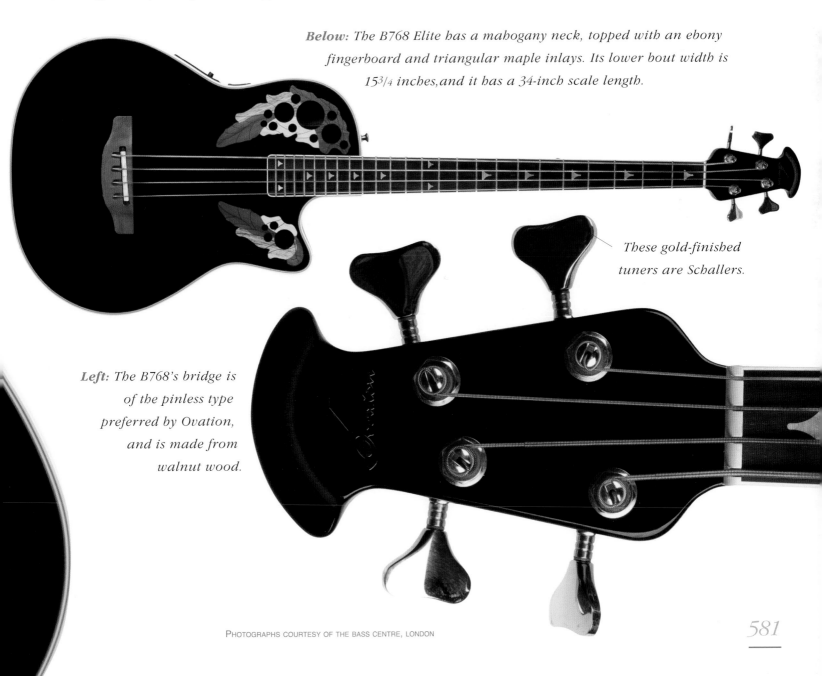

Below: The B768 Elite has a mahogany neck, topped with an ebony fingerboard and triangular maple inlays. Its lower bout width is 15³/₄ inches, and it has a 34-inch scale length.

These gold-finished tuners are Schallers.

Left: The B768's bridge is of the pinless type preferred by Ovation, and is made from walnut wood.

Right: Signals from the 6- and 12-string sections of the guitar are routed to the OP24+ preamp via a toggle swtich on the instrument's shoulder.

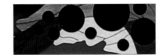

OVATION CSD225-BCB DOUBLENECK

DOUBLE-NECKED GUITARS have a long history: as early as 1902, the Martin company had produced a two-necked harp guitar (though its second neck had no frets, and served only to support the instrument's twelve "drone" strings); and by the 1930s, Gibson was making electric Hawaiian models with twin necks that could each be tuned differently in order to expand the instrument's harmonic capabilities. Leo Fender later took this concept even further, with his mid-1950s three- and four-necked Stringmaster Hawaiians, while pedal steel instruments are also frequently made in paired-neck configurations.

doubleneck acoustics or electrics. Among this brave minority is Ovation, which has recently introduced the production-model Celebrity Deluxe Doubleneck shown in our photos at the comparatively modest price of just over $1,400. Aware of the problems with size and weight that often dog the design of these guitars, the company has developed a scaled-down roundback body (approximately three-quarter size) for it. Care has

"Dots and diamonds" inlays grace the guitar's twin necks.

Gold-plated tuners are fitted to the CSD-225.

"Spanish-style" doublenecks (i.e. those held upright, rather than placed on the player's lap or on a stand) are most usually 6-/12-stringers (see earlier entry for an electric Gibson SG double), although the additional

Left: The two necks have rosewood fingerboards, and a 25¹/₄-inch scale length. The guitar's bridge is walnut.

neck sometimes carries bass guitar or even mandolin strings, and a few triplenecks, created by specialists like Hugh Manson or the Canadian luthier Linda Manzer, are also in circulation. The more exotic and elaborate of such instruments tend, for obvious reasons, to be custom-built, and only a handful of manufacturers currently supply "off-the-shelf"

also been taken with the central cutaway, which allows easy access to the upper, 12-string neck; and the guitar has been fitted with a modified version of Ovation's OP24+ preamp system that controls the pickup output from either or both of the necks. The top is made from laminated spruce, and the Celebrity Deluxe is finished in "Black Cherryburst."

OVATION TANGENT M.O.B.

PREMIUM-PRICE OVATIONS, which carry the Ovation and Adamas names, are built at Kaman's Connecticut headquarters; but the corporation's cheapest, Applause-brand guitars are made in China, while its mid-price Pinnacle and Celebrity ranges, as well as Tangent models like the "M.O.B." seen in these photographs, originate from Korea. The M.O.B. initials stand for "My Other Board," and Ovation's publicity

Below: The M.O.B.'s rosewood bridge is wave-shaped, while its soundholes and fret markers resemble surfboards!

Above: *The guitar's preamp offers switchable three-band EQ, plus a "pre-shape" setting that boosts bass and treble, while reducing unwanting low frequencies. There is also an onboard chromatic tuner.*

Right: *The M.O.B. has an unusually configured headstock, with four of its six gray gun-metal tuners mounted on the treble side.*

describes it as "a rugged axe [that] can stand up to the stage, the beach and the street better than any other pro-quality acoustic."

The guitar's "Blue Surf Burst" finish and board-shaped soundholes contribute to its informal, fun-looking image, but it is unquestionably a serious instrument, with no shortage of bright, powerful tone—especially when plugged into an amp or PA that can do justice to its impressively specified internal pickup system and OP30 preamp. Like most Ovations, it boasts a slimline neck (made from a single piece of nato—also known as eastern mahogany) that will please players accustomed to the easy feel of electric guitars, and its laminated spruce top is braced in Ovation's unique "Quintad" pattern, which uses nine internal lengthwise struts rather than the X-bracing more commonly found on acoustics.

The M.O.B. is available in two different Lyrachord bowlback sizes: "mid-depth" (providing optimum acoustic sound) or "super-shallow."

The Progress III Deluxe bass seen here has two output sockets mounted on the right edge of its body: a standard jack and a 3-pin XLR.

This rear shot shows the instrument's "neck-through-body" construction, with two "wings" on either side of the central neck section.

OVERWATER PROGRESS III

FOUNDED BY DESIGNER, MUSICIAN and craftsman Chris May in 1979, Overwater operates from a converted Victorian mill in the Cumbrian city of Carlisle, near the English/Scottish border. Over the last quarter of a century the company has produced more than three thousand basses, and specializes in high-end models, aimed principally at professionals and serious amateurs. Overwater makes a wide variety of instruments, including bolt-on neck and semi-acoustic models. The bass in our photographs, however, comes from the firm's Progress range, described by Chris May as his "flagship series" of through-neck designs. These are produced in 4-, 5-, 6- and 7-string versions; the "deluxe" 5-stringer seen here is tuned (bottom to top) BEADG. It has an Indian mahogany body, with a top facing of figured jarrah, and a five-piece maple and walnut neck section. Its electronics include low-noise twin-coil pickups and a 3-band onboard EQ.

Right: The instrument's solid brass bridge is set into its body to maximize sustain.

The 24-fret neck has a 36-inch scale length; its fingerboard is made from Indian rosewood.

OZARK MODEL 3616 RESONATOR

A FEW DECADES AGO, budding players interested in taking up the resonator guitar would have struggled to find affordable instruments. Today, thankfully, the state of the market is very different, with a number of firms supplying excellent quality National- and Dobro-style models aimed primarily at entry-level and intermediate pickers. One of these is the UK-based Stentor Music Company, which, since the 1980s, has been the worldwide distributor of Korean made, "Ozark" branded resonator guitars; the Ozark range also includes banjos, mandolins, bouzoukis and mandolas, and is available throughout the USA and Europe.

The Ozark guitar in our pictures is a deluxe single resonator model, with a "biscuit" bridge and a deliberately "aged" body made from bronze-cored bell brass. Brass was one of the materials used in the construction of the pre-war Nationals created by John Dopyera (see National section), and

Above: The Ozark's open headstock resembles those appearing on many pre-war National models.
Both left: The guitar has a mahogany neck; its decorated brass body contains a single-cone aluminum resonator.

the Ozark has many similarities with these classic designs: it even sports a Hawaiian beach scene etching on its back, inspired by the "tropical" engravings found on its famous predecessors. Its powerful tone is ideal for blues, country or rock, and it is robust enough to give years of service. Among Ozark's other guitars are several electro-acoustic resonators, as well as a metal-bodied, single-cone bass.

JUAN PAGÉS, 1802

JUAN PAGÉS (d.1821) made his instruments in the southwestern Spanish port of Cádiz; the one shown in our photographs was built there in 1802, and is believed to have been the property of the great artist Goya—Francisco José de Goya y Lucientes (1746-1828)—who was a keen player, and frequently included images of guitars in his work.

Despite being made some four years after the 6-string Giovanni Battista Fabricatore model seen earlier in this book, the Pagés is strung in old-style "courses" (pairs); only the top (E) string is undoubled. There are two probable reasons for this: the longer survival of older playing traditions in Spain, which, as guitar historian James Westbrook has written, "was the only country [still] producing music for this type of guitar";

and the conservative influence of the Spanish craft guild system, which actively discouraged innovation among its members.

While its stringing is old-fashioned, the instrument also has some more progressive features, though these are invisible without x-rays. Pagés is widely recognized

Left: The initials on this pearl plaque are "FG"—do they stand for Francisco Goya, the guitar's supposed owner?

Below: Unlike many older guitars, the Pagés is still in playable condition, and has recently been used at a concert.

PHOTOGRAPHS COURTESY OF JAMES WESTBROOK

for the improvements to internal strutting he instigated during his career, and the elaborate "fan-bracing" used to reinforce the spruce top on this model was later taken up and further refined by other major luthiers. The guitar's back and sides are of rosewood, divided by strips of purfling, and the neck is made from mahogany, with a rosewood-veneered headstock and a rosewood fingerboard.

Bottom: *This picture shows the purfling dividing the rosewood "ribs" that make up the instrument's sides.*

Above: *The "floral" decorations beneath the bridge were created with ebony and mother-of-pearl.*

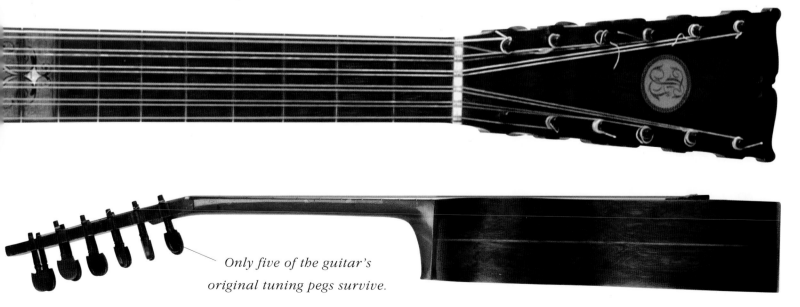

Only five of the guitar's original tuning pegs survive.

LOUIS PANORMO, 1831

LOUIS PANORMO (1784-1862) was born in Paris, where his Italian father, Vicenzo, worked as a guitar maker. Both Louis and his older brothers, Joseph and George, were trained as luthiers by Vicenzo; later, all three siblings moved to England, and in 1819, Louis—already the best known of them—set up his own workshop in the fashionable London district of Bloomsbury.

The printed labels on Louis Panormo's instruments proclaim him to be "the only maker of guitars in the Spanish style" (in England, at any rate!) Many of his designs, such as the example shown here, incorporate internal "fan-bracing" of the kind developed by Juan Pagés of Cádiz (see previous entry), and share some similarities of shape with older Spanish models. However, Panormo also produced other, more experimental guitars, including at least one with a highly unusual oval body.

He left London for New Zealand, where one of his sons lived, in the mid-1850s, but the Panormo name was to remain prominent in British guitar-playing circles for several decades to come, thanks to the continuing activities of other members of his family.

Right: This style of body and decoration can be seen on a good many of Panormo's guitars.

Left: Spruce is used for the instrument's top; its back and sides are made from rosewood.

These elegant machine heads still work well, despite their age.

   PHOTOGRAPHS COURTESY OF JAMES WESTBROOK

ANTONIO RAYA PARDO, 1982

THE SPANISH CITY OF GRANADA is a long established center for lutherie: it was here that the young Andrés Segovia (1893-1987) acquired his first guitar—an inexpensive model from the workshop of Benito Ferrer, which the budding player continued to use until he made his concert debut in Madrid at the age of 19 in 1912. Ferrer (1845-1925) was a key figure in what came to be known as the "Granada School" of luthiers, whose classical and flamenco instruments were renowned for their clear response and sweet, balanced tone. Among his apprentices was his nephew, Eduardo Ferrer, who later became a distinguished guitar maker in his own right, and was responsible for training one of today's most celebrated "Granada School" luthiers, Antonio Raya Pardo.

Pardo was born in 1950, and has been described, in Maurice J. Summerfield's book *The Classical Guitar: Its Evolution, Players and Personalities*, as "one of

Below: Like many hand-made guitars, this model carries its maker's signature on its soundhole label.

Below: The fingerboard on this outstanding flamenco guitar is made from mahogany.

the finest classical guitar makers since 1800." He went on to marry Eduardo Ferrer's granddaughter, and his own son, Antonio Raya Ferrer (b.1980), is the most recent member of the Ferrer/Pardo dynasty to distinguish himself in the family profession.

The many virtues of the Granada School are readily apparent in the Antonio Raya Pardo guitar shown here. A flamenco model dating from 1982, it has a top of German spruce, and back and sides of cypress—a wood both lighter in weight and brighter in tone than the rosewood traditionally used on standard classical instruments. The British dealer who recently offered it for sale commented that "twenty-three years of careful playing have left [it] delightfully open and tonal," and there seems little doubt that it will improve further in the coming decades!

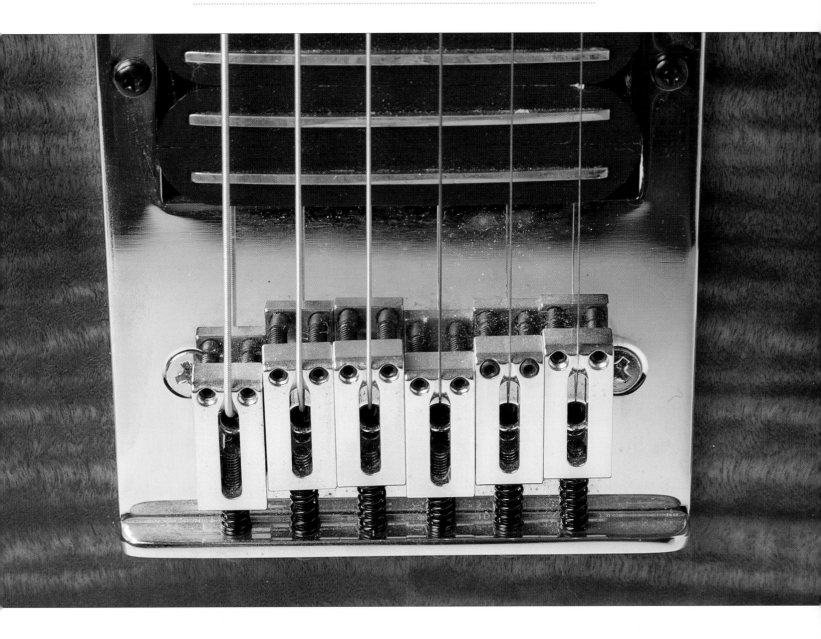

Left: The Cropper Classic's pickups are selected via this three-way switch. The coil-tap control for the bridge pickup appears in our main photograph.

Top: Above the guitar's gold-plated bridge is the "Db 4" bridge humbucker, three of whose four polepieces can be seen in the close-up.

Left: Pau Ferro ("iron wood") is used for the Grind's fingerboard.

PEAVEY GRIND 5-STRING BASS

OVER THE LAST four decades, Peavey has won countless awards and accolades for its instruments and sound reinforcement gear, and its basses—which include student, mid-price and professional models—are perennial best-sellers. The 5-string Grind shown here was introduced in 2001; like the 4-string Grind that debuted at the same time, it has an alder body and two passive, humbucking pickups. The transducers fitted to the 5-string are Peavey "J-styles" (named in tribute to the Fender Jazz Bass), while the 4-stringer boasts both a J-style and a staggered-coil "P-style" unit inspired by those found on Fender's Precision Basses. Though the pickups themselves are passive, the Grind has an active, three-band EQ system, as well as treble boost, master volume and blend controls. Its maple neck is bolted on, and there is a 24-fret fingerboard with a 34-inch scale.

More recent Grind models boast a neck-through-body design, and carry the self-explanatory suffix NTB. The choice of woods has also changed—the center section is now mahogany and maple, with the body "wings" now being made from attractively striped Imbuya wood imported from Brazil—and the range has been augmented by a 6-string Grind.

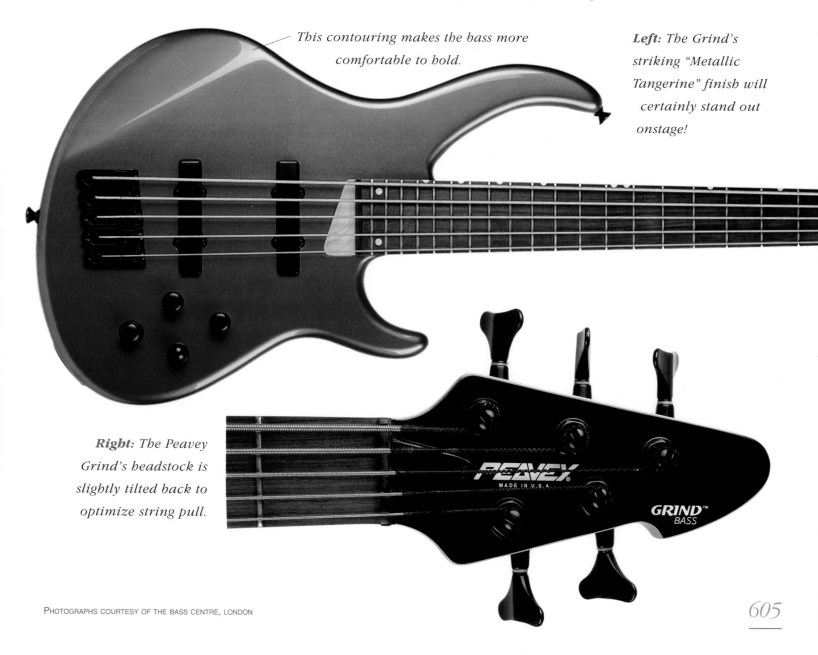

This contouring makes the bass more comfortable to hold.

Left: *The Grind's striking "Metallic Tangerine" finish will certainly stand out onstage!*

Right: *The Peavey Grind's headstock is slightly tilted back to optimize string pull.*

PEAVEY JD-AG1

Below: This dreadnought-style acoustic boasts a rosewood fretboard with an "Old No.7" inlay at its 12th fret.

IN 2004, Peavey announced that it had obtained an exclusive license to produce musical instruments and related equipment bearing the trademark of one of America's most celebrated whiskey makers, Jack Daniel's of Lynchburg, Tennessee. It is not known whether Mr. Jack himself—who lived from 1850 to 1911, and took over the still that was produce his "smooth sippin'" liquor at the age of just 13—was especially partial to music. However, he would surely have been pleased to see his brand promoted so ingeniously, and the Peavey-manufactured, Daniel's-adorned guitars and amps that began appearing in Summer 2005 certainly have novelty value! Pictured here is the one of three currently available Peavey/Daniel's acoustics, the JD-AG1. It has a spruce top, mahogany back, neck and sides, and a built-in piezo pickup, and is intended, in Peavey's words, to appeal to "Jack Daniel's enthusiasts, avid music fans, serious collectors and dedicated musicians alike."

Below: Guitar builder and whiskey maker share the credits on the JD-AG1's smart black headstock.

Note the Jack Daniel's filigree on the soundhole above.

RADIOTONE ARCHTOP, c.1935

THE INTRODUCTION of the Gibson L-5 archtop acoustic in 1922 opened up a new role for the guitar as a rhythm and solo instrument in jazz and swing ensembles—and European manufacturers, like Gibson's American competitors, were soon turning out archtops of their own that replicated some of its features. Germany, with its long tradition of lutherie, was a significant producer of such guitars, and the mid-1930s Radiotone seen in our photographs is likely to have been made there.

Opposite page: The Radiotone has a spruce top, and back and sides of maple. Its fingerboard is ebony.

Definite information about the provenance of the brand is hard to find; Radiotone ukuleles are known to have been in circulation in Britain before World War II, and our Radiotone, which was purchased in the UK, has a telltale "foreign make" marker, just visible on its headstock, that identifies it as an import. An elegantly finished, high quality guitar, it would have suited a busy professional who lacked the funds for a Gibson or an Epiphone. At least one "name" British performer, Jack McKechnie, used a Radiotone for a while in the 1930s, and instruments similar to the model shown here could be seen and heard throughout Europe during the post-war period.

Left and right: Note the fancy tuners—and the "foreign make" stamp below the headstock logo.

JOSÉ RAMÍREZ FLAMENCO

FOR WELL OVER A CENTURY, José Ramírez has been one of the most highly revered names in classical guitar lutherie. The first José, who was born in 1858, set up as a "constructor de guitarras" in the Spanish capital, Madrid, in 1882, and worked for some years alongside his younger brother, Manuel, whom he trained as an instrument maker. However, the siblings parted company following a series of disputes in the

1890s: Manuel went on to establish his own guitar-making business, while José—who had become especially renowned for his thin-topped, powerful sounding flamenco models—eventually handed control of the José Ramírez workshop to his own son, José II. It has remained in the family ever since, and is currently headed by Amalia Ramírez, daughter of José Ramírez III (1922-1994). Amalia was born in 1955, and took over the firm following the early death of her brother, José IV, in 2000.

The fine Ramírez guitar seen here is a flamenco model dating from 1975. It is one of eighteen instruments recently sold, via London dealer Chandlers, by Mike Oldfield, who first gained international fame for his 1973 album *Tubular Bells*.

Dual scratchplates protect the top from over-vigorous playing.

Left: Like many flamenco guitars, this model has a cypress top (giving extra tonal brilliance), and a cedar back and sides.

Left: Traditionally, flamenco models are fitted with simple, ungeared tuning pegs instead of machine heads.

Right: The guitar's label carries the signature of José Ramírez III.

This Regal model has a laminated wood body. Regal/Saga also produces all-metal instruments.

REGAL SQUARE-NECK RESONATOR

THE REGAL TRADEMARK has one of the most convoluted histories of all U.S. fretted instrument brands. An Indianapolis music storeowner and wholesaler, Emil Wulschner, first used it in the late 1890s. In the wake of a slump in the sales of Regal products, the marque was next acquired by the Chicago-based firm Lyon & Healy, which began producing Regal guitars in the Windy City in 1908. Over the next six decades, the Regal marque changed hands several more times, and its product lines varied considerably. The company's most historically significant guitars were the Dobro resonators (created by John Dopyera) that it built under license from National-Dobro between 1934 and about 1940. Like most manufacturers of non-essential goods, Regal suspended guitar production for the duration of World War II, but although it resumed instrument making after 1945, its Dobros were never reintroduced.

During the 1950s and 60s, the company made guitars for third parties such as Harmony; however its Chicago factory closed in 1968, and the Regal trademark remained dormant until 1987, when a San Francisco-based firm, Saga Musical Instruments, took it over and went on to apply it to a range of instruments manufactured in the Far East.

Regal/Saga currently offers an impressive selection of inexpensive resonator guitars, including the square-neck, Dobro-type instrument shown here.

Below: With its square neck profile and raised strings, the Regal in our pictures is designed for lap-style playing.

The Regal brand originated in the 19th century, and has appeared on a wide variety of instruments.

Right: These upward pointing machine head buttons make it easy to tune the Regal when it is in a horizontal position.

RELIANCE ARCHTOP

THE FINELY PRESERVED ARCHTOP shown here is believed to date from the mid-1920s. Like the Radiotone model featured on pages 622-3, it was originally purchased in Britain, but was made in mainland Europe, probably at a factory in the Sudetenland (now part of the Czech Republic). This same region was the original home of the famous Höfner company, and of the craftsmen who later built instruments for Framus (see separate entries).

Its name reveals little about its provenance or history. "Reliance" may well have been a "house brand," used by a particular retailer or wholesaler for guitars bought in from a third-party manufacturer. Some such models were exclusive to a single store, and, if not produced in significant quantities, can be almost impossible to trace.

This author has seen only one other guitar with a "Reliance" logo—a battered single-cone resonator that may have no connection with our mystery archtop—and the make is not known to have been favored by any very well-known players.

This elderly archtop has been well cared for.

Above, left and below: The Reliance's neck has recently been refretted, and its floating bridge replaced, but it is otherwise original.

RICKENBACKER 4001 BASS

RICKENBACKER'S FIRST electric bass, the 4000, was a single-pickup model with a comparatively unadorned appearance. It was introduced in 1957, and was joined just four years later by the twin-pickup 4001, which boasted neck and body bindings, as well as triangular fingerboard markers (the 4000 had only dot inlays). From around 1963, the 4001 also featured the latest version of the company's distinctive string mute, whose dampers, located in the instrument's bridge/tailpiece assembly, could be raised and lowered by means of two thumbscrews (unfortunately the 4001 in our photographs has lost one of these).

The 4001, like Rickenbacker's 6-string guitars,

benefited considerably from its association with The Beatles. Paul McCartney was given one of the basses by the firm's President, F.C. Hall, in 1964; he went on to feature it on several of the group's LPs, and remained faithful to Rickenbackers during his post-Beatles projects in the 1970s. Among the 4001's numerous US devotees was Rush's Geddy Lee, and in 1977 it appeared in a Playboy centerfold, when Star Stowe (the then-girlfriend of KISS frontman—and non-Rickenbacker user—Gene Simmons) posed with it as that year's "Miss February."

Though the first 4001s were offered only in "Fireglo," more options were eventually added;

Below: The 4001 has a 33½-inch scale. Its neck is reinforced with two steel truss rods.

"Checkering" enhances the look of the 4001's body binding.

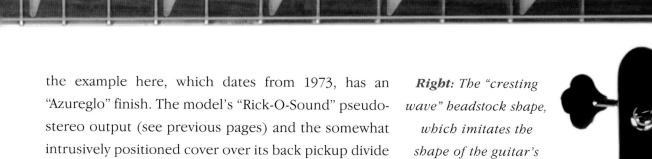

the example here, which dates from 1973, has an "Azureglo" finish. The model's "Rick-O-Sound" pseudo-stereo output (see previous pages) and the somewhat intrusively positioned cover over its back pickup divide opinion among players; however, the former is easy to ignore, and the latter can be removed without unduly affecting the character of this classic 1960s design.

Right: The "cresting wave" headstock shape, which imitates the shape of the guitar's body cutaways, is found on many Rickenbackers.

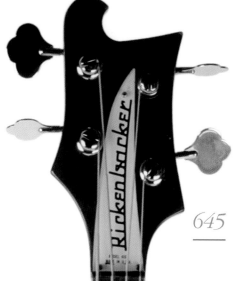

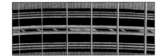

MANUEL RODRIGUEZ EMC1 "GITANO"

MANUEL RODRIGUEZ began studying lutherie as a teenage apprentice in Spain. He subsequently lived and worked in Los Angeles for fifteen years before returning to the Spanish capital, Madrid, where he set up his current company. This is renowned for producing fine classical and flamenco guitars; however, the Rodriguez shown here, an EMC1 "Gitano," is a Maccaferri-style steel-strung model, based on the Maccaferri-Selmer style instruments used by the great Django Reinhardt (see Dell' Arte entry for further background). Built with a "grande bouche" D-shaped soundhole ("petite bouche" instruments have smaller, oval holes), it offers all the features expected by a Reinhardt-style player, including rich tone, strong

Below: Spruce is used for this guitar's top; its back and sides are rosewood, and its neck is made from African mahogany.

This "built-out" fingerboard gives the E and B strings a two-octave range.

PHOTOGRAPHS COURTESY OF PEACH, BLAKE END, BRAINTREE

Above: *The Rodriguez's impressive brass tailpiece is very similar to the units found on the original Mario Maccaferri guitars.*

These machine heads are gold-plated.

projection, and additional high notes provided by the fingerboard extension serving the top two strings (see photograph and caption). Manuel's sons, also luthiers, are now part of the family firm, and thanks to a distribution deal with Fender, Rodriguez guitars are becoming ever more widely known.

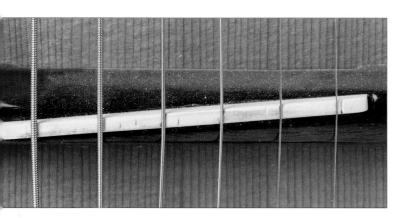

Left: *The long "mustache" bridge is another feature derived from Maccaferri instruments.*

SANDBERG CALIFORNIA PM 4 BASS

THE SANDBERG COMPANY is based southeast of the German city of Hannover, in the town of Braunschweig. It makes an extensive range of both guitars and basses, and high-profile users of its instruments include Richard Jones of The Stereophonics, as well as top session man Ken Taylor. In both 2004 and 2005, the firm received awards for its basses from the influential British magazine *Guitar & Bass*; its products are now readily available across the USA, thanks to a recent distribution deal.

The Sandberg California PM 4 bass shown in our

Delano as combining "'oomph' and greasy swamp bottom," "grinding wire attitude," and "a slight Delano twist to enhance dynamics and articulation!" In the bridge position is a PowerHB humbucker.

The Sandberg's bolted-on neck, which has a 34-inch scale, is Canadian maple, with a rosewood (or, optionally, maple) fingerboard. Our PM 4 has an alder body, but ash is used on some examples. The California range also features JM models incorporating Fender Jazz Bass-type pickups, and both PMs and JMs are produced as 4- or 5-stringers.

Left: The PM 4's outline is reminiscent of Fender's Precision bass.

pictures has a "Tobacco" body coloring ("Aged White" and "Voodoo" finishes can also be supplied), and may be used in active or passive modes. Its pickups are designed and built by another leading German manufacturer, Delano: the upper, spilt-coil unit is a PC 4, modeled on the classic Fender Precision bass transducer, with a sound graphically described by

Below: Six bolts fasten the PM 4's neck to its body; to their left is the compartment for the battery that powers the bass's active electronics.

SANTA CRUZ H STUDIO MODEL

RICHARD HOOVER first became involved in guitar-making during the late 1960s; he settled in the Monterey Bay-side city of Santa Cruz, California, in 1972, and co-founded the Santa Cruz Guitar Company four years later, in partnership with Bruce Ross and William Davis. Richard is now the business's sole owner, supervising a small, dedicated team of luthiers that produces its high-end acoustics. Among SCGC's customers is a long list of distinguished musicians, including Tony Rice, David Crosby, Joan Baez, Kenny Loggins, Janis Ian, and Elvis Costello.

In an interview with this author first published in 1999, Richard explained that one of his aims in setting up Santa Cruz was to create "a small company that is building superior instruments and [can be] really responsive to the players' needs"—positioning itself between the solo builder, with his or her inevitably limited production capacity, and the larger, more

Below: Sitka spruce is used for the H Studio Model's top; its back and sides are Indian rosewood.

The Bluestick transducer's manufacturers describe it as "the equivalent of a studio-grade microphone under [the] guitar's saddle."

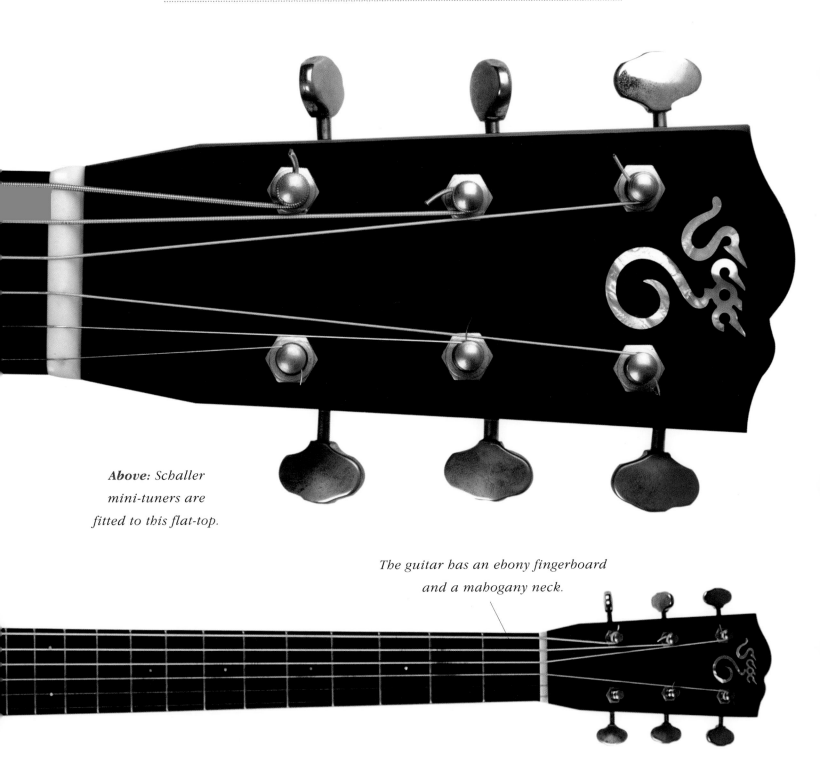

Above: Schaller mini-tuners are fitted to this flat-top.

The guitar has an ebony fingerboard and a mahogany neck.

impersonal manufacturer. SCGC's impressive reputation is clear evidence of his success, and of the efficacy of what he has since described on the Santa Cruz website as his "bench style" approach to guitar construction. This replaces a standard production line with a more collaborative environment in which each of his craftspeople "not only performs [their] own specialty, but also reviews the work of those who have completed stages before [them]."

The H Studio flat-top in our photographs is a fine example of Santa Cruz's recent output. Its rich, powerful sound belies the comparatively small size of its top (just 14^6/$_{10}$ inches), while its cutaway and pre-installed Schertler Bluestick undersaddle transducer are both boons to the working musician. Its high quality woods and finish perfectly complement its sonic performance. The model is also made in an alternative, thinner-body version.

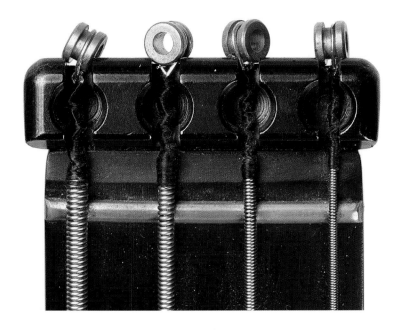

adopted a more radical solution: the complete removal of the peghead, and the repositioning of the tuners at the instrument's bridge end. He was also dissatisfied with the sound produced by wooden basses, and was soon fabricating prototypes from graphite-reinforced epoxy resin.

The outcome of Steinberger's experiments was his "headless," single-pickup L1 bass, unveiled at the NAMM (National Association of Music Merchants) trade show in 1979, and marketed the following year; the dual-pickup L2 seen here first appeared in 1981.

Above: The Steinberger's nut is also a string anchor.

The L2's small, symmetrical body maximizes comfort and balance...but when the instrument debuted in the 1980s, it surprised and shocked players used to more conventional shapes.

Above: The Steinberger has no neck joint, as its neck and body are formed from a single piece of resin.

STEINBERGER L2 FRETLESS BASS

NED STEINBERGER'S bold L1 and L2 bass designs quickly attracted interest from prominent musicians: among the first players to purchase them were John Entwistle of The Who, and King Crimson star Tony Levin. Their enthusiastic advocacy, combined with widespread press and media attention (in 1981, the L2 was declared one of the "Five Best Designs" of the year by *Time* magazine), generated huge demand for Steinbergers; this was to grow even greater following the introduction of a number of new models, including a headless 6-string guitar, and a fretless bass similar to the one shown in our photos.

In 1980, Ned Steinberger and a small group of partners had set up the Steinberger Sound Corporation to produce the L1. Within three years, SSC had been obliged to move to larger premises in order

Below: *This fretless L2 is fitted with two EMG humbucking pickups.*

PHOTOGRAPHS COURTESY OF GUITAR CLASSICS, LONDON

These are position markers, not frets!

Above: *A removable leg rest provides a comfortable support for seated Steinberger players*

to cope with its expanded product line, and as the decade progressed, managing the company became an increasingly onerous task for its founder. As he explained to Jim Reilly on the nedsteinberger.com website, "We weren't really making money....we were just breaking even and having all kinds of capital problems." Ned decided to turn to Henry Juszkiewicz, who had recently taken charge at Gibson, for some business advice; their discussions led, in 1987, to the purchase of Steinberger by the Nashville-based guitar giant, which continues to supervise the production of both US-made and imported Steinberger models.

TACOMA PAPOOSE

TACOMA GUITARS, now the third largest US acoustic guitar manufacturer (after Martin and Taylor), had its origins in a Japanese-owned wood processing firm, the Sound Mill, set up in the early 1990s in Tacoma, Washington State, to produce soundboards for pianos. It also supplied woods to luthiers throughout America, and, in 1997, launched its own Tacoma brand guitars. The first of these was the model shown here, the Papoose—an unusual, small-bodied instrument that sounds a perfect fourth (five half-steps) higher than a standard guitar; from bottom to top, its open strings are tuned to ADGCEA.

It is not only the Papoose's raised pitch (playing it provides a similar effect to using a regular acoustic with a capo at its fifth fret) that sets it apart. Like nearly all Tacomas, it boasts an offset, "paisley"-shaped

Above: Tacoma's distinctive bridge plate is also found on the normal-size guitars in the company's range.

PHOTOGRAPHS COURTESY OF PEACH, BLAKE END, BRAINTREE

soundhole and a characteristically contoured bridge, and is built using a combination of traditional craftsmanship and state-of-the-art computer numeric control (CNC) technology that guarantees both high productivity and maximum consistency.

Tacoma's instruments (including mandolins and acoustic basses as well as guitars) have gone on to find favor with amateur and professional players; among the leading performers who have used them onstage and in the studio are Bob Dylan, the Dixie Chicks, Bonnie Raitt, and Jackson Browne. In 2003 the firm, which had gained independence from its Japanese parent four years previously, won the Marco Polo award: this, in the words of its sponsors, the Russell Investment Group, is given to small and medium-sized businesses "for first-time success and accomplish-ments in international trade."

By now, Tacoma was selling no less than 60 different

Right: Despite its small size, the Papoose presents no problems for players used to standard-pitched guitars. It has a 19¹/₁₀-inch scale length, and 15 frets clear of its body.

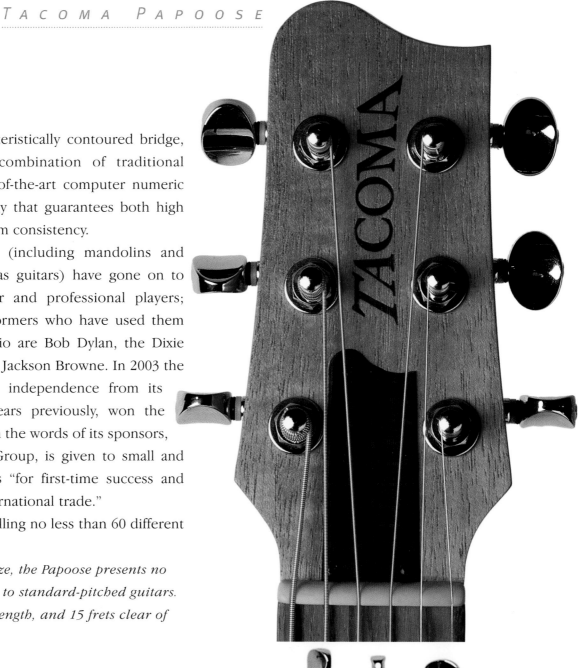

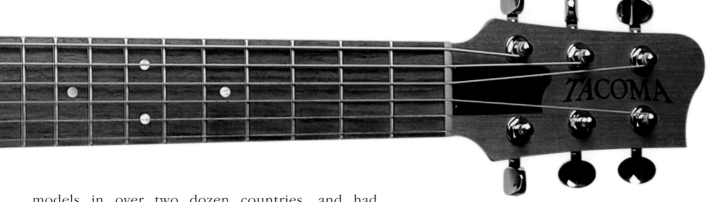

models in over two dozen countries, and had established a network of 450 dealers throughout the USA. In 2004, the company was bought by Fender, but it still operates from its own factory in the Pacific North-West, and seems set to continue delivering high-quality guitars to a growing number of customers at home and abroad.

Above: Standard Papooses like this one have cedar tops, a mhogany neck, back and sides, and a rosewood fingerboard; more exotic woods are also available.

The Papoose is produced in both 6-string and 12-string configurations.

669

TACOMA CHIEF

THE PAPOOSE'S distinctive soundhole, and the special top construction that goes with it, are shared by the other members of Tacoma's "Wing" range of acoustic instruments. The company's reason for placing its characteristically shaped vents on the upper bass bouts of these models is that this unusual location is an area of low inherent tension (unlike the high torque middle section of the top), where the soundhole can be "naturally supported by the sides and neck block." With no central cutout to be reinforced, the top itself can, therefore, be less rigidly braced and more flexible at its edges—and the result, according to Tacoma, is a "significant improvement in its...tonal response and volume."

These theories, already tested and proved on the Papoose, are borne out further by the impressive performance of the guitar that appears in our photos, the Chief. A single cutaway "mini-jumbo" with a solid Western cedar top, plus a back and sides of solid mahogany, it delivers a powerful sound that belies its

Below: The Tacoma Chief's natural coloring is enhanced by what the company terms a "light satin finish."

Above: Thanks to the Chief's unconventional soundhole shape and location, its label has had to be resited!

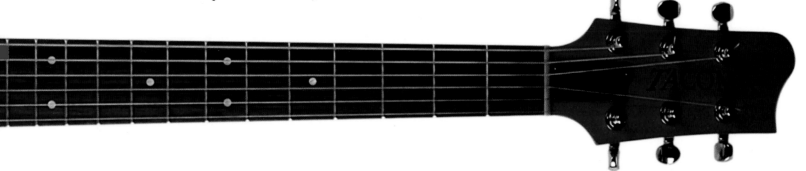

relatively small size. Its bridge and 22-fret fingerboard are rosewood, its tuning machines chrome, and its bolted-on neck mahogany. The standard version, seen here, has a natural finish and no on-board electronics; other colors are available as optional extras, and the Chief can be supplied with three different pickup systems (by, respectively, L.R. Baggs, Fishman and B-Band), at an additional cost of between $150 and $250.

The Tacoma "Wing" series also includes larger-bodied regular and baritone guitars and basses, as well as two mandolins. The company describes them collectively as "highly unique instruments featuring innovative designs and…technology, for players who want their voice to be just a little different." Examples of Tacoma guitars with conventional soundholes can be found on the next four pages.

TACOMA DR14

TACOMA DESCRIBES ITS "14" SERIES of flat-tops as a combination of "tradition and innovation." Like all its guitars, the DR14 Dreadnought seen here is fitted with an asymmetrical "tone-shaped" bridge, whose bass side is carved low and wide in order, as the company puts it, to "engage a large area of the top, and reproduce low frequencies more easily." Conversely, the bridge's treble end is narrower, and shaped to play its part in "dispersing string energy…in the most efficient possible way," while its edges are rounded in order to minimize potentially harmful concentrations of stress on the top. The D14 also features triangular bracing, instead of the more standard X-braces found on most acoustics, and, like other Tacomas, it boasts a precision-fitted bolted neck (the majority of its competitors glue their necks in) attached with a pressure washer to maximize solidity.

The DR14's woods and finish are less radical than some aspects of its construction. Its top is made from solid sitka spruce, its back and sides are rosewood, and ebony is used for its all-important bridge as well as its 20-fret fingerboard.

The model can be supplied in an alternative, cutaway version (the DR14C), and among the other "14" instruments is a second Dreadnought (the DM14), and a cutaway "little jumbo," the EM14C.

Below: Abalone is used for the DR14's headstock inlays and fingerboard position markers, as well as for the decorations around its soundhole.

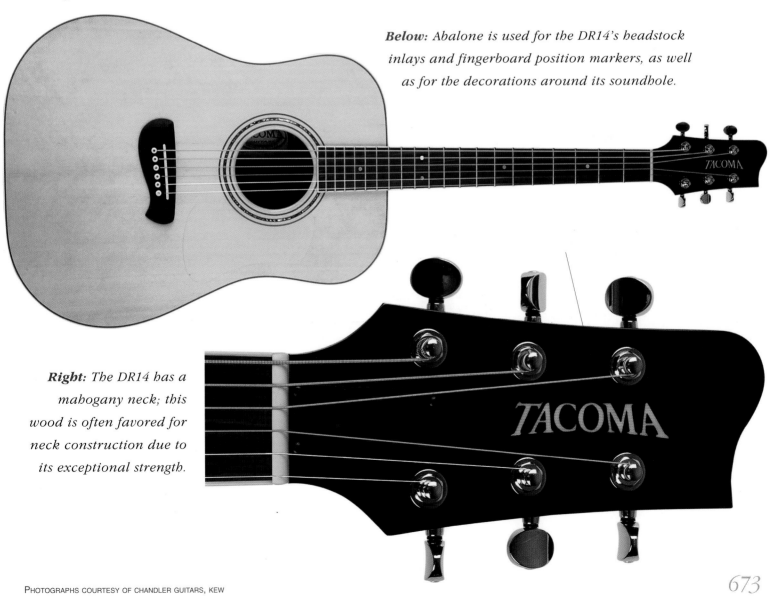

Right: The DR14 has a mahogany neck; this wood is often favored for neck construction due to its exceptional strength.

TACOMA PM28

TACOMA'S "28" RANGE has been described by the company as "perfect for professional players [whatever] their style," and all the guitars in the series share luxury features such as gold tuners and ebony bridges and fretboards. Among the "28s" are no less than four dreadnoughts, two regular-size jumbos and a cutaway "little jumbo," while the "baby" of the line in terms of size is the PM28 parlor model shown here.

As explained earlier (see pages 600-1), gut-strung European parlor guitars became popular in the early to mid-19th century, and were often elaborately embellished. Similarly sized American instruments were being made by Martin from the 1850s, but tended to have a simpler, more restrained look, as did the designs produced by other US manufacturers in the following decades—although some of Lyon & Healy's Washburn parlor models from the 1890s boasted fancier inlays. The gentle tone of these guitars was adequate for domestic use, but would have been insufficient in other contexts; however, modern parlor flat-tops like Tacoma's, while retaining the understated appearance of some of their predecessors, are more

Below: Spruce is used for the PM28's top, whose soundhole rosette is decorated with abalone. The guitar's back and sides are mahogany.

Below: These "leaf" fingerboard inlays are created with abalone ginko.

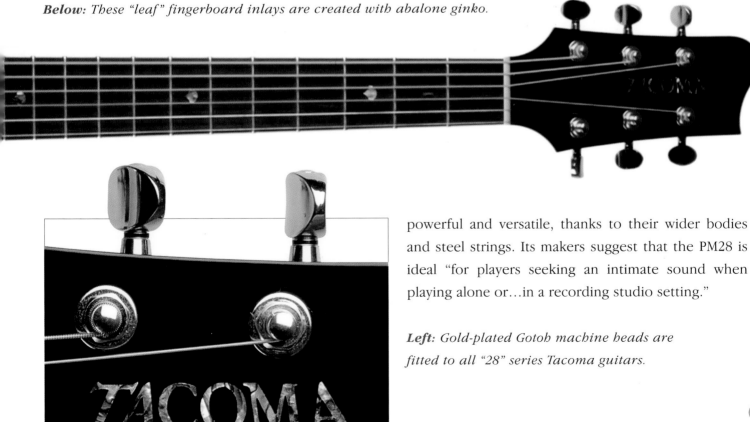

powerful and versatile, thanks to their wider bodies and steel strings. Its makers suggest that the PM28 is ideal "for players seeking an intimate sound when playing alone or...in a recording studio setting."

Left: Gold-plated Gotoh machine heads are fitted to all "28" series Tacoma guitars.

TAKAMINE ENV360SCX

MANY GUITAR ENTHUSIASTS first had their attention drawn to the Takamine brand by a sleevenote acknowledgement on Ry Cooder's classic 1979 album *Bop Till You Drop* (also notable for being one of the first records to be recorded and mixed digitally), thanking the company's boss Mass K. Hirade. At the time, Takamine, named for the mountain in Japan's Toyama Prefecture at whose foot the company's headquarters is located, was little known in the USA, although Mr. Hirade had been shaping its policy and products since 1968, developing a range of fine nylon-strung guitars, and going on to spearhead the firm's introduction of flat-top acoustics with integral piezo-type pickups and onboard preamps—still something of a novelty when the acoustic-electric "Taks" made their debut in 1978.

The instruments' high quality, and the convenience they offered to acoustic players, who were now able to

Below: The ENV360SCX's spruce top is decorated with abalone. Its back and sides are made from Indian rosewood.

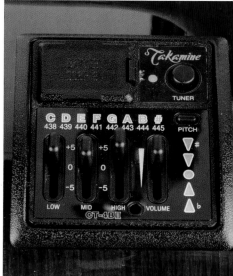

Left: Japan's Mount Takamine is pictured on the guitar's soundhole label.

Above: The preamp's control panel provides 3-band equalization and includes a tuning device.

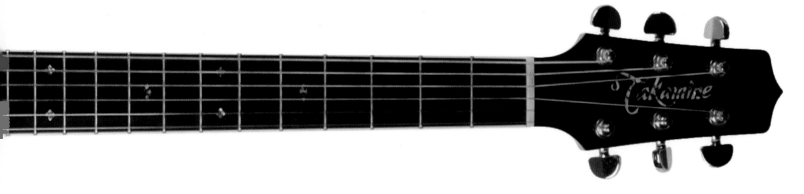

"plug in" and roam around on stage instead of being obliged to stay close to a microphone, led to a surge in Takamine's sales and reputation in the 1980s and 90s. Their profile was also boosted when a number of big-name stars, apprehensive about exposing their treasured high-end instruments to the hazards of live gigs, took to using Takamines on tour, only bringing out their vintage Gibsons and Martins in the studio! Despite this trend, however, it would be misguided to think of "Taks" only as "workhorses" or stand-ins. The firm's finest guitars have earned the respect of numerous pickers and critics, and the Dreadnought-bodied model shown here, the cutaway, "bear claw" spruce-top ENV360SCX incorporating a CT-4B preamp system, is part of the company's high-end Nashville series, described by Takamine as being "as close to a luthier-built instrument as you will find from an international guitarmaker."

TAKAMINE EC132SCX NYLON-STRUNG

MASS HIRADE'S original inspiration for the nylon-strung guitars that he and his team of Takamine craftsmen began producing in 1968 was the great Spanish luthier Antonio de Torres (see separate entry). Torres' instruments, built in Seville and later in his hometown of Almería in the mid- and late nineteenth century, had an immense influence both on his contemporaries and on almost all subsequent luthiers and classical players, and Hirade's blueprints, still used for a number of Takamine classics, contain many elements derived from his great predecessor.

However, musical styles and conditions of performance have changed radically since Torres' day, and Takamine's guitars have moved with the times. Consequently, the firm's more "purist," "concert classic" models co-exist in its catalog with ones offering features borrowed from other branches of lutherie, such as cutaways and built-in transducers and preamplifiers. The cedar-topped EC132SCX belongs in this latter category: it has a six-element pickup embedded in its bridge, plus a "SoundChoice" CT-4B preamp with with three-band equalization and a tuner.

Below: The EC132SCX has a rosewood back and sides; the same wood is used for its fingerboard.

PHOTOGRAPHS COURTESY OF CHANDLER GUITARS, KEW

Above: This elegant soundhole rosette is produced using marquetry techniques.

Bottom of page: The invisible pickup beneath the bridge has no effect on the guitar's acoustic performance.

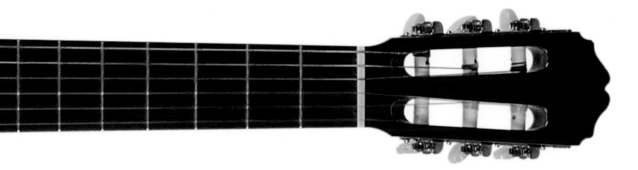

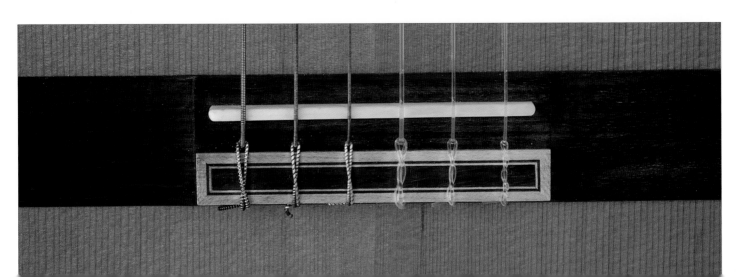

TANGLEWOOD TW 47B

TANGLEWOOD BRAND GUITARS first appeared in the United Kingdom in the 1990s; they are produced under the auspices of the British-based European Music Company, which is responsible for the instruments' design, and has them manufactured in China. The Tanglewood product line is extensive, including acoustics and electrics, as well as banjos and ukuleles, and has proved highly popular, especially with beginners and intermediate players.

Thanks to a distribution deal made in 2004 with Musiquip, Inc., of Dorval, Quebec, musicians from the USA and Canada now also have access to Tanglewood flat-tops. Three categories of these are currently available in North America: the moderately priced Indianas; the mid-range Premiere models (launched at the 2005 National Association of Music Merchants show, and described by Musiquip's Jeff Sazant as "an incredibly exciting addition to the Tanglewood

Below: The TW 47B is made from solid mahogany, and has celluloid binding on its top, back and headstock.

Long-lasting Elixir strings are fitted as standard on Tanglewood's Sundance models..

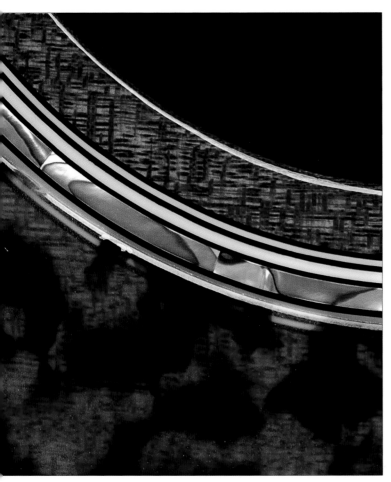

family… jam packed with high end features, yet [with] prices of $499 and below"); and the Sundance Pro series, all of which sport solid tops and are aimed, to quote the company's publicity, at "the discerning acoustic guitarist who is looking for a superb playing experience… on stage…or in a recording studio." The TW 47B shown here belongs to this third, higher end group; it has a "super folk size" body providing easy access to its 20-fret fingerboard, and is fitted with an under-bridge saddle piezo pickup and preamp made by the Finnish firm B-Band.

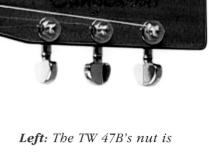

Left: *The TW 47B's nut is hand carved from bone; the same material is used for the guitar's bridge saddle.*

TAYLOR XXV-GA

THE TAYLOR COMPANY WAS FOUNDED in 1974 by two friends, Bob Taylor and Kurt Listug, who, since the previous year, had been working side by side at the American Dream guitar-making shop in Lemon Grove, near San Diego, California. When American Dream's proprietor, Sam Redding, sold his business, Taylor, Listug and a third partner, Steve Schemmer, took it over and changed its name—first to the Westland Music Company, and then to Taylor Guitars.

Times were hard during the firm's early years, but Taylor gradually gained a well-deserved reputation for the excellence of its acoustics, and major names such as John Prine and 12-string virtuoso Leo Kottke began using them. Following a period of steady growth from the mid-1980s onwards, the company (minus Schemmer, who left in 1983) relocated to larger premises in Santee, a few miles northeast of Lemon Grove, and in 1992, it established its current headquarters in nearby El Cajon. Here, Taylor has installed state-of-the-art Computer Numeric Control (CNC) technology, which streamlines production, ensures precision and consistency in the manufacturing process, and reduces costs, allowing staff to, as Bob Taylor himself puts it, "deliver more guitars to people at reasonable prices that really give them what they're hoping to have."

Taylor is now recognized as one of the world's premier guitar makers, and the instruments featured on the following pages demonstrate the range and quality of its designs. The model shown here is one of the limited edition XXV-GA Grand Auditorium models issued to mark the firm's 25th anniversary in 1999.

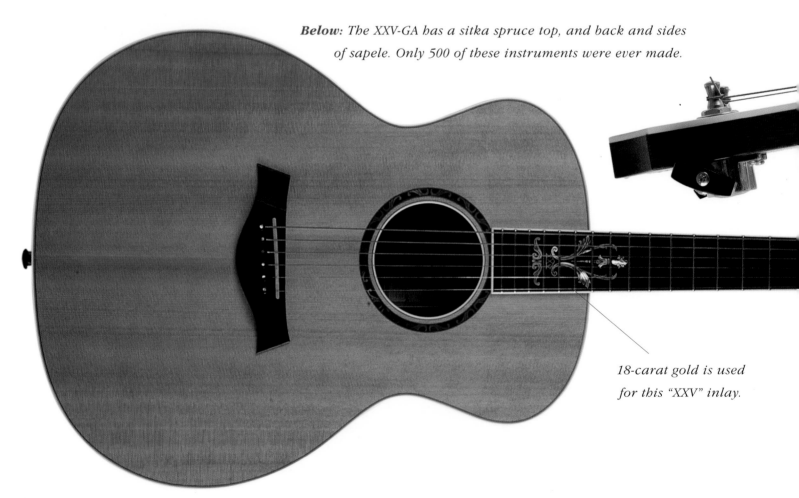

Below: The XXV-GA has a sitka spruce top, and back and sides of sapele. Only 500 of these instruments were ever made.

18-carat gold is used for this "XXV" inlay.

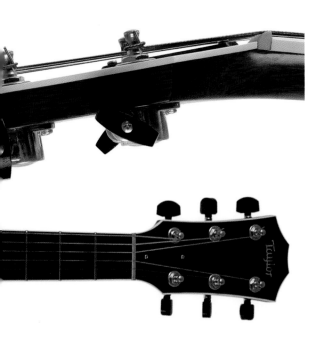

Right: The XXV-GA's soundhole rosette is embellished with koa and tropical padouk woods.

TAYLOR 110

TAYLOR CATEGORIZES its guitars by "series." In company parlance, a series is a group of instruments made from the same tonewoods, and sharing identical inlays and hardware; it is usually identified by the first digit of an individual model's three-figure catalog number. The simplest and least expensive full-size Taylors belong to the 100 series: these have solid sitka spruce tops, as well as backs and sides made from laminated sapele (most commonly sourced from the rain forests of West Africa, though it also grows as far east as Uganda and Tanzania), and comparatively plain decorative features such as wood fiber soundhole rosettes and pearloid fingerboard dots. The second digit in the model number indicates whether the guitar is a 6-string (1) or a 12-string (5), while the final figure refers to the body shape, with 0 representing a dreadnought, 2 a Grand Concert, 4 a Grand Auditorium, and 5 a Jumbo.

Below: Like all Taylor dreadnoughts, the 110 is 16 inches wide, with a body depth of 4⁵/8 inches.

Above: The sapele used for the 110's sides has a distinctive grain.

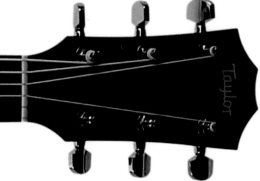

This key reveals that the Taylor 110 in our photos is a Series 1 6-string dreadnought—a modest looking, but highly durable instrument that provides outstanding performance and playability at a surprisingly low cost.

Left: This headstock is faced with black Lexan thermoplastic.

TAYLOR 310

WHILE THE TAYLOR 100 and 200 series offer only a restricted choice of instruments, the 300 category includes a full range of body types, as well as both 6- and 12-string guitars. All 300s have solid sitka spruce tops; until a few years ago, their backs and sides were made from solid sapele, but Taylor now uses a more exotic timber, African mahogany (***khaya ivorensis***), for them. Its sound, characterized by the company as "warm and open," combines with the "bright and snappy" qualities of spruce to deliver the highly distinctive tone quality for which the 300 series has been very widely praised.

310 dreadnoughts like the one shown here are full-fledged professional models; in Summer 2002, Taylor's own quarterly journal ***Wood & Steel*** carried a profile of San Diego-based musician Dennis Caplinger, who bought a 310 for his studio work because he liked the timbre provided by its mahogany (as he told interviewer Andy Robinson, "all my banjos are mahogany too"), and used it "on every acoustic guitar

Below: The Taylor 310 has a gloss finish to its top. Black fiber provides its body binding.

Above: Both the 310's fingerboard and bridge are made from ebony.

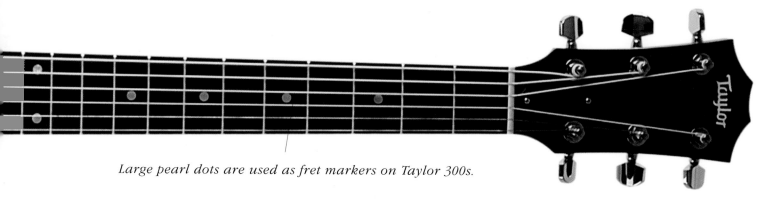

Large pearl dots are used as fret markers on Taylor 300s.

session [I did] for five or six years." After it was stolen, Caplinger immediately replaced it with another one, which continues to give him good service, and has been heard on several episodes of **The Simpsons**, as well as on numerous other TV and ad soundtracks.

Taylor also produces a cutaway version of the 310 with built-in electronics, the 310CE.

687

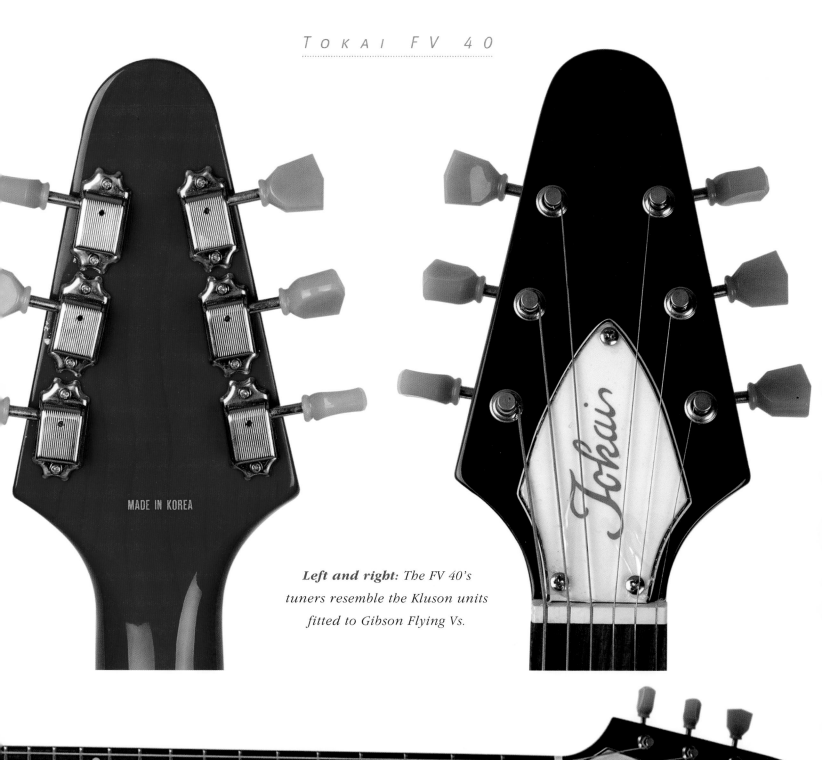

Left and right: *The FV 40's tuners resemble the Kluson units fitted to Gibson Flying Vs.*

copies, which were sometimes termed "traditional" or "classic reissues" in its catalogs.

After a period out of the limelight, Tokai is currently undergoing something of a renaissance, and the Flying V-like FV 40 in our photographs comes from an extensive batch of electrics and acoustics recently released by the company.

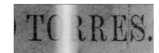

ANTONIO DE TORRES, 1889

ANTONIO DE TORRES (1817-1892) laid the foundations for modern classical guitar design, and surviving examples of his work are highly prized by historians and collectors. Born in the southeastern Spanish province of Almería, where he trained as a carpenter, Torres did not begin his guitar-making career until the 1850s, by which time he had moved northwest to Seville. There, his friendship with the distinguished player Julián Arcas inspired what is known as his "first epoch" of activity as a luthier. It lasted until 1869, and established him as a craftsman of the first rank; however, following his decision to return to Almería, his instrument building came to a temporary halt—perhaps, as some experts have suggested, because he was finding it impossible to make a living from it.

In about 1875, Torres took up lutherie once again: however, during this "second epoch" (which lasted until his death), his increasing poverty obliged him to combine it with other activities, and, sometimes, to use low-quality woods. Significantly, the 1889 guitar featured here contains a plugged nail hole, and may have been made from recycled furniture—though these inferior materials do not detract from the beauty of the finished instrument. It is one of about 88 authenticated Torres guitars still in existence.

Below: The guitar has a pine top; its soundhole rosette is made from 27 concentric circles of inlaid wood.

PHOTOGRAPHS COURTESY OF JAMES WESTBROOK

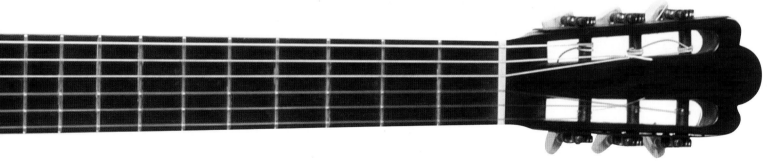

Above: The guitar's label gives the date and place of its construction.
Left: Strips of mahogany and walnut make up the Torres' side "ribs."

705

VIGIER ARPÈGE

PATRICE VIGIER'S DECISION to set up the guitar- and bass-making company that bears his name in 1980 came after several years of experience as an instrument repairer—and as a result of growing dissatisfaction with the major-name models that were ending up on his workbench.

From the start, the designs produced by his firm in Grigny, France, were bold and challenging: they included the Surfreter fretless electric (Vigier himself had previously built a prototype nylon-strung fretless with a glass fingerboard, which quickly shattered!), and the Arpège bass, a more recent example of which is pictured here; versions of both remain in production to this day. Among the key features that make Vigier basses like the Arpège special are their pickups (highly responsive units designed by the late Michel

Above: According to Vigier publicity, its Grigny HQ "builds as many guitars in a year [as] an industrial manufacturer does in a few days. [Hence], our guitars receive the attention that an expert musician looks for."

Left: Vigier Arpège basses are produced as 4-, 5-, or 6-stringers; all have a neck-through-body construction.

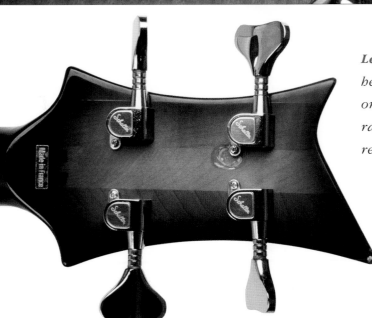

Left: *This distinctive headstock shape appears on both the Vigier Arpège range and the company's related Passion basses.*

Above: *The Arpège's twin pickups work in tandem with powerful active electronics that offer twelve preset tone settings.*

Bottom left: *Vigier necks are leveled to tolerances of one hundredth of a millimeter.*

Benedetti), and the composition of their necks, which are made from 90% wood and 10% carbon—the latter material taking the place of a conventional truss-rod.

High-profile Vigier players include Adam Clayton of U2 and Roger Glover of Deep Purple.

707

VOX PHANTOM BASS

IN 1957, Tom Jennings and Dick Denney, the co-proprietors of a thriving music store in the southern English county of Kent, began manufacturing "Vox" branded guitar amplifiers. Their first model was the AC15 15-watt combo, and it was followed, two years later, by the 30-watt AC30, which became a favorite with countless pop groups.

Buoyed by this success, Jennings and Denney decided to diversify, and launched their first guitars in the early 1960s. Initially, these were made in England, but by 1962—the year Vox introduced its distinctively shaped Phantom solid electric—production of some instrument components had moved to Italy, and before long, all Vox guitars were being built overseas. The Phantom line expanded to include both guitars and basses: some (including the original 1962 6-string, and the mid-60s Phantom bass shown in our photographs) had five-sided bodies, while others, such as those used by Brian Jones and Bill Wyman of the Rolling Stones, were made in a lute-inspired "teardrop" shape.

Like many European electrics of the period, the Phantoms featured a proliferation of on-board electronics (see captions for details) that now makes them seem somewhat dated; Vox amps, in contrast, are

Above: A distortion switch, plus an adjustable treble/bass boost, add to the Phantom's complexity.

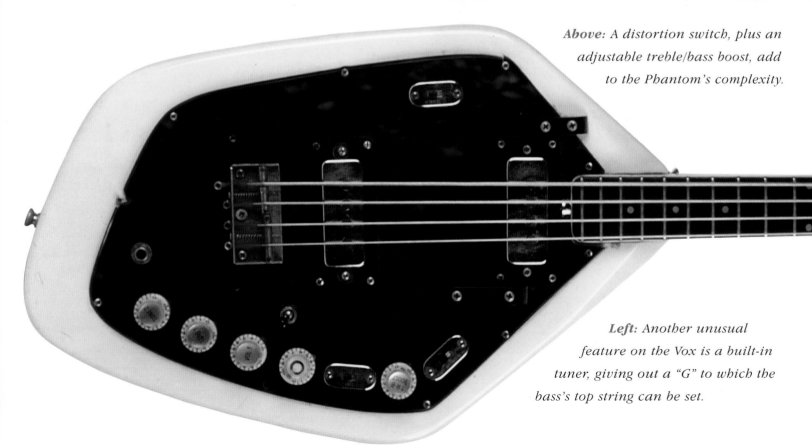

Left: Another unusual feature on the Vox is a built-in tuner, giving out a "G" to which the bass's top string can be set.

Left: *Unsealed tuners can suffer from the effects of wear and grime; however, these are in excellent condition, despite being some 40 years old.*

Below: *Vox models like this one were manufactured at the Eko guitar factory in Recanati, Italy.*

still regarded as classics. The company's history since the late 1960s is a complex saga of takeovers and relaunches: since 1998, a series of US-made Phantom-type models has been available, although trademark restrictions prevent them from being officially named Phantoms or Teardrops. Significantly, they lack many of the "gizmos" seen on our authentic '60s bass.

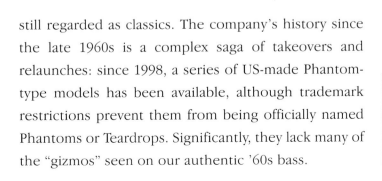

Made in Italy by Vox

K. YAIRI DY 40

YAIRI FLAT-TOPS are endorsed by a host of major popular music names. Some of them, like Grateful Dead rhythm guitarist Bob Weir, have played Yairis for many years: the company released its first Weir "Signature" model back in 1991, and has recently produced the WY1BW, a replica of the instrument's original prototype. Other notable Yairi users include the singer-songwriter Ani DiFranco, whose ADY1G acoustic/electric cutaway has a specially widened scratchplate to protect the guitar's finish from her famously vigorous picking hand!

These steel-strung instruments come in various categories and sizes: the one seen here is a DY 40 dreadnought incorporating the firm's innovative "Direct Coupled Bridge" system, also fitted to much of the rest of its acoustic range. This patented design is intended to stop the problem of upward string pull encountered on conventional bridges (which can lead

Below: The DY 40's woods are perennial favorites: spruce for the top, and mahogany for the back and sides.

PHOTOGRAPHS COURTESY OF THE LONDON RESONATOR CENTRE

Left: *Ivory and pearl are used for the DY 40's body bindings and decorations.*

Above: *The strings are inserted into the top through this ebony "reinforcement" plate.*

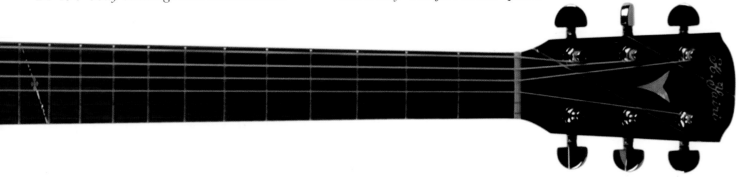

to the bridge becoming unglued from the guitar's top) by anchoring the strings behind rather than within the bridge unit itself. It also has the effect of steepening the angle at which the strings meet the saddle, thereby, in Yairi's words, making for "a maximum transfer of string vibration energy" that improves the instrument's tone and sustain.

K. YAIRI FY 94

IN ADDITION TO CLASSICAL ("CY"-prefixed) and dreadnought ("DY") instruments like the ones shown on the previous pages, K. Yairi, known as Alvarez Yairi in the USA, produces several other categories of guitar—such as WY acoustic-electrics (all fitted with piezo transducers and Yairi's own System 600T preamps), and a range of small-body models that, as the company's publicity puts it, "comes in all flavors." This group includes two cedar-topped "parlor" guitars, the RAG 6 and the cutaway FY 6C, as

Below: This flat-top, which has recently been discontinued, has a spruce top and mahogany back and sides.

PHOTOGRAPHS COURTESY OF THE LONDON RESONATOR CENTRE

Below: The Yairi's 20-fret fingerboard (with 14 frets clear of the body) is made from rosewood.

Above: The FY 94 boasts gold die-cast machine heads.

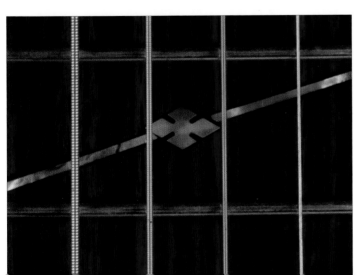

well as the slightly larger FY 94 featured in our photographs. Inspired by the OM-style flat-tops originally developed in the late 1920s by Martin, the FY 94 is especially designed for fingerpicking, and, like other similarly dimensioned Yairis, provides a rich yet delicate tone perfect for folk, blues or country-style playing; many musicians also find it ideal for recording.

Left: *Sadly, the Zenith logo on the instrument's headstock has almost completely worn away.*

These inlays are very similar to those on the Framus archtop featured earlier in this book.

GUITARS BY MAKER AND PAGE NUMBER

ACKNOWLEDGEMENTS

This book could not have been produced without the kind and generous cooperation of the guitar store proprietors, collectors, musicians and luthiers who allowed their instruments to appear in it, and the author would like to express his sincere thanks to all of them. Some of those who assisted in this way have asked to remain anonymous; the others include:

Guitar Village, Farnham *(www.guitarvillage.co.uk)*
Guitar Junction, Worthing *(www.guitarjunction.co.uk)*
The American Guitar Centre & Bassworld *(www.psst.co.uk/americanguitars/)*
Peach, Blake End, Braintree *(www.peachideas.co.uk)*
Chandler Guitars, Kew *(www.chandlerguitars.co.uk)*
The House of Guitars, London
(www.acousticcentre.com and www.basscentre.co.uk)
Guitar Classics, London *(www.guitar-classics.co.uk)*
Tom Anfield *(www.ukguitars.com)*
The London Resonator Centre *(www.resocentre.com)*
Nevada Music, Portsmouth *(www.nevadamusic.co.uk)*
The Ivor Mairants Musicentre, London *(www.ivormairants.co.uk)*
James Westbrook, The Guitar Museum, Hove *(www.theguitarmuseum.com)*

Thanks also to Colin Gower, Marie Clayton, Charles Alexander, Gary Boner, Roger Hurrell, Andy Robinson, Taro Takeuchi and Ulrich Wedemeier, and to Neil Sutherland (who photographed all the guitars with his customary skill) and designer Phil Clucas.